GUARDIANS
OF THE GALAXY

"THE FINAL GAUNTLET"

DONNY CATES
writer

GEOFF SHAW
artist

MARTE GRACIA [#1-3] & **DAVID CURIEL** [#4-6]
colorists

VC's CORY PETIT
letterer

DAVID MARQUEZ & DEAN WHITE
cover artists

DANNY KHAZEM & LAUREN AMARO
assistant editors

DARREN SHAN
editor

JORDAN D. WHITE
senior editor

collection editor JENNIFER GRÜNWALD
assistant editor CAITLIN O'CONNELL
associate managing editor KATERI WOODY
editor, special projects MARK D. BEAZLEY
vp production & special projects JEFF YOUNGQUIST
book designer: ADAM DEL RE

svp print, sales & marketing DAVID GABRIEL
director, licensed publishing: SVEN LARSEN
editor in chief C.B. CEBULSKI
chief creative officer JOE QUESADA
president DAN BUCKLEY
executive producer ALAN FINE

GUARDIANS OF THE GALAXY VOL. 1: THE FINAL GAUNTLET. Contains material originally published in magazine form as GUARDIANS OF THE GALAXY #1-6. First printing 2019. ISBN 978-1-302-91588-9. Published by MARVEL WORLDWIDE, INC., a subsidiary of MARVEL ENTERTAINMENT, LLC. OFFICE OF PUBLICATION: 135 West 50th Street, New York, NY 10020. © 2019 MARVEL No similarity between any of the names, characters, persons, and/or institutions in this magazine with those of any living or dead person or institution is intended, and any such similarity which may exist is purely coincidental. **Printed in the U.S.A.** DAN BUCKLEY, President, Marvel Entertainment; JOHN NEE, Publisher; JOE QUESADA, Chief Creative Officer; TOM BREVOORT, SVP of Publishing; DAVID BOGART, Associate Publisher & SVP of Talent Affairs; DAVID GABRIEL, SVP of Sales & Marketing, Publishing; JEFF YOUNGQUIST, VP of Production & Special Projects; DAN CARR, Executive Director of Publishing Technology; ALEX MORALES, Director of Publishing Operations; DAN EDINGTON, Managing Editor; SUSAN CRESPI, Production Manager; STAN LEE, Chairman Emeritus. For information regarding advertising in Marvel Comics or on Marvel.com, please contact Vit DeBellis, Custom Solutions & Integrated Advertising Manager, at vdebellis@marvel.com. For Marvel subscription inquiries, please call 888-511-5480. **Manufactured between 6/21/2019 and 7/23/2019 by LSC COMMUNICATIONS INC., KENDALLVILLE, IN, USA.**

10 9 8 7 6 5 4 3 2 1

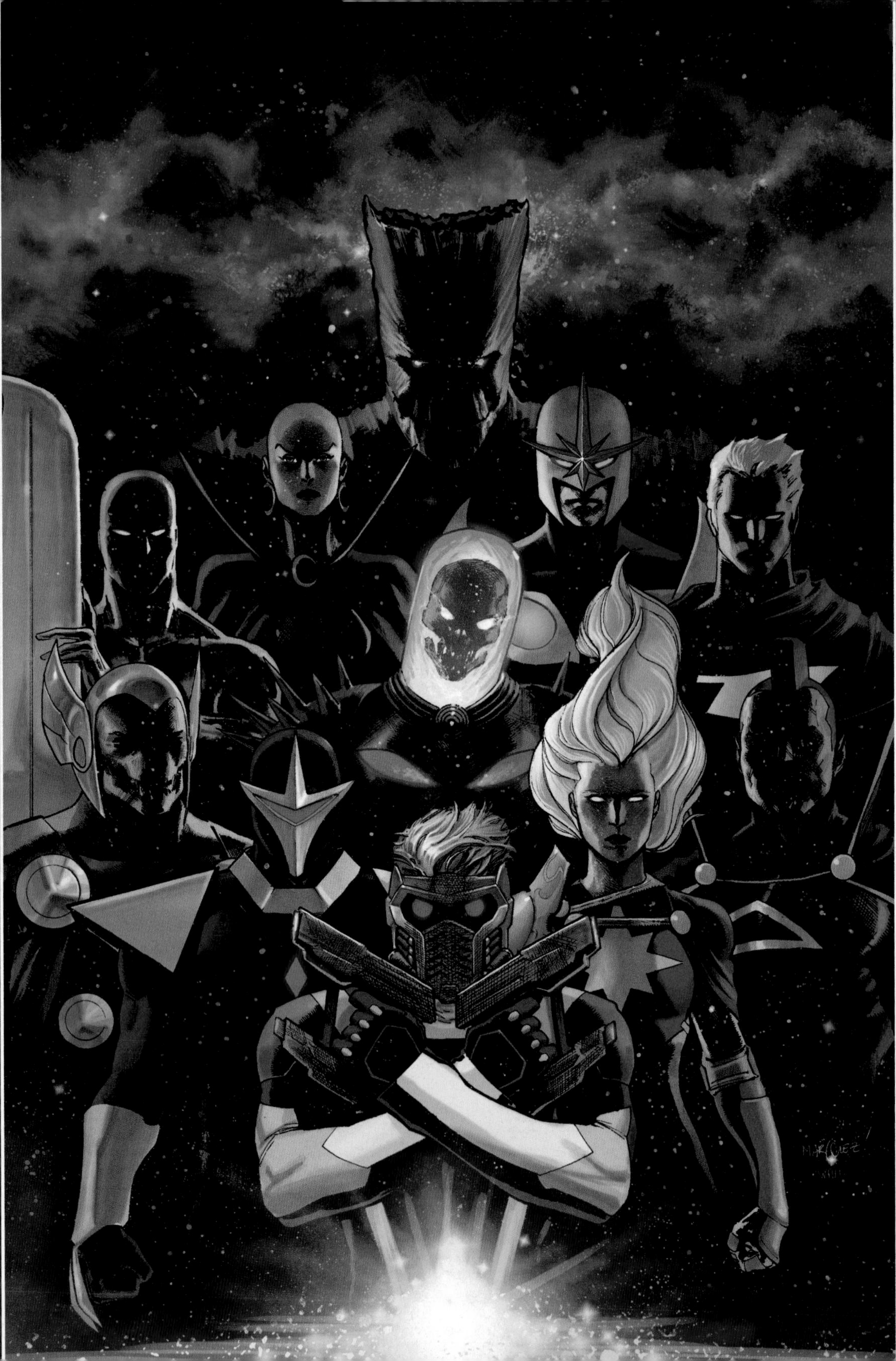

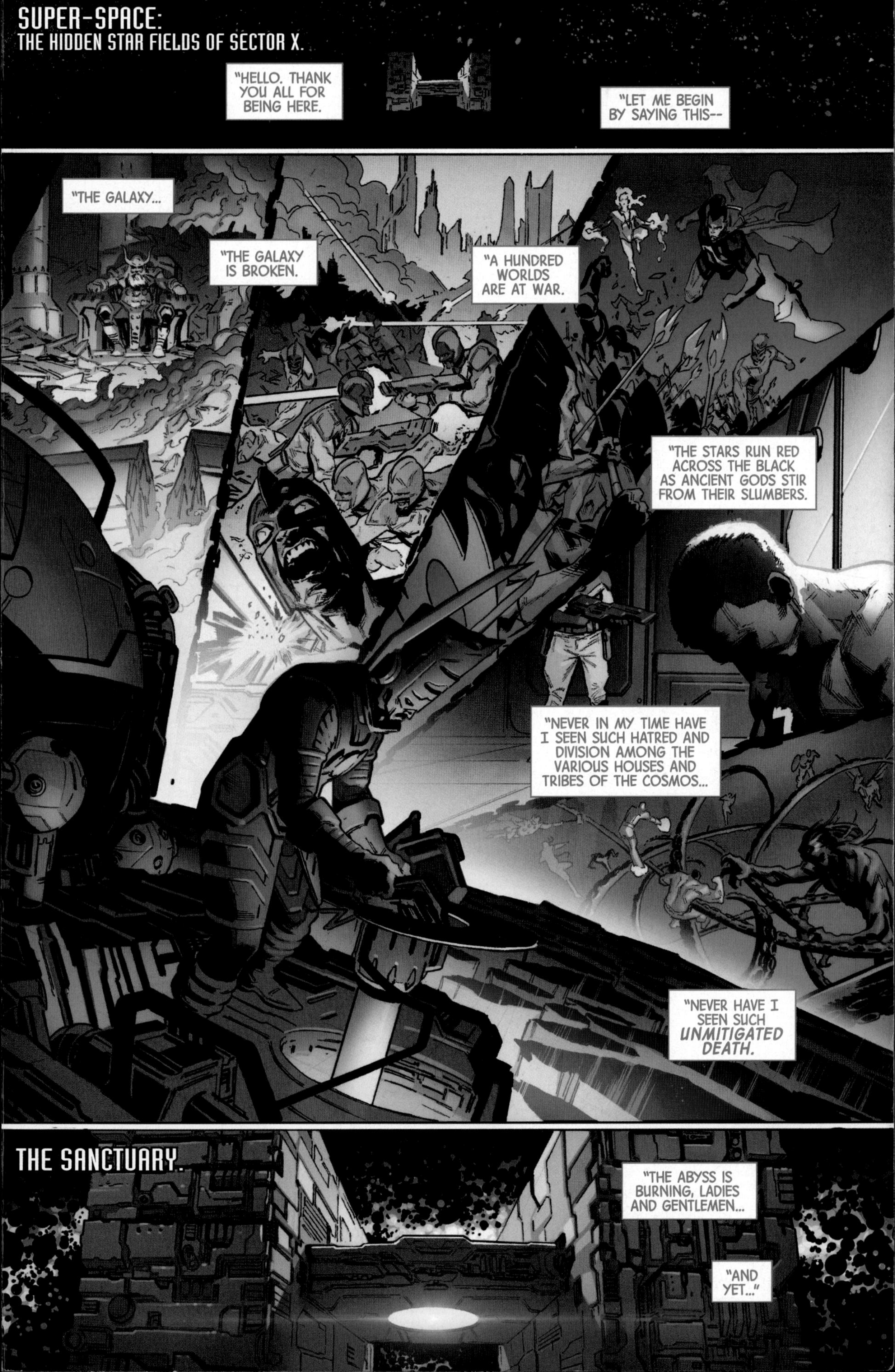
SUPER-SPACE:
THE HIDDEN STAR FIELDS OF SECTOR X.
"HELLO. THANK YOU ALL FOR BEING HERE.
"LET ME BEGIN BY SAYING THIS--
"THE GALAXY...
"THE GALAXY IS BROKEN.
"A HUNDRED WORLDS ARE AT WAR.
"THE STARS RUN RED ACROSS THE BLACK AS ANCIENT GODS STIR FROM THEIR SLUMBERS.
"NEVER IN MY TIME HAVE I SEEN SUCH HATRED AND DIVISION AMONG THE VARIOUS HOUSES AND TRIBES OF THE COSMOS...
"NEVER HAVE I SEEN SUCH UNMITIGATED DEATH.
THE SANCTUARY.
"THE ABYSS IS BURNING, LADIES AND GENTLEMEN...
"AND YET..."

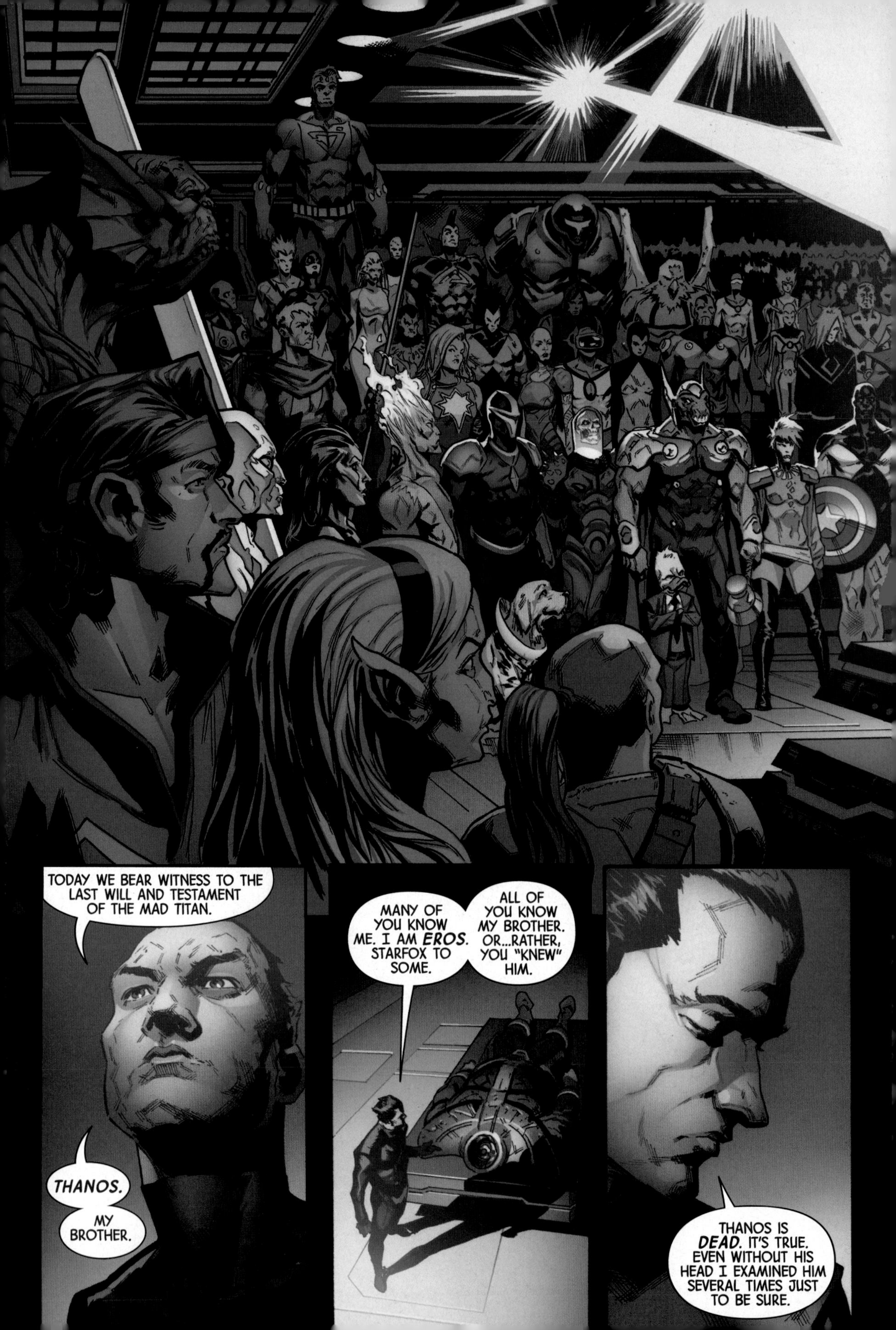
TODAY WE BEAR WITNESS TO THE LAST WILL AND TESTAMENT OF THE MAD TITAN.
THANOS.
MY BROTHER.
MANY OF YOU KNOW ME. I AM EROS. STARFOX TO SOME.
ALL OF YOU KNOW MY BROTHER. OR...RATHER, YOU "KNEW" HIM.
THANOS IS DEAD. IT'S TRUE. EVEN WITHOUT HIS HEAD I EXAMINED HIM SEVERAL TIMES JUST TO BE SURE.

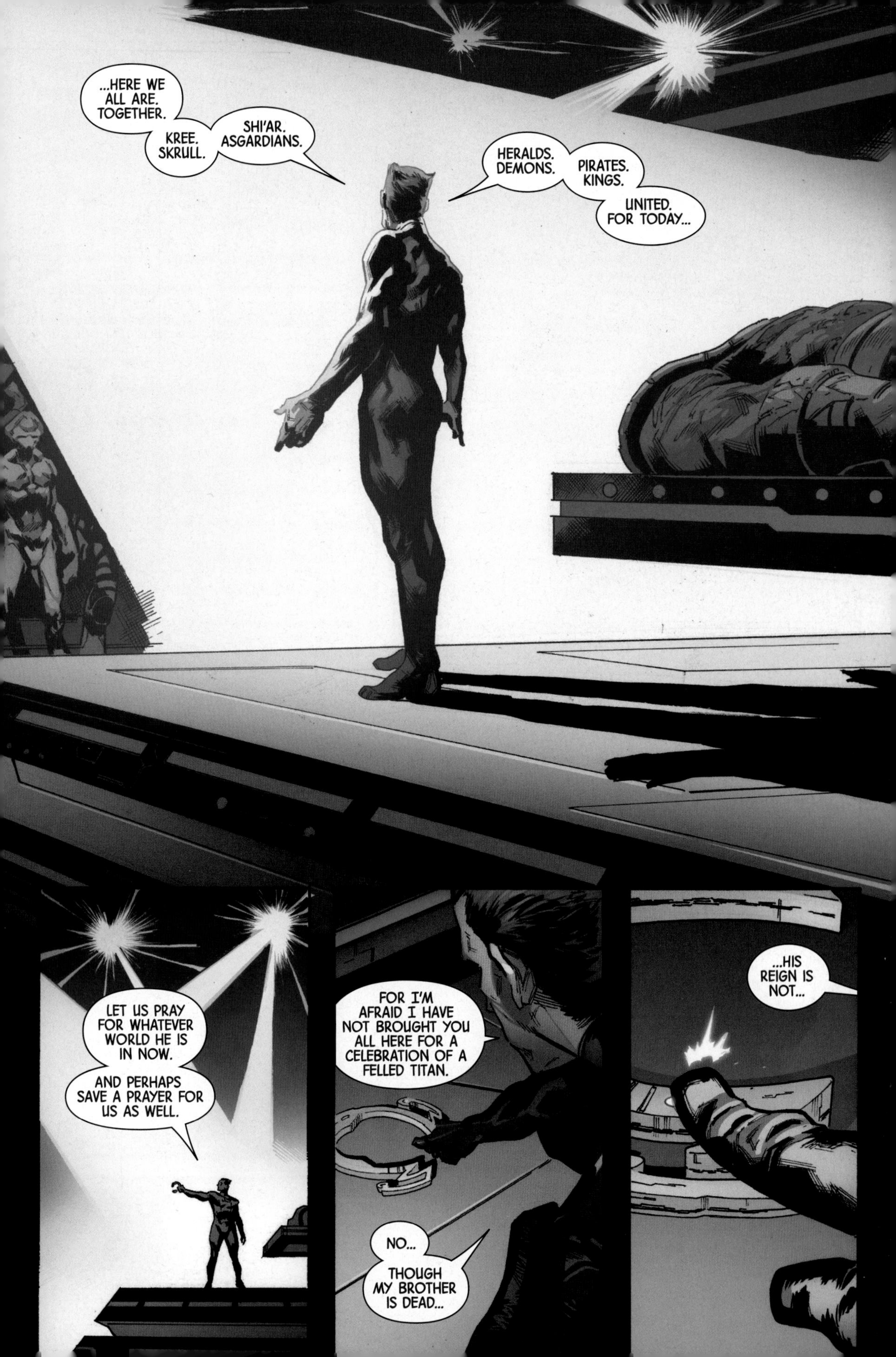
...HERE WE ALL ARE. TOGETHER.
KREE. SKRULL.
SHI'AR. ASGARDIANS.
HERALDS. DEMONS.
PIRATES. KINGS.
UNITED. FOR TODAY...
LET US PRAY FOR WHATEVER WORLD HE IS IN NOW.
AND PERHAPS SAVE A PRAYER FOR US AS WELL.
FOR I'M AFRAID I HAVE NOT BROUGHT YOU ALL HERE FOR A CELEBRATION OF A FELLED TITAN.
NO...
THOUGH MY BROTHER IS DEAD...
...HIS REIGN IS NOT...

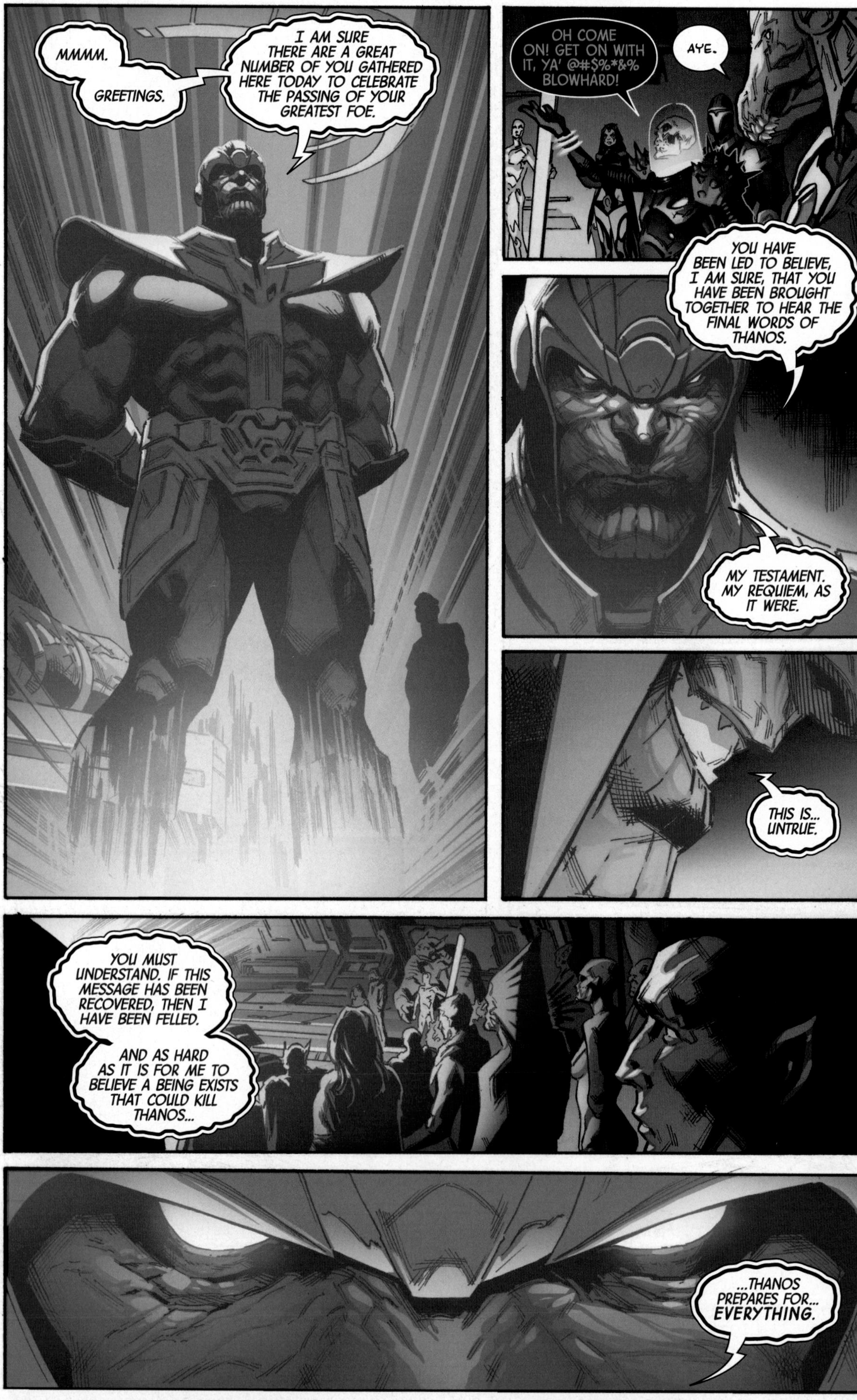
MMMM.
GREETINGS.
I AM SURE THERE ARE A GREAT NUMBER OF YOU GATHERED HERE TODAY TO CELEBRATE THE PASSING OF YOUR GREATEST FOE.
OH COME ON! GET ON WITH IT, YA' @#$%*&% BLOWHARD!
AYE.
YOU HAVE BEEN LED TO BELIEVE, I AM SURE, THAT YOU HAVE BEEN BROUGHT TOGETHER TO HEAR THE FINAL WORDS OF THANOS.
MY TESTAMENT. MY REQUIEM, AS IT WERE.
THIS IS... UNTRUE.
YOU MUST UNDERSTAND. IF THIS MESSAGE HAS BEEN RECOVERED, THEN I HAVE BEEN FELLED.
AND AS HARD AS IT IS FOR ME TO BELIEVE A BEING EXISTS THAT COULD KILL THANOS...
...THANOS PREPARES FOR... EVERYTHING.

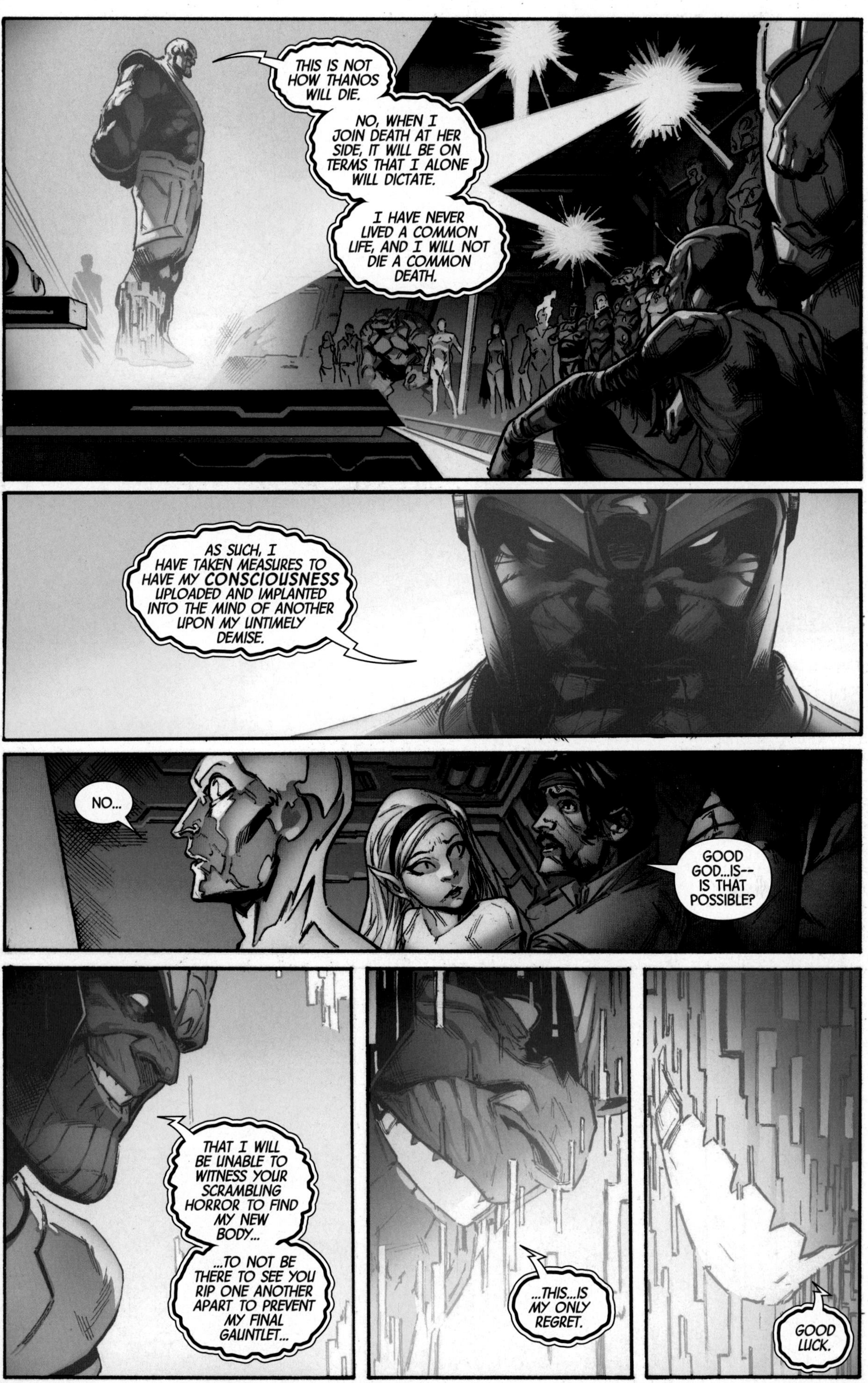
THIS IS NOT HOW THANOS WILL DIE.
NO, WHEN I JOIN DEATH AT HER SIDE, IT WILL BE ON TERMS THAT I ALONE WILL DICTATE.
I HAVE NEVER LIVED A COMMON LIFE, AND I WILL NOT DIE A COMMON DEATH.
AS SUCH, I HAVE TAKEN MEASURES TO HAVE MY CONSCIOUSNESS UPLOADED AND IMPLANTED INTO THE MIND OF ANOTHER UPON MY UNTIMELY DEMISE.
NO...
GOOD GOD...IS-- IS THAT POSSIBLE?
THAT I WILL BE UNABLE TO WITNESS YOUR SCRAMBLING HORROR TO FIND MY NEW BODY...
...TO NOT BE THERE TO SEE YOU RIP ONE ANOTHER APART TO PREVENT MY FINAL GAUNTLET...
...THIS...IS MY ONLY REGRET.
GOOD LUCK.

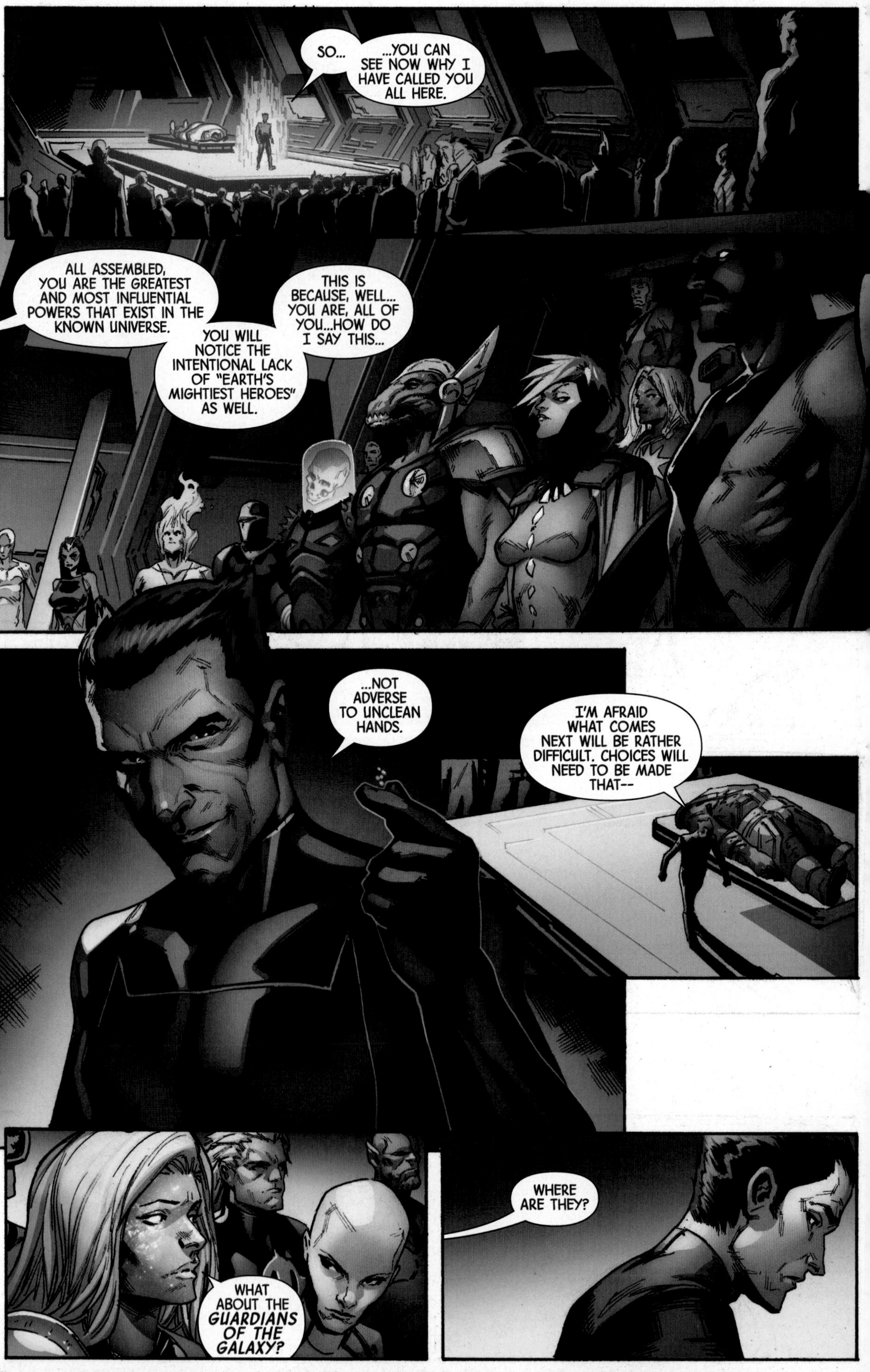
SO...
...YOU CAN SEE NOW WHY I HAVE CALLED YOU ALL HERE.
ALL ASSEMBLED, YOU ARE THE GREATEST AND MOST INFLUENTIAL POWERS THAT EXIST IN THE KNOWN UNIVERSE.
YOU WILL NOTICE THE INTENTIONAL LACK OF "EARTH'S MIGHTIEST HEROES" AS WELL.
THIS IS BECAUSE, WELL... YOU ARE, ALL OF YOU...HOW DO I SAY THIS...
...NOT ADVERSE TO UNCLEAN HANDS.
I'M AFRAID WHAT COMES NEXT WILL BE RATHER DIFFICULT. CHOICES WILL NEED TO BE MADE THAT--
WHAT ABOUT THE *GUARDIANS OF THE GALAXY?*
WHERE ARE THEY?

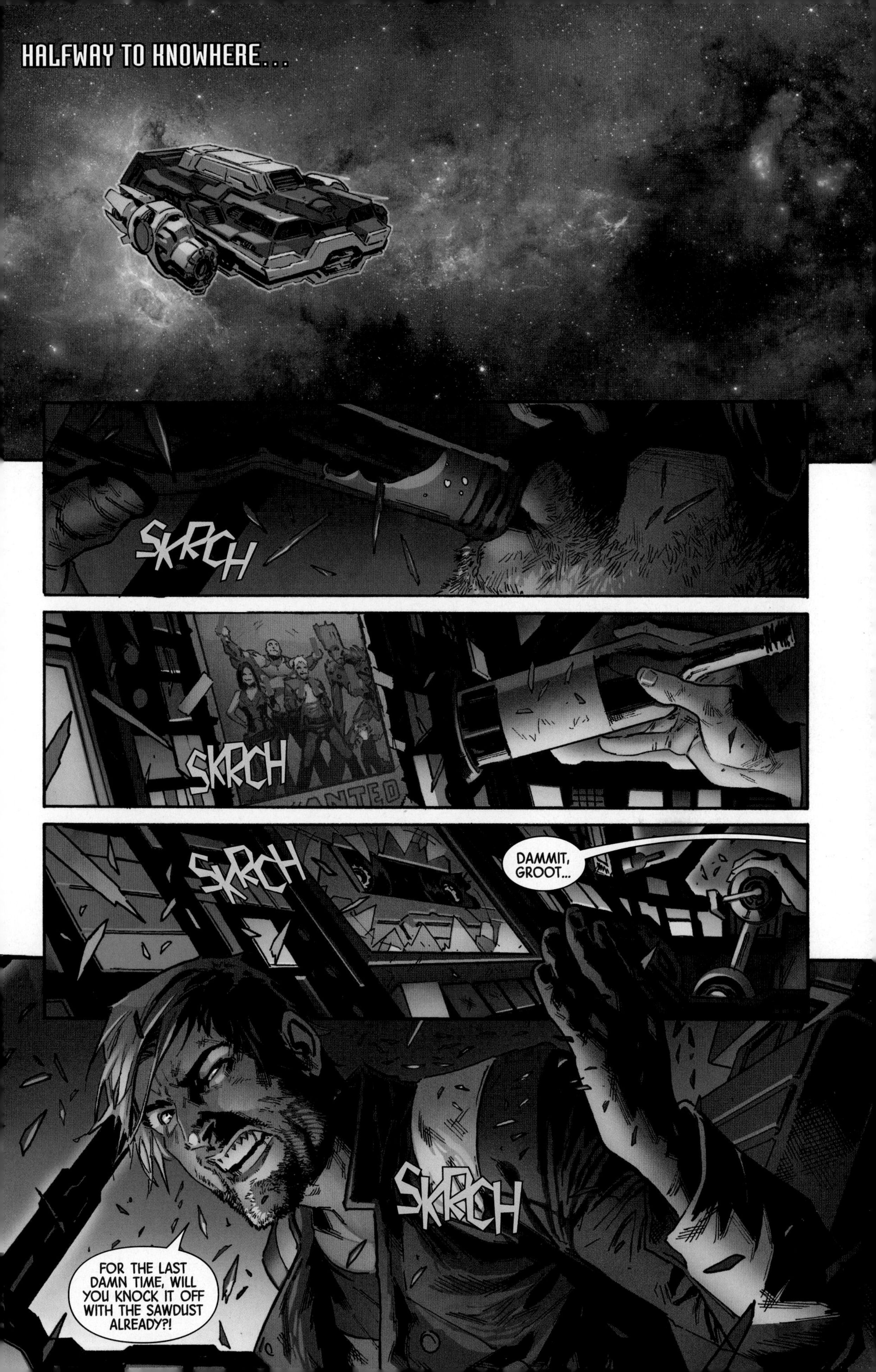
HALFWAY TO KNOWHERE...
SKRCH
SKRCH
SKRCH
DAMMIT, GROOT...
SKRCH
FOR THE LAST DAMN TIME, WILL YOU KNOCK IT OFF WITH THE SAWDUST ALREADY?!

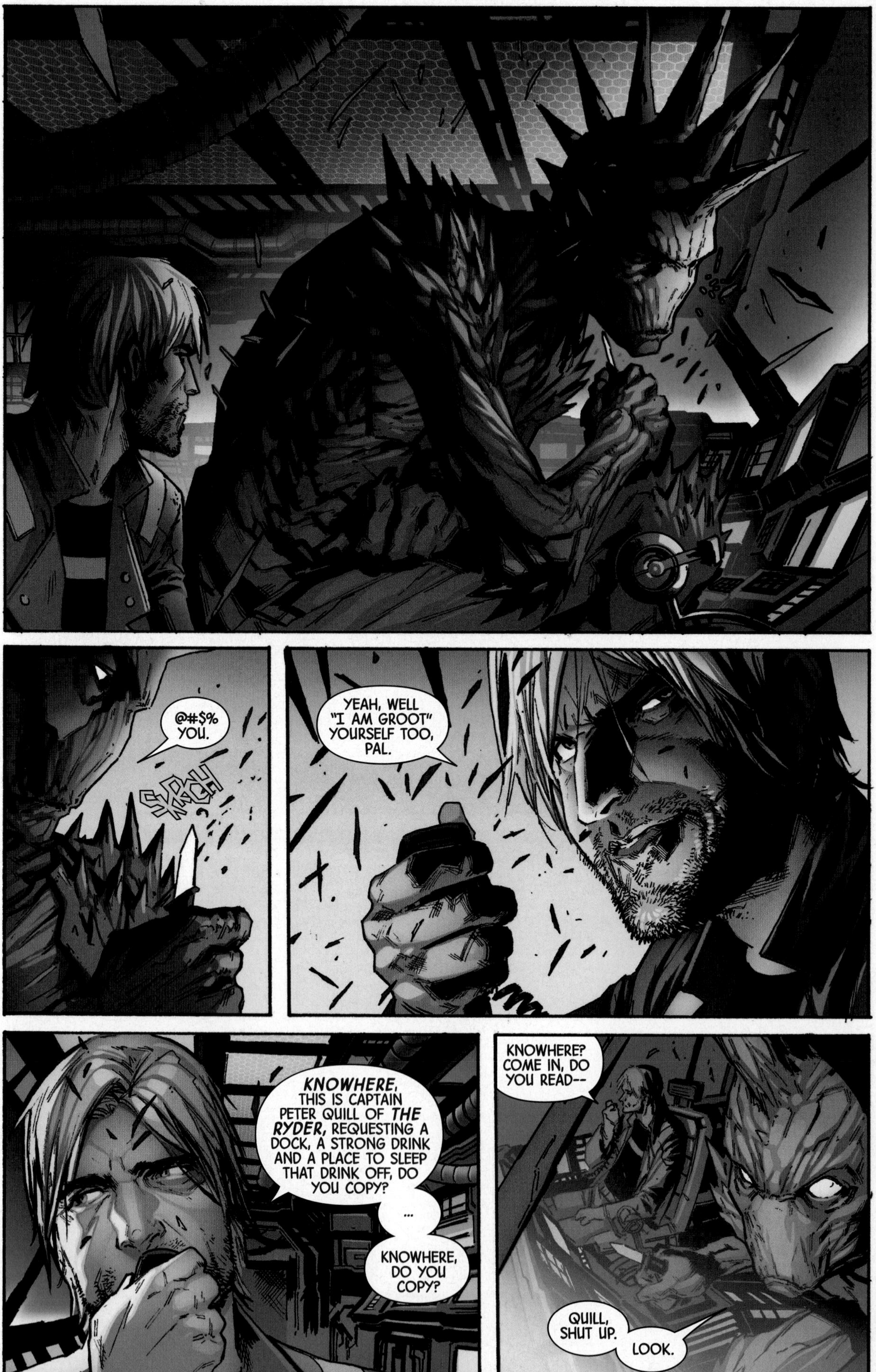
@#$% YOU.
SKRICH
YEAH, WELL "I AM GROOT" YOURSELF TOO, PAL.
KNOWHERE, THIS IS CAPTAIN PETER QUILL OF THE RYDER, REQUESTING A DOCK, A STRONG DRINK AND A PLACE TO SLEEP THAT DRINK OFF, DO YOU COPY?
...
KNOWHERE, DO YOU COPY?
KNOWHERE? COME IN, DO YOU READ--
QUILL, SHUT UP.
LOOK.

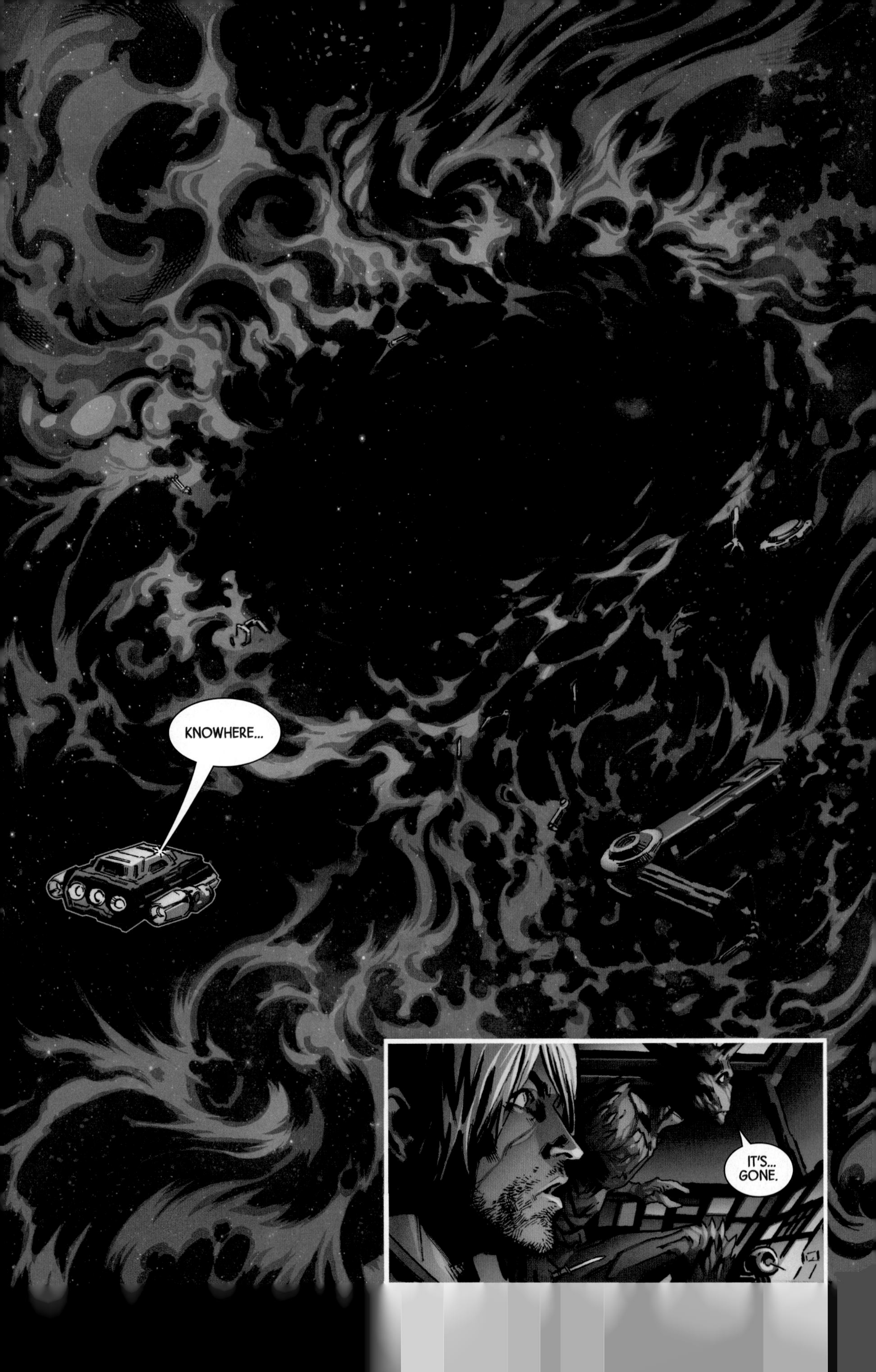
KNOWHERE...
IT'S... GONE.

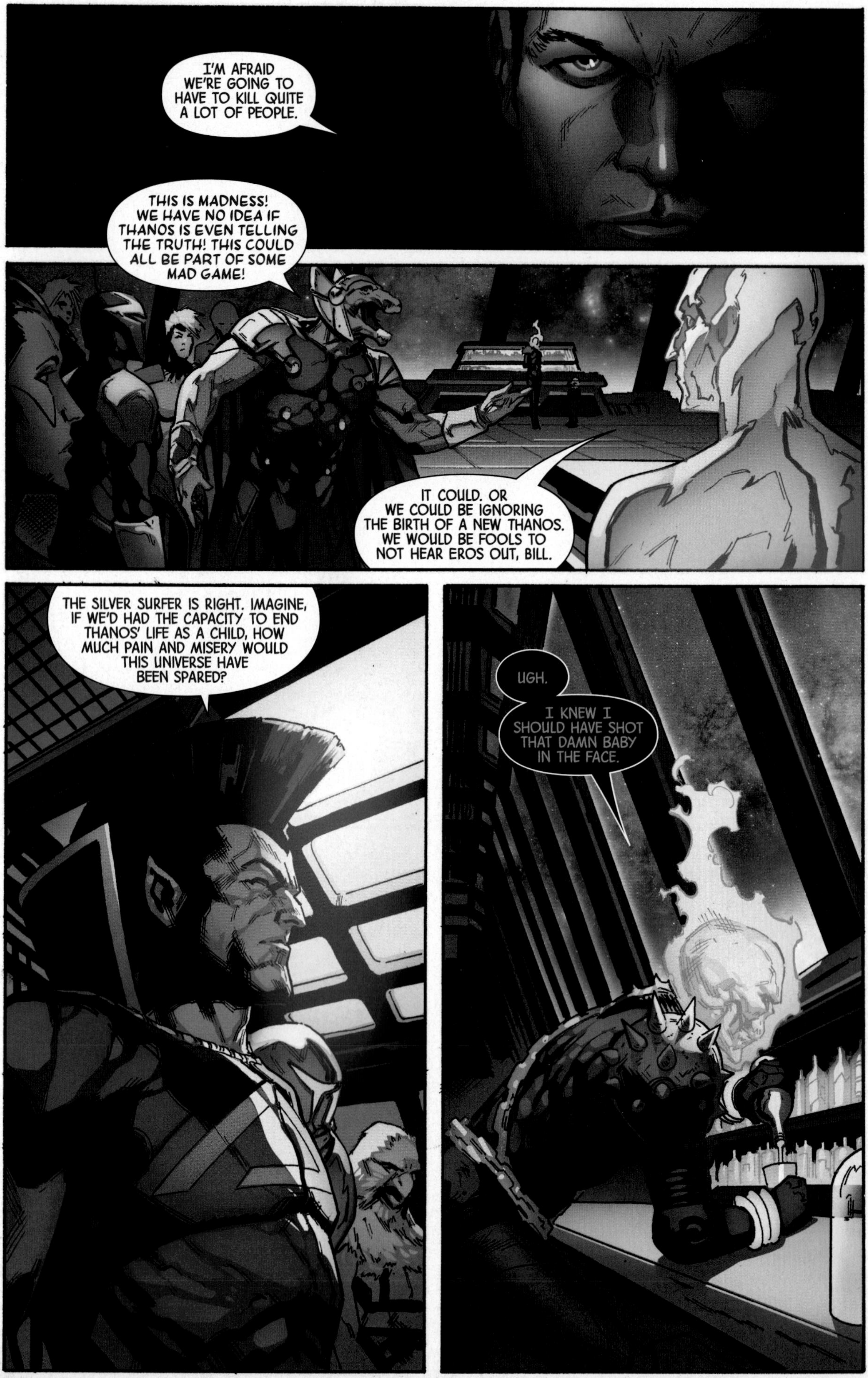
I'M AFRAID WE'RE GOING TO HAVE TO KILL QUITE A LOT OF PEOPLE.
THIS IS MADNESS! WE HAVE NO IDEA IF THANOS IS EVEN TELLING THE TRUTH! THIS COULD ALL BE PART OF SOME MAD GAME!
IT COULD. OR WE COULD BE IGNORING THE BIRTH OF A NEW THANOS. WE WOULD BE FOOLS TO NOT HEAR EROS OUT, BILL.
THE SILVER SURFER IS RIGHT. IMAGINE, IF WE'D HAD THE CAPACITY TO END THANOS' LIFE AS A CHILD, HOW MUCH PAIN AND MISERY WOULD THIS UNIVERSE HAVE BEEN SPARED?
UGH.
I KNEW I SHOULD HAVE SHOT THAT DAMN BABY IN THE FACE.

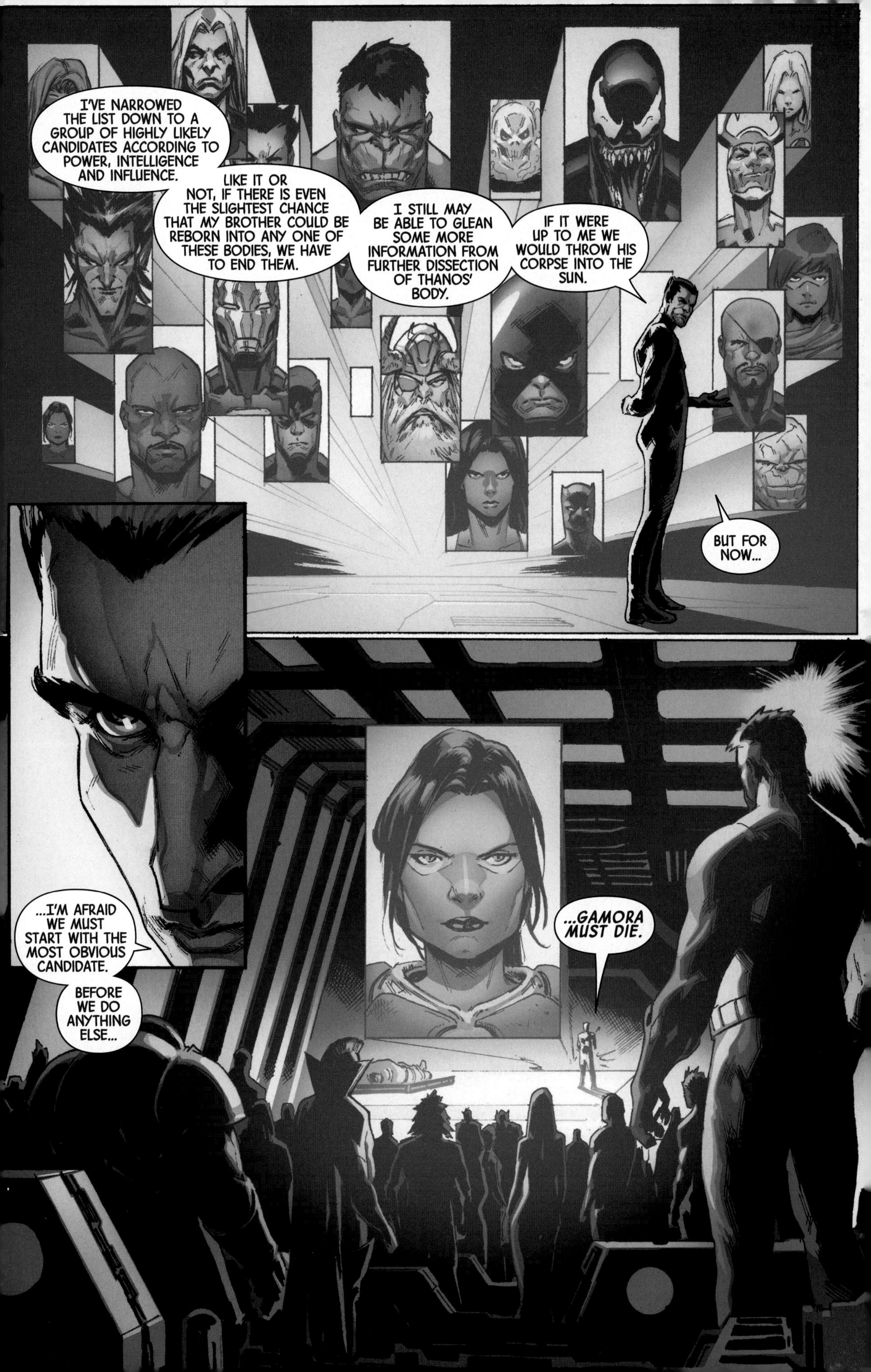
I'VE NARROWED THE LIST DOWN TO A GROUP OF HIGHLY LIKELY CANDIDATES ACCORDING TO POWER, INTELLIGENCE AND INFLUENCE.
LIKE IT OR NOT, IF THERE IS EVEN THE SLIGHTEST CHANCE THAT MY BROTHER COULD BE REBORN INTO ANY ONE OF THESE BODIES, WE HAVE TO END THEM.
I STILL MAY BE ABLE TO GLEAN SOME MORE INFORMATION FROM FURTHER DISSECTION OF THANOS' BODY.
IF IT WERE UP TO ME WE WOULD THROW HIS CORPSE INTO THE SUN.
BUT FOR NOW...
...I'M AFRAID WE MUST START WITH THE MOST OBVIOUS CANDIDATE.
BEFORE WE DO ANYTHING ELSE...
...GAMORA MUST DIE.

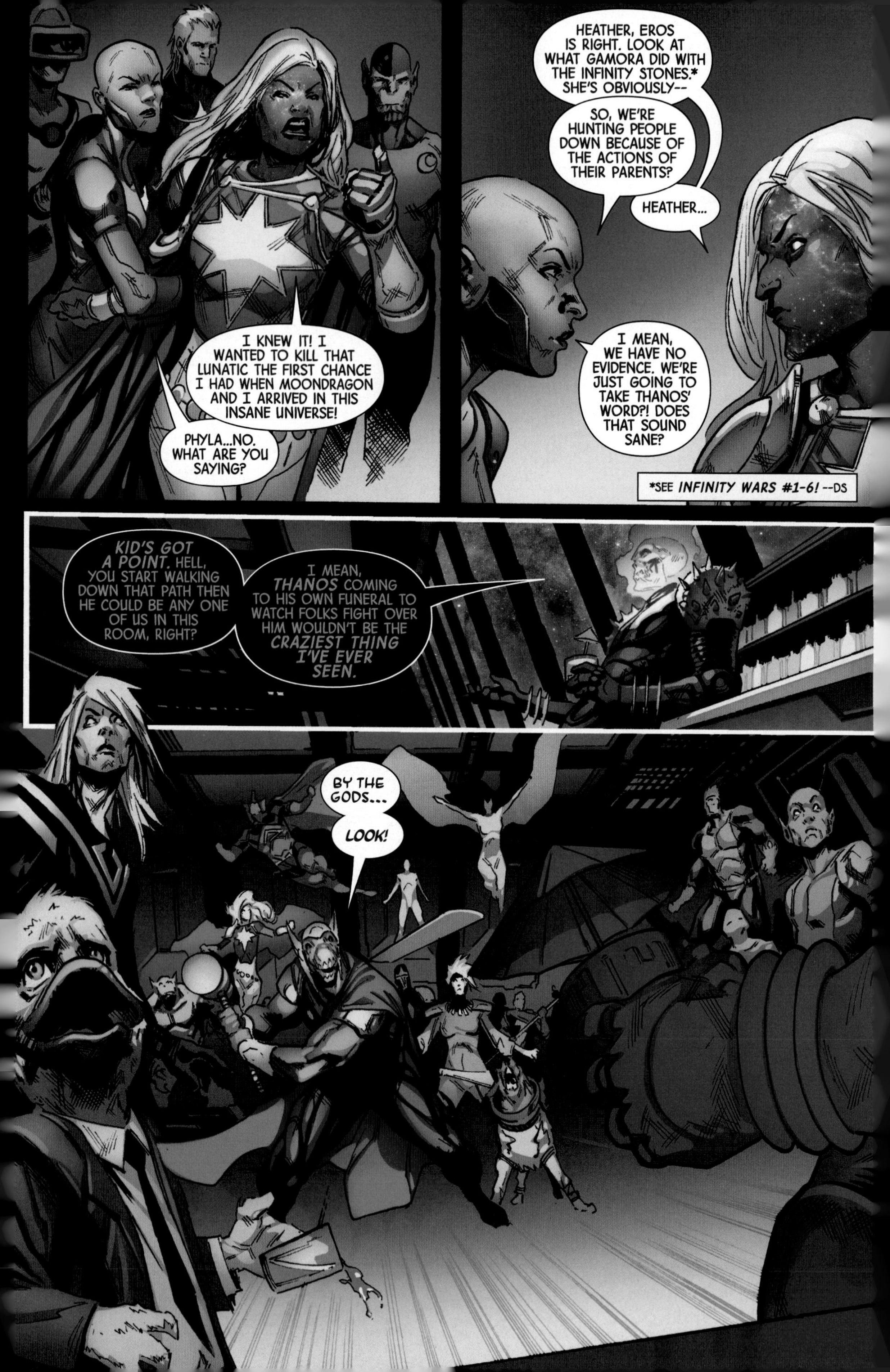
I KNEW IT! I WANTED TO KILL THAT LUNATIC THE FIRST CHANCE I HAD WHEN MOONDRAGON AND I ARRIVED IN THIS INSANE UNIVERSE!
PHYLA...NO. WHAT ARE YOU SAYING?
HEATHER, EROS IS RIGHT. LOOK AT WHAT GAMORA DID WITH THE INFINITY STONES.* SHE'S OBVIOUSLY--
SO, WE'RE HUNTING PEOPLE DOWN BECAUSE OF THE ACTIONS OF THEIR PARENTS?
HEATHER...
I MEAN, WE HAVE NO EVIDENCE. WE'RE JUST GOING TO TAKE THANOS' WORD?! DOES THAT SOUND SANE?
*SEE INFINITY WARS #1-6! --DS
KID'S GOT A POINT. HELL, YOU START WALKING DOWN THAT PATH THEN HE COULD BE ANY ONE OF US IN THIS ROOM, RIGHT?
I MEAN, THANOS COMING TO HIS OWN FUNERAL TO WATCH FOLKS FIGHT OVER HIM WOULDN'T BE THE CRAZIEST THING I'VE EVER SEEN.
BY THE GODS...
LOOK!

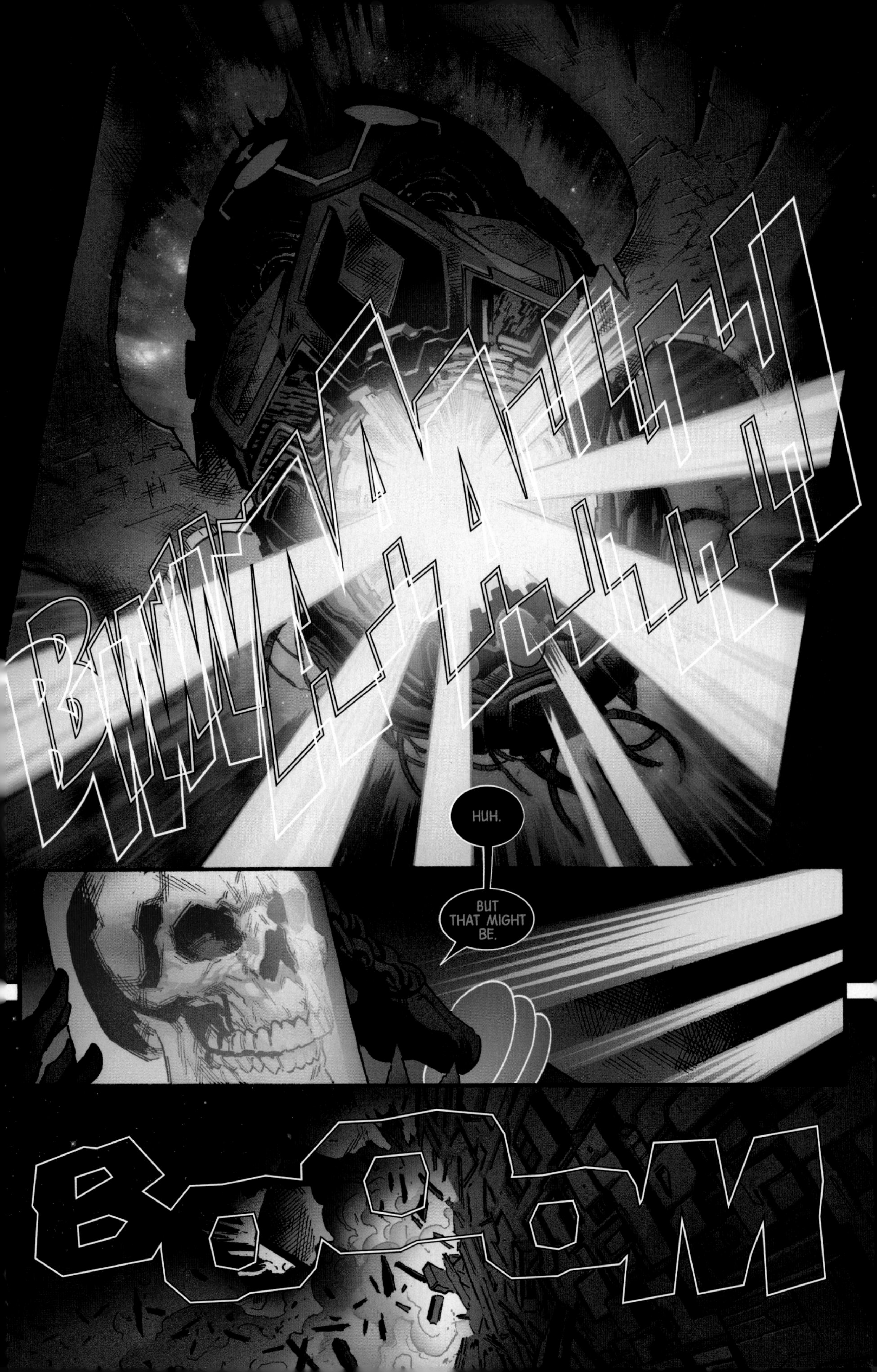
BWWAAAAAAAAAAAAHHHH
HUH.
BUT THAT MIGHT BE.
BOOOM

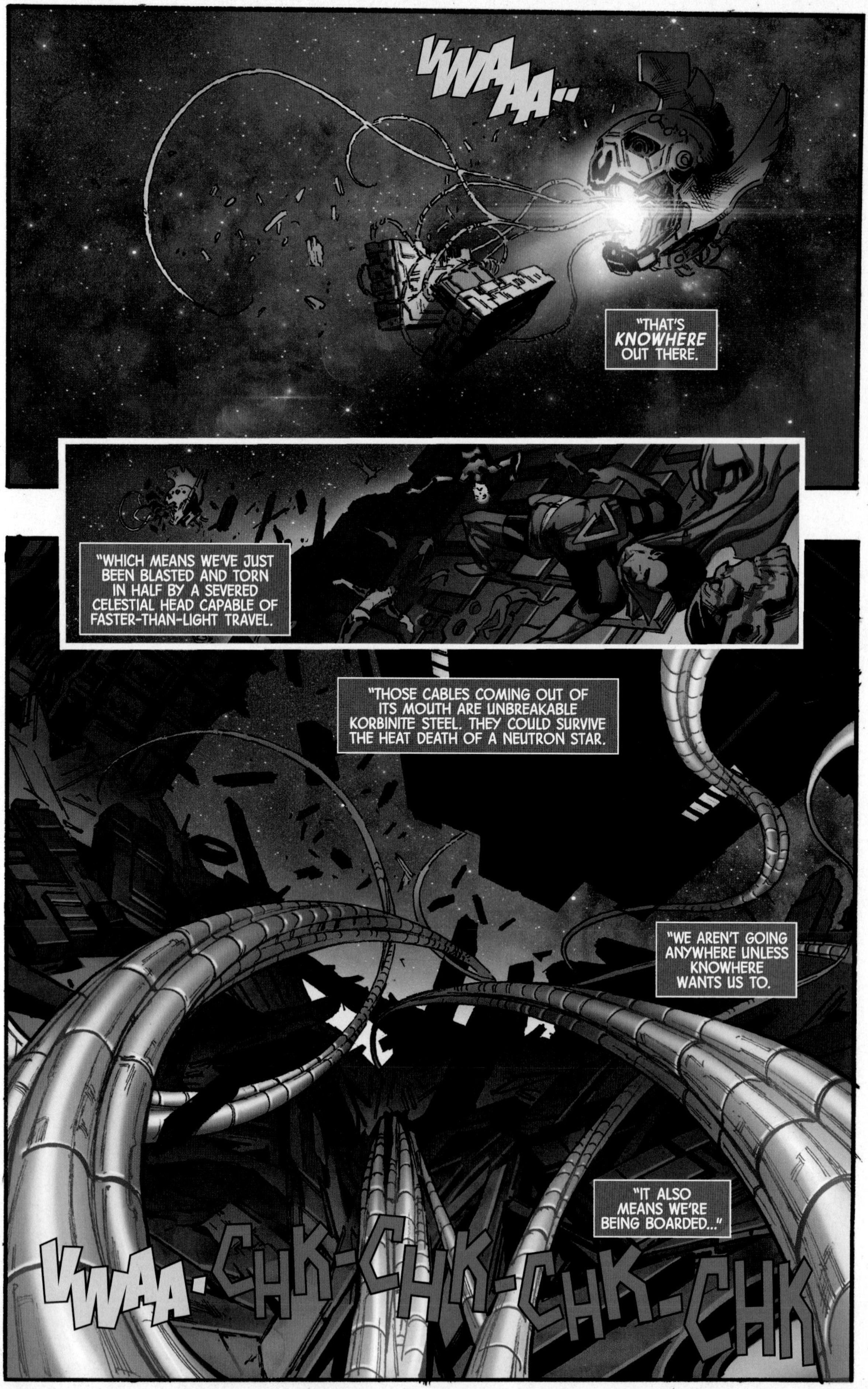
VWAAA..
"THAT'S KNOWHERE OUT THERE.
"WHICH MEANS WE'VE JUST BEEN BLASTED AND TORN IN HALF BY A SEVERED CELESTIAL HEAD CAPABLE OF FASTER-THAN-LIGHT TRAVEL.
"THOSE CABLES COMING OUT OF ITS MOUTH ARE UNBREAKABLE KORBINITE STEEL. THEY COULD SURVIVE THE HEAT DEATH OF A NEUTRON STAR.
"WE AREN'T GOING ANYWHERE UNLESS KNOWHERE WANTS US TO.
"IT ALSO MEANS WE'RE BEING BOARDED..."
VWAA-CHK-CHK-CHK-CHK

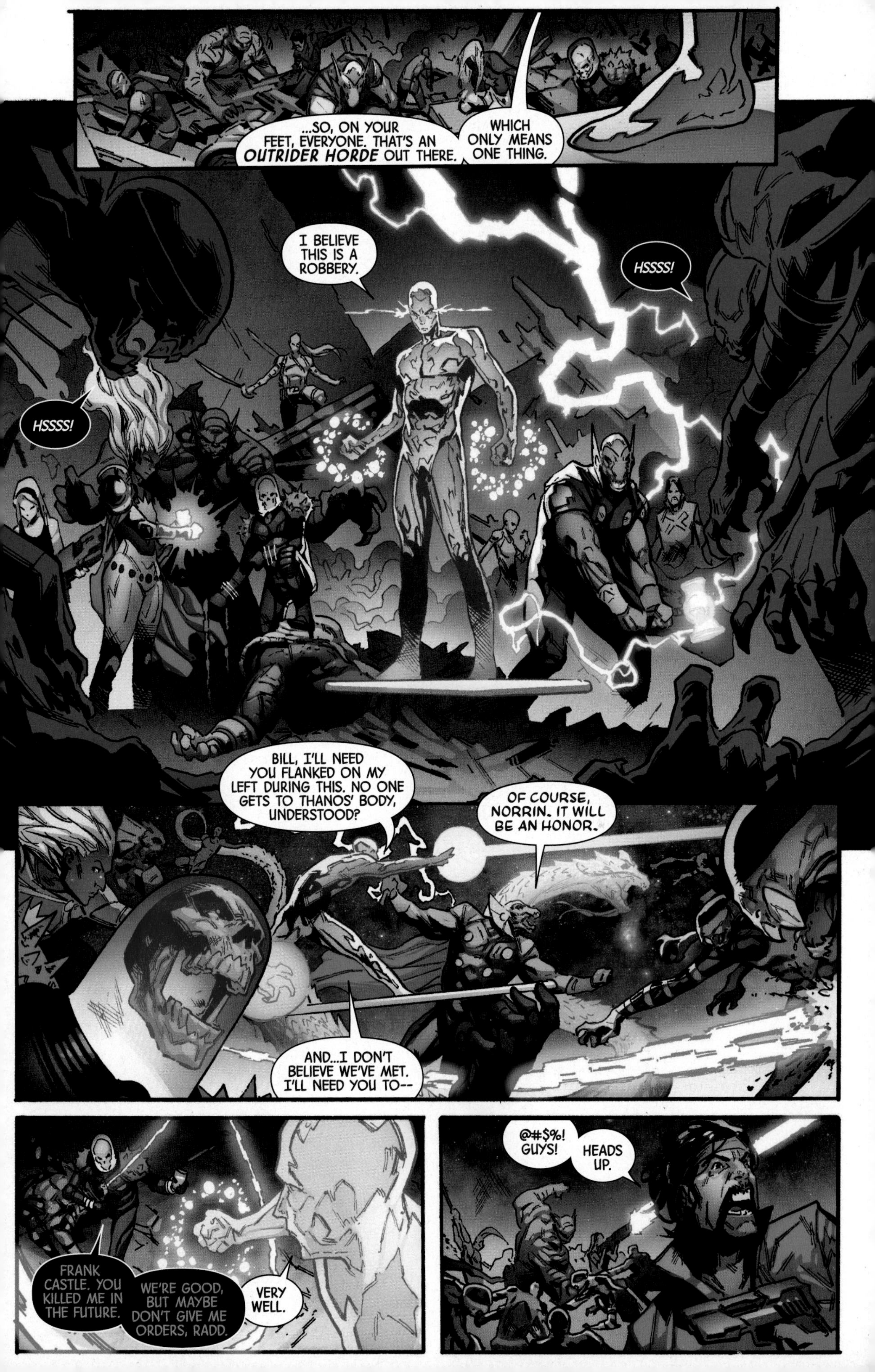
...SO, ON YOUR FEET, EVERYONE. THAT'S AN OUTRIDER HORDE OUT THERE.
WHICH ONLY MEANS ONE THING.
I BELIEVE THIS IS A ROBBERY.
HSSSS!
HSSSS!
BILL, I'LL NEED YOU FLANKED ON MY LEFT DURING THIS. NO ONE GETS TO THANOS' BODY, UNDERSTOOD?
OF COURSE, NORRIN. IT WILL BE AN HONOR.
AND...I DON'T BELIEVE WE'VE MET. I'LL NEED YOU TO--
FRANK CASTLE. YOU KILLED ME IN THE FUTURE.
WE'RE GOOD, BUT MAYBE DON'T GIVE ME ORDERS, RADD.
VERY WELL.
@#$%! GUYS!
HEADS UP.

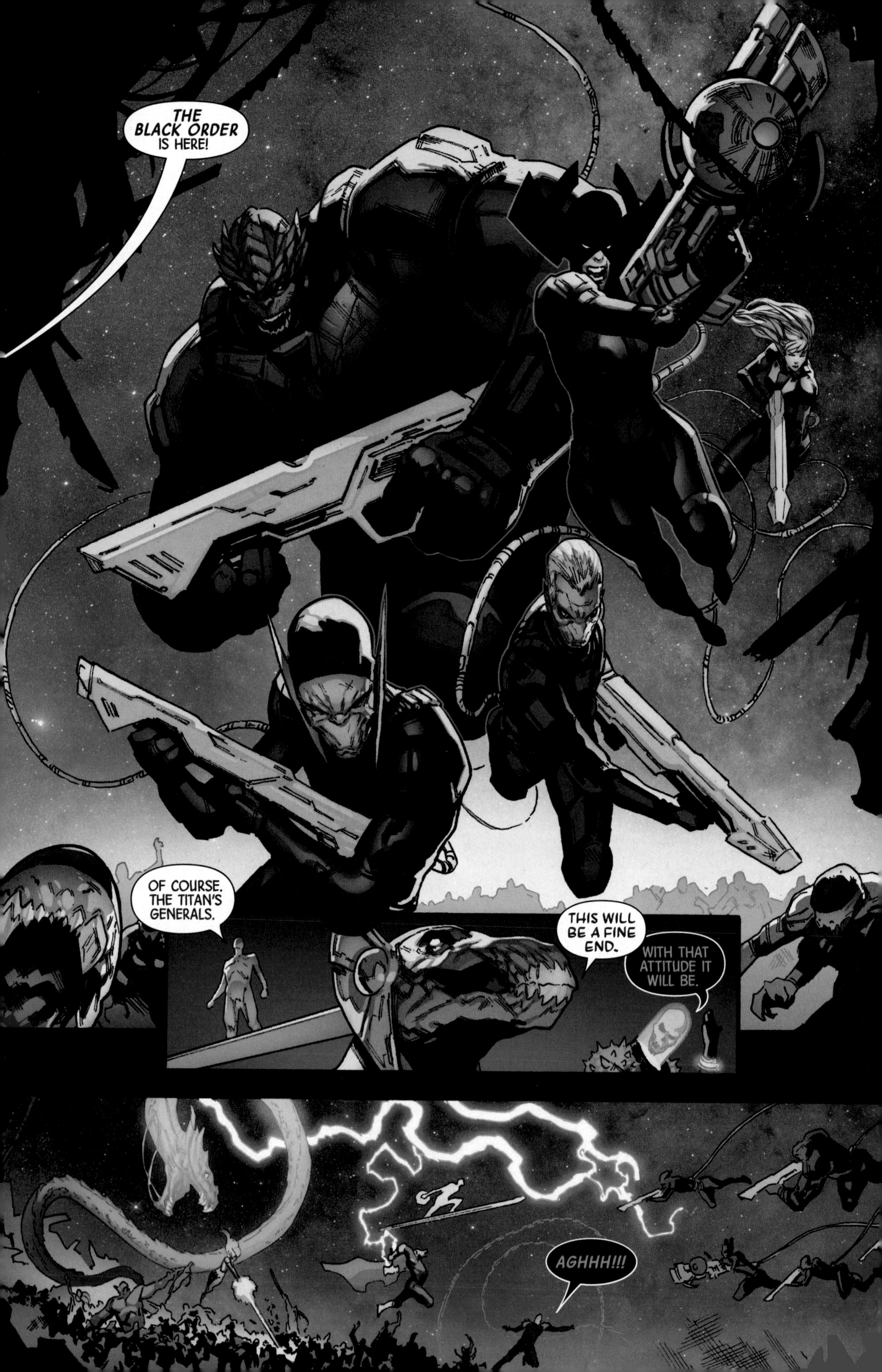
THE BLACK ORDER IS HERE!
OF COURSE. THE TITAN'S GENERALS.
THIS WILL BE A FINE END.
WITH THAT ATTITUDE IT WILL BE.
AGHHH!!!

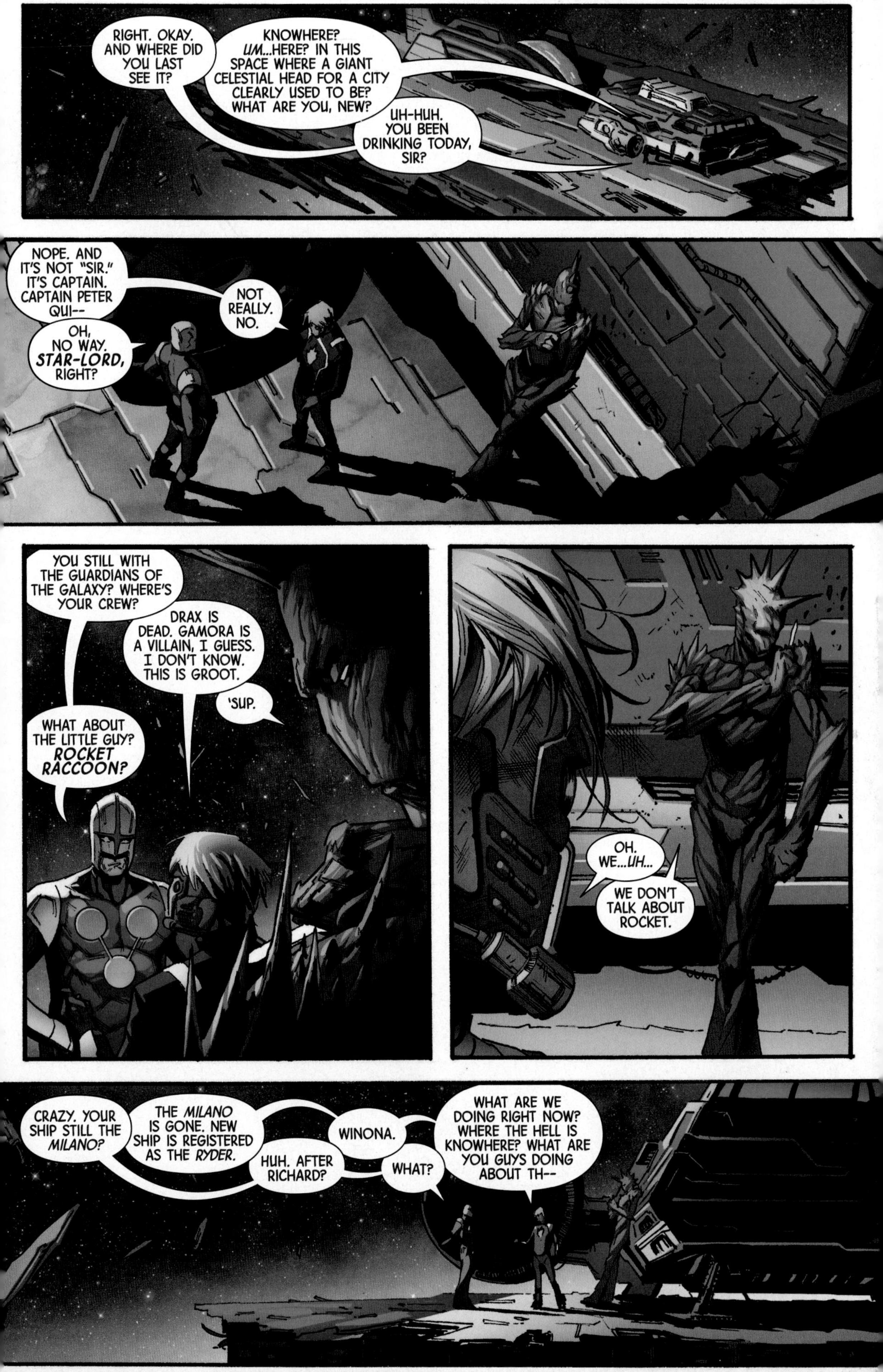
RIGHT. OKAY. AND WHERE DID YOU LAST SEE IT?
KNOWHERE? *UM*...HERE? IN THIS SPACE WHERE A GIANT CELESTIAL HEAD FOR A CITY CLEARLY USED TO BE? WHAT ARE YOU, NEW?
UH-HUH. YOU BEEN DRINKING TODAY, SIR?
NOPE. AND IT'S NOT "SIR." IT'S CAPTAIN. CAPTAIN PETER QUI--
OH, NO WAY. ***STAR-LORD,*** RIGHT?
NOT REALLY. NO.
YOU STILL WITH THE GUARDIANS OF THE GALAXY? WHERE'S YOUR CREW?
DRAX IS DEAD. GAMORA IS A VILLAIN, I GUESS. I DON'T KNOW. THIS IS GROOT.
'SUP.
WHAT ABOUT THE LITTLE GUY? ***ROCKET RACCOON?***
OH. WE...*UH*...
WE DON'T TALK ABOUT ROCKET.
CRAZY. YOUR SHIP STILL THE *MILANO?*
THE *MILANO* IS GONE. NEW SHIP IS REGISTERED AS THE *RYDER*.
HUH. AFTER RICHARD?
WINONA.
WHAT?
WHAT ARE WE DOING RIGHT NOW? WHERE THE HELL IS KNOWHERE? WHAT ARE YOU GUYS DOING ABOUT TH--

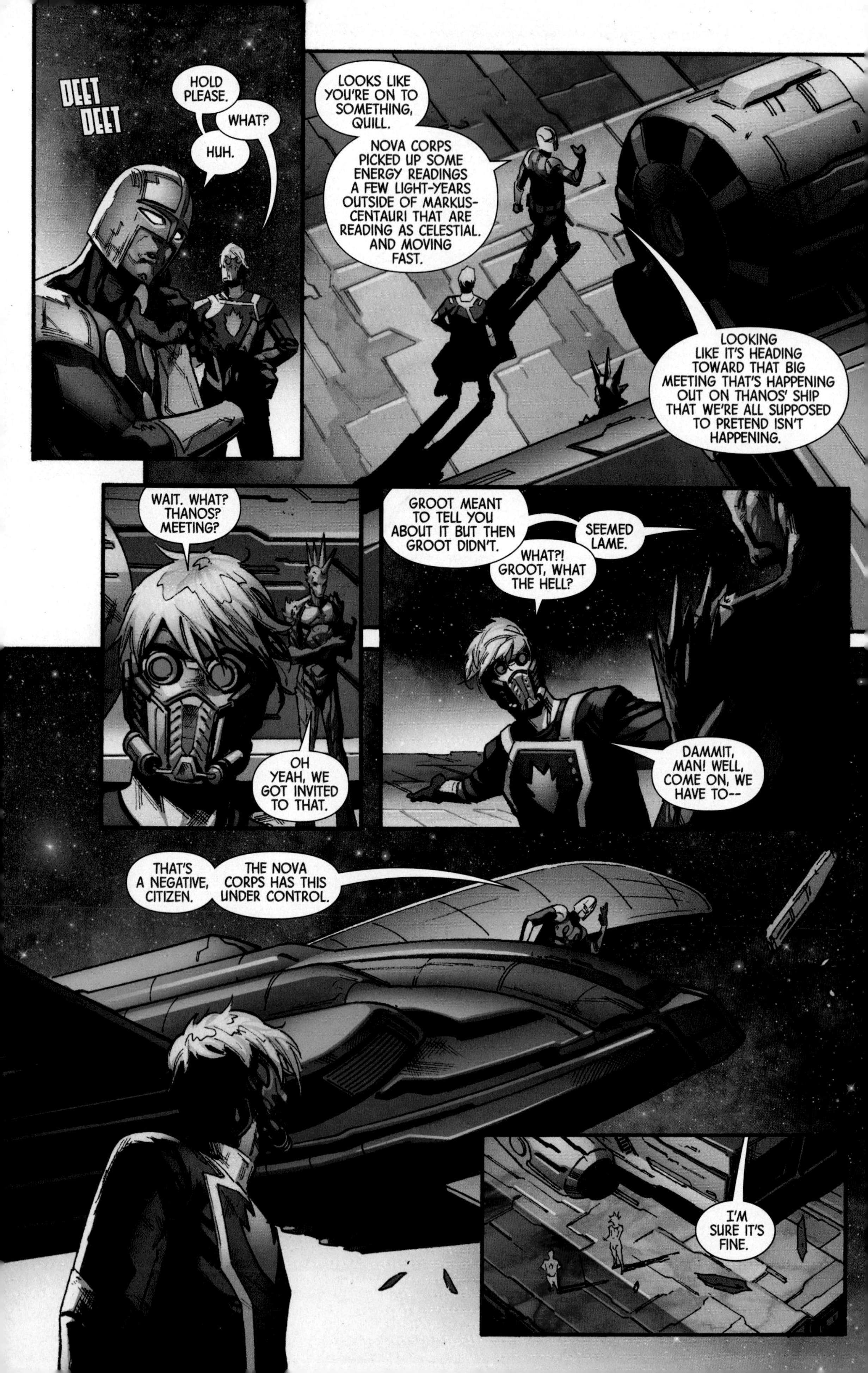
DEET DEET
HOLD PLEASE.
WHAT?
HUH.
LOOKS LIKE YOU'RE ON TO SOMETHING, QUILL.
NOVA CORPS PICKED UP SOME ENERGY READINGS A FEW LIGHT-YEARS OUTSIDE OF MARKUS-CENTAURI THAT ARE READING AS CELESTIAL. AND MOVING FAST.
LOOKING LIKE IT'S HEADING TOWARD THAT BIG MEETING THAT'S HAPPENING OUT ON THANOS' SHIP THAT WE'RE ALL SUPPOSED TO PRETEND ISN'T HAPPENING.
WAIT. WHAT? THANOS? MEETING?
OH YEAH, WE GOT INVITED TO THAT.
GROOT MEANT TO TELL YOU ABOUT IT BUT THEN GROOT DIDN'T.
SEEMED LAME.
WHAT?! GROOT, WHAT THE HELL?
DAMMIT, MAN! WELL, COME ON, WE HAVE TO--
THAT'S A NEGATIVE, CITIZEN.
THE NOVA CORPS HAS THIS UNDER CONTROL.
I'M SURE IT'S FINE.

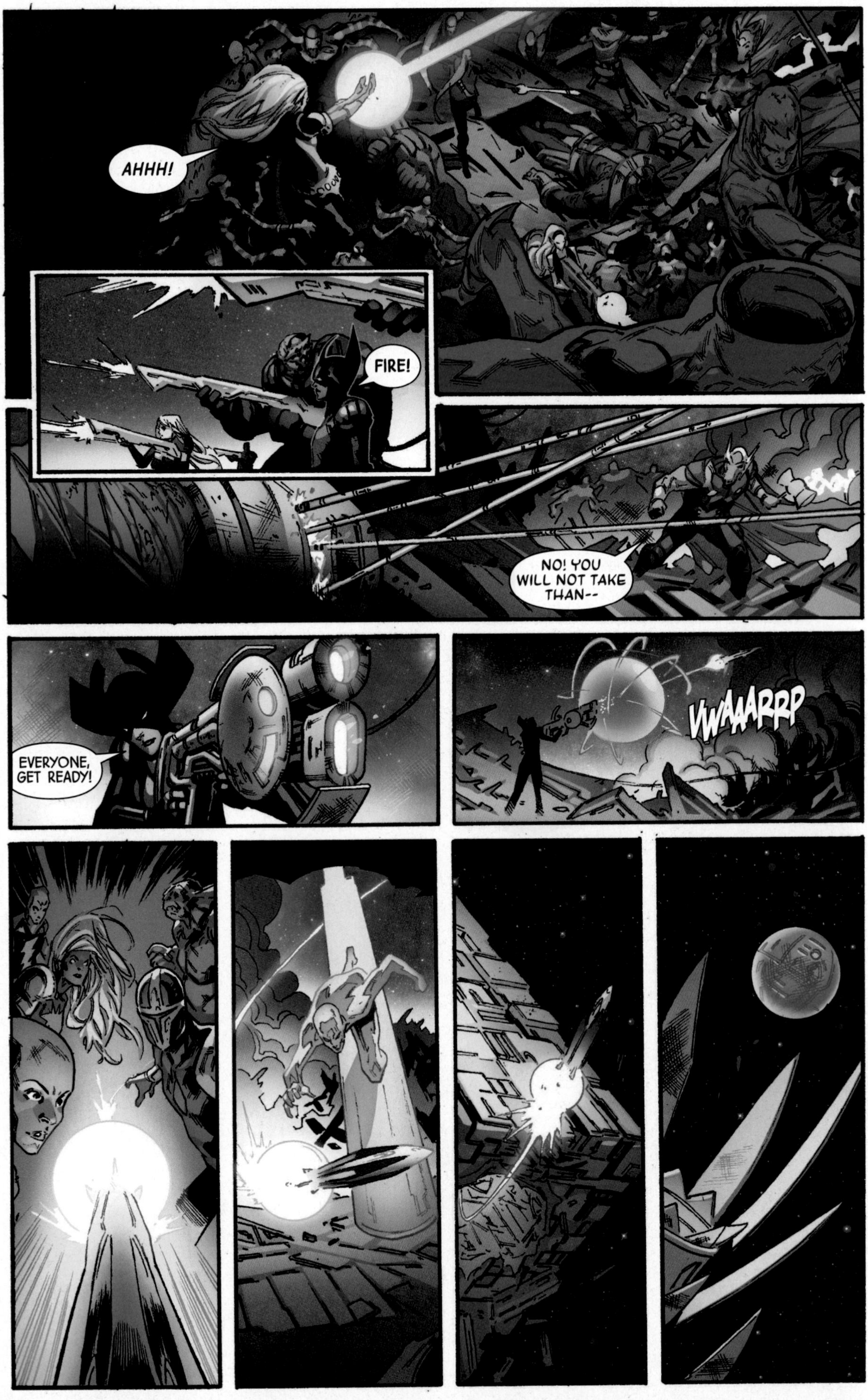
AHHH!
FIRE!
NO! YOU WILL NOT TAKE THAN--
EVERYONE, GET READY!
VWAAARRP

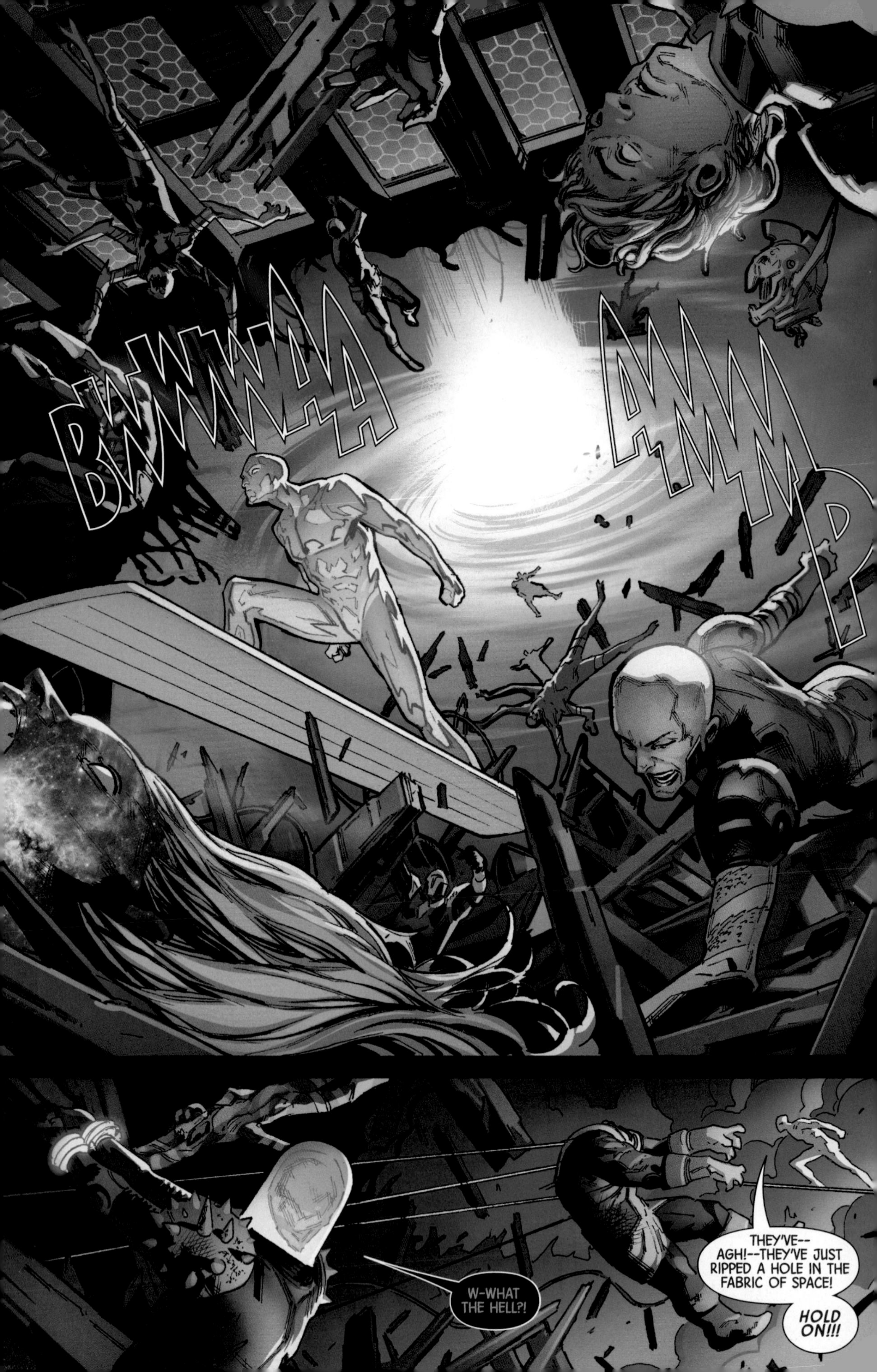
BWWWAAAAAMP
W-WHAT THE HELL?!
THEY'VE-- AGH!--THEY'VE JUST RIPPED A HOLE IN THE FABRIC OF SPACE!
HOLD ON!!!

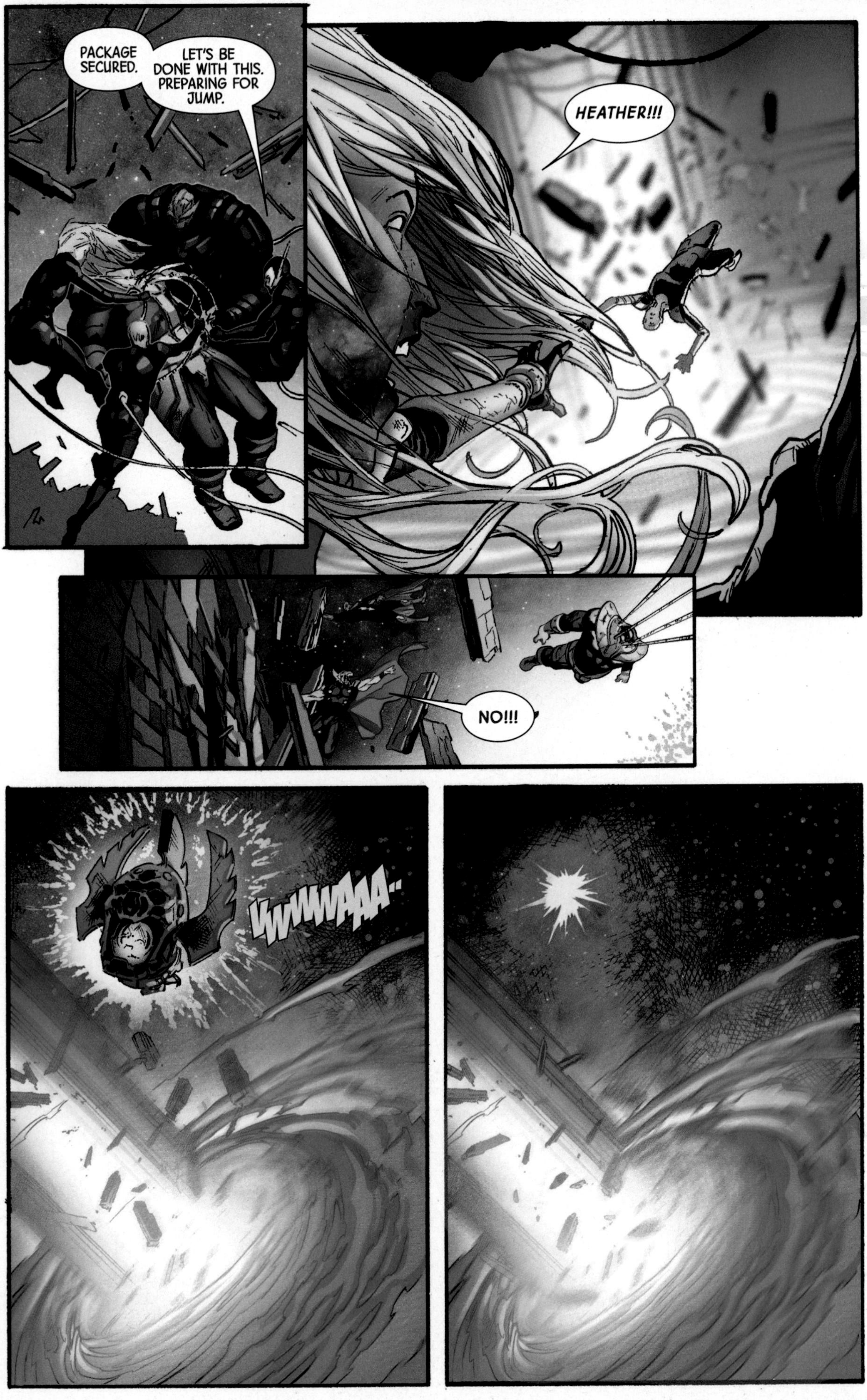
PACKAGE SECURED.
LET'S BE DONE WITH THIS. PREPARING FOR JUMP.
HEATHER!!!
NO!!!
VWWWAAA--

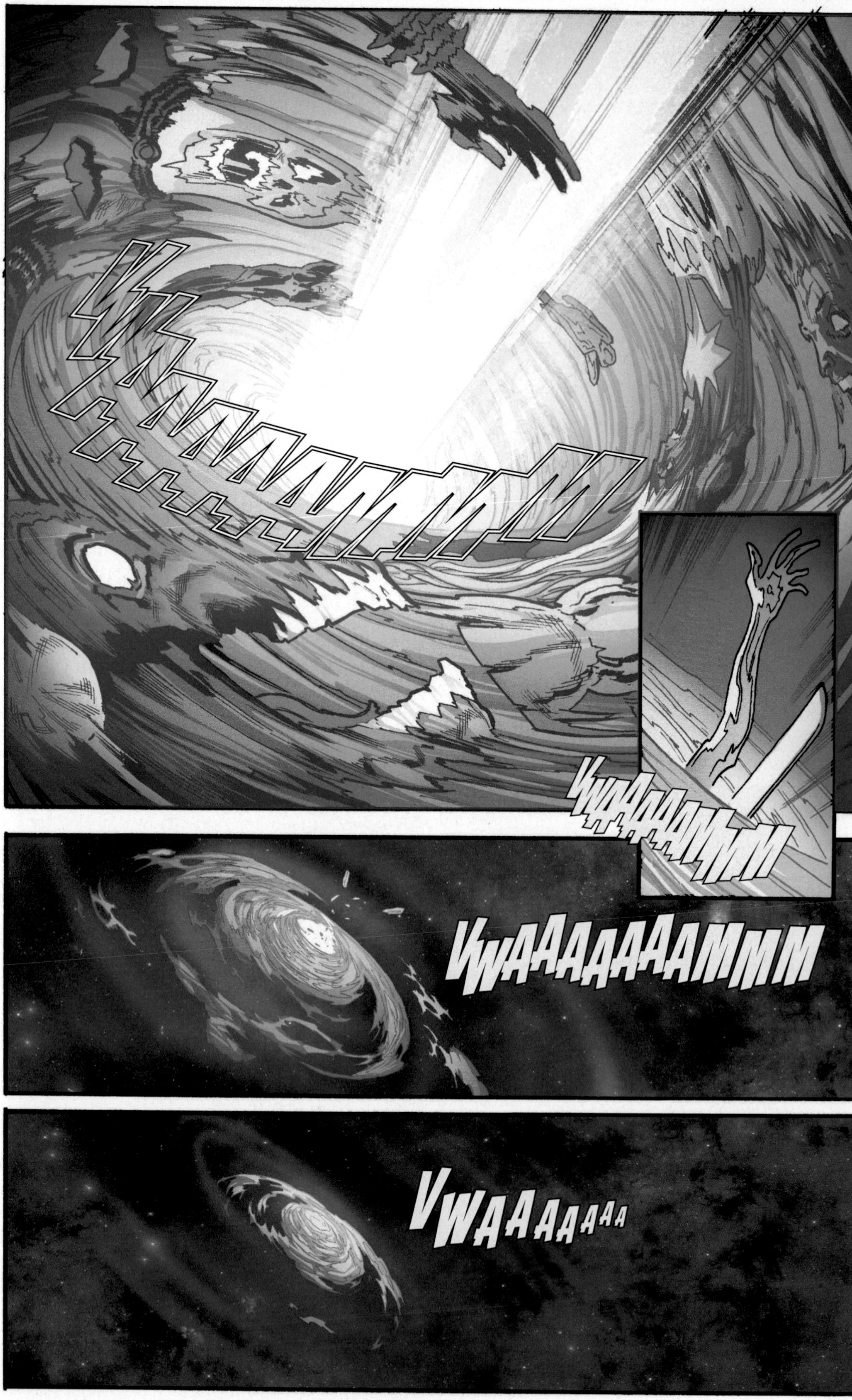
VWAAAAAMMM
VWAAAAMMM
VWAAAAAAAMMM
VWAAAAAA

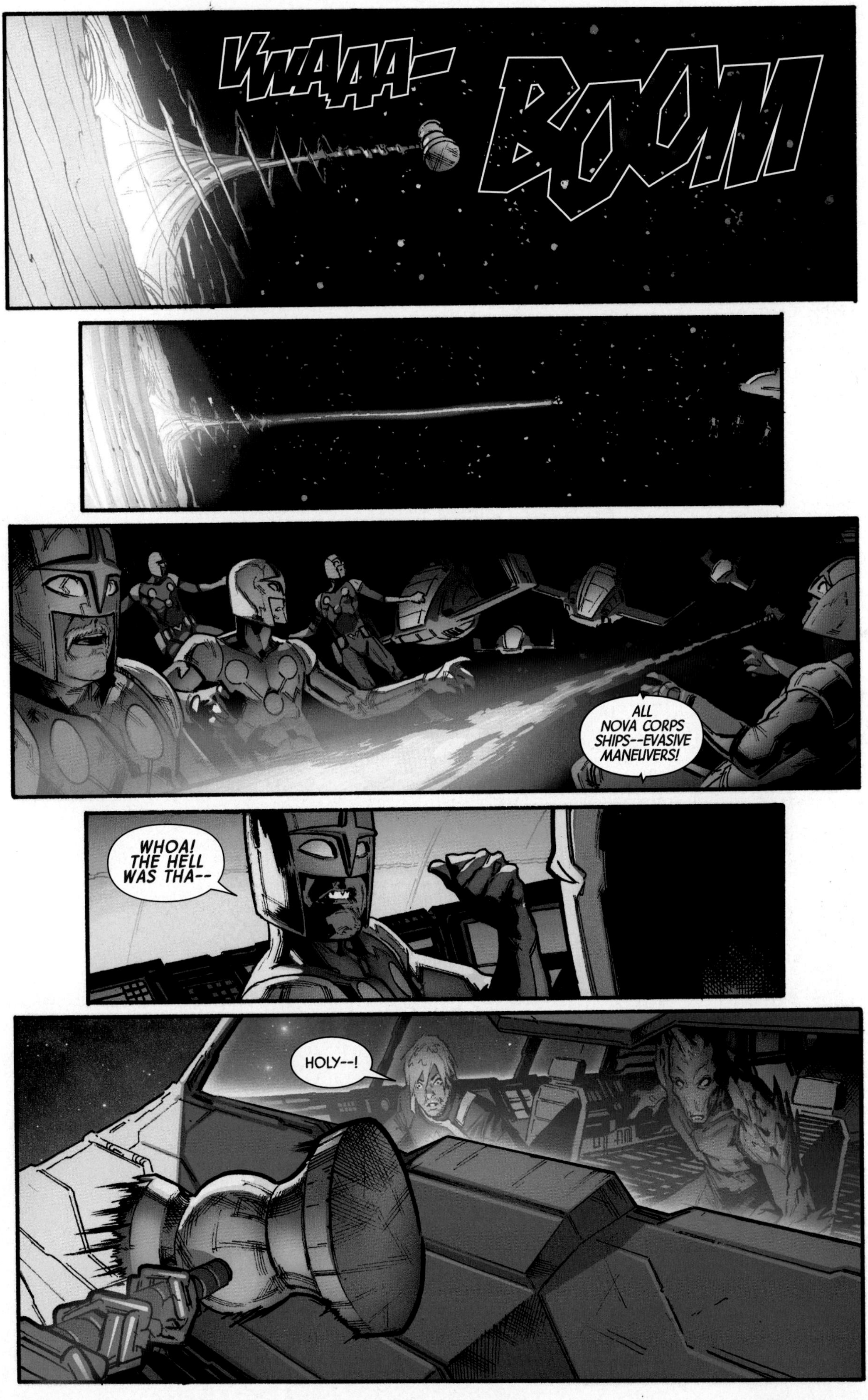

KWAAA-
BOOM
ALL NOVA CORPS SHIPS--EVASIVE MANEUVERS!
WHOA! THE HELL WAS THA--
HOLY--!

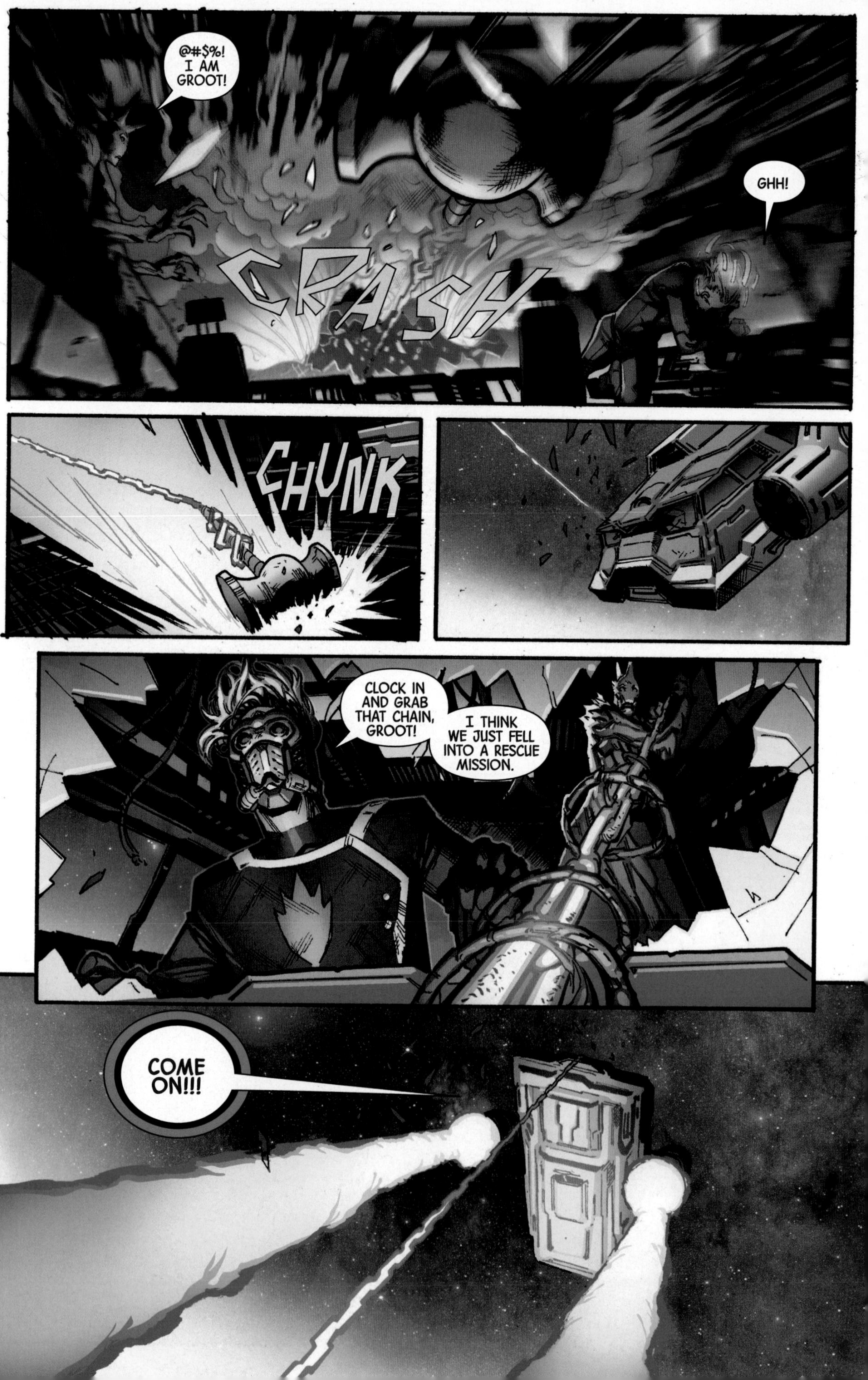
@#$%! I AM GROOT!
CRASH
GHH!
CHUNK
CLOCK IN AND GRAB THAT CHAIN, GROOT!
I THINK WE JUST FELL INTO A RESCUE MISSION.
COME ON!!!

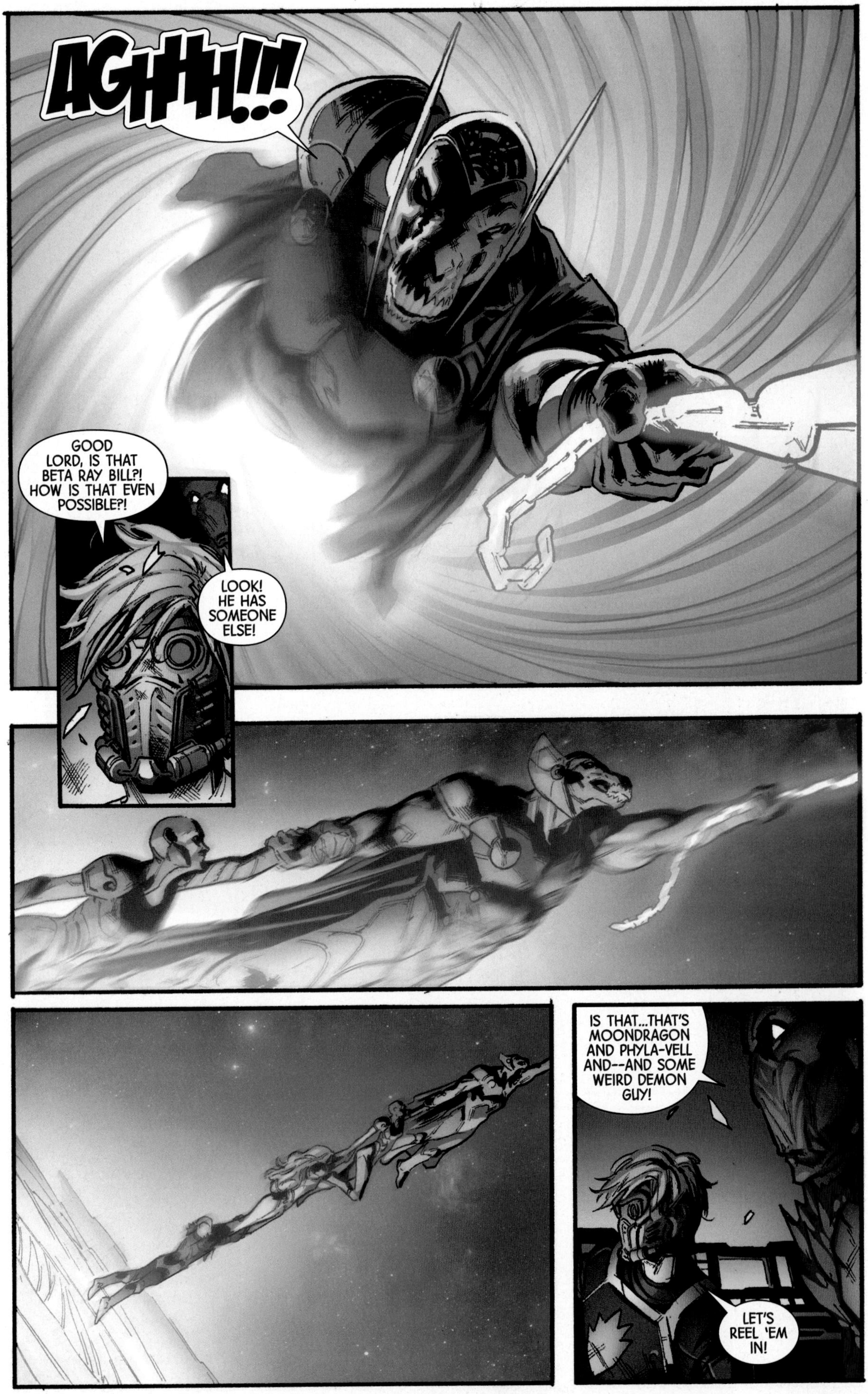
AGHHH!!!
GOOD LORD, IS THAT BETA RAY BILL?! HOW IS THAT EVEN POSSIBLE?!
LOOK! HE HAS SOMEONE ELSE!
IS THAT...THAT'S MOONDRAGON AND PHYLA-VELL AND--AND SOME WEIRD DEMON GUY!
LET'S REEL 'EM IN!

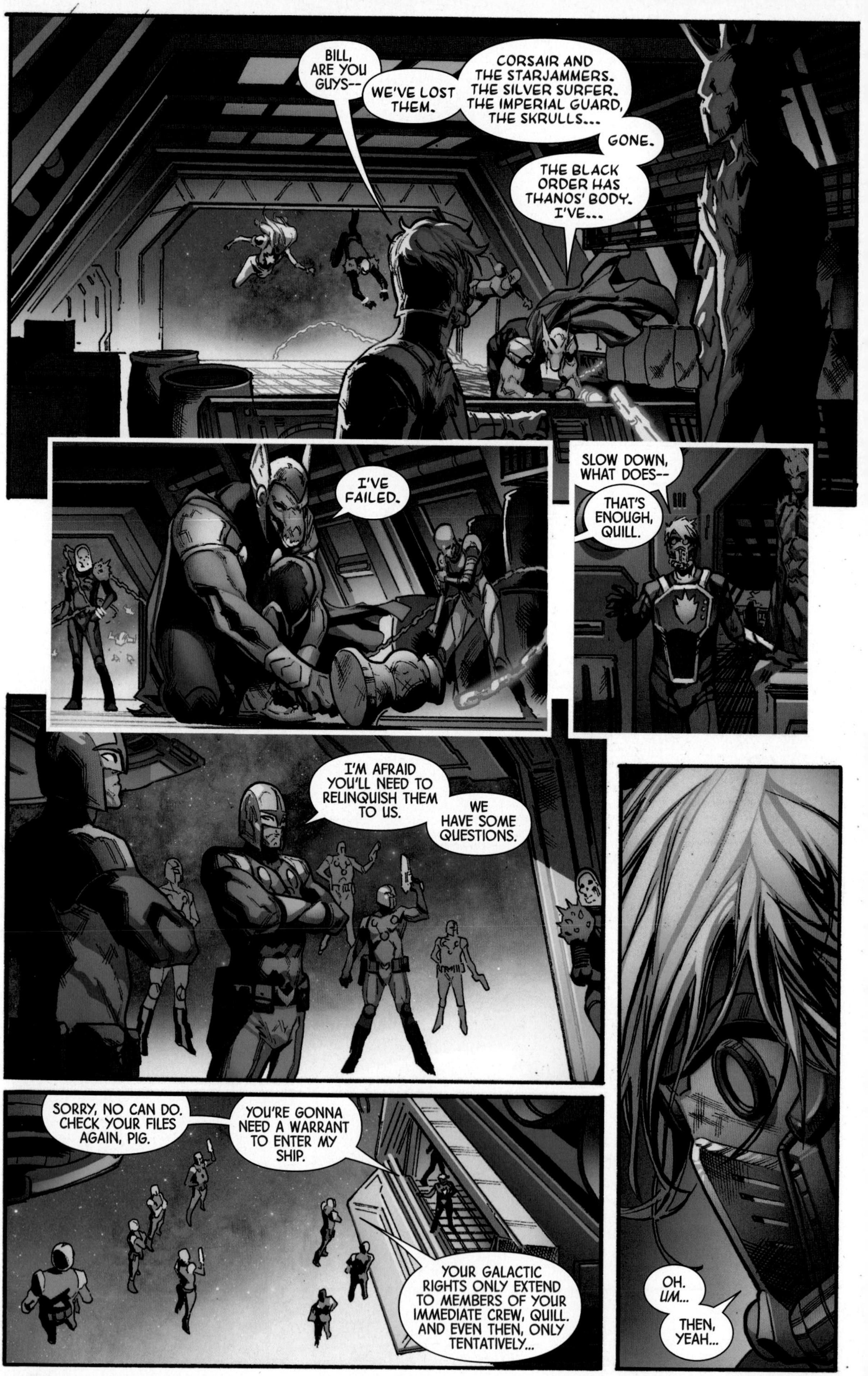
BILL, ARE YOU GUYS--
WE'VE LOST THEM.
CORSAIR AND THE STARJAMMERS. THE SILVER SURFER. THE IMPERIAL GUARD, THE SKRULLS...
GONE.
THE BLACK ORDER HAS THANOS' BODY. I'VE...
I'VE FAILED.
SLOW DOWN, WHAT DOES--
THAT'S ENOUGH, QUILL.
I'M AFRAID YOU'LL NEED TO RELINQUISH THEM TO US.
WE HAVE SOME QUESTIONS.
SORRY, NO CAN DO. CHECK YOUR FILES AGAIN, PIG.
YOU'RE GONNA NEED A WARRANT TO ENTER MY SHIP.
YOUR GALACTIC RIGHTS ONLY EXTEND TO MEMBERS OF YOUR IMMEDIATE CREW, QUILL. AND EVEN THEN, ONLY TENTATIVELY...
OH. UM...
THEN, YEAH...

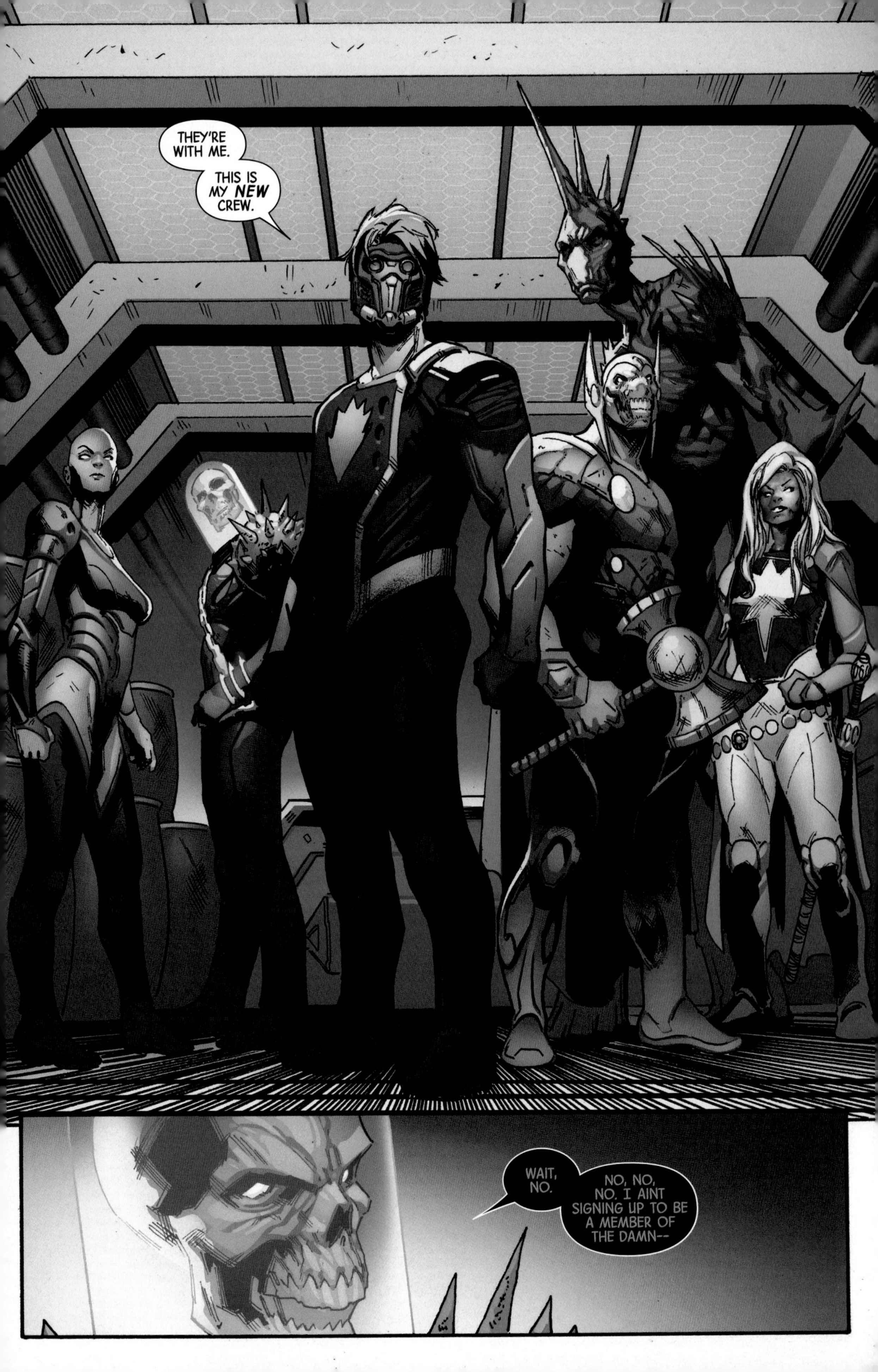
THEY'RE WITH ME.
THIS IS MY NEW CREW.
WAIT, NO.
NO, NO, NO. I AINT SIGNING UP TO BE A MEMBER OF THE DAMN--

GUAR
OF THE

DIANS
GALAXY

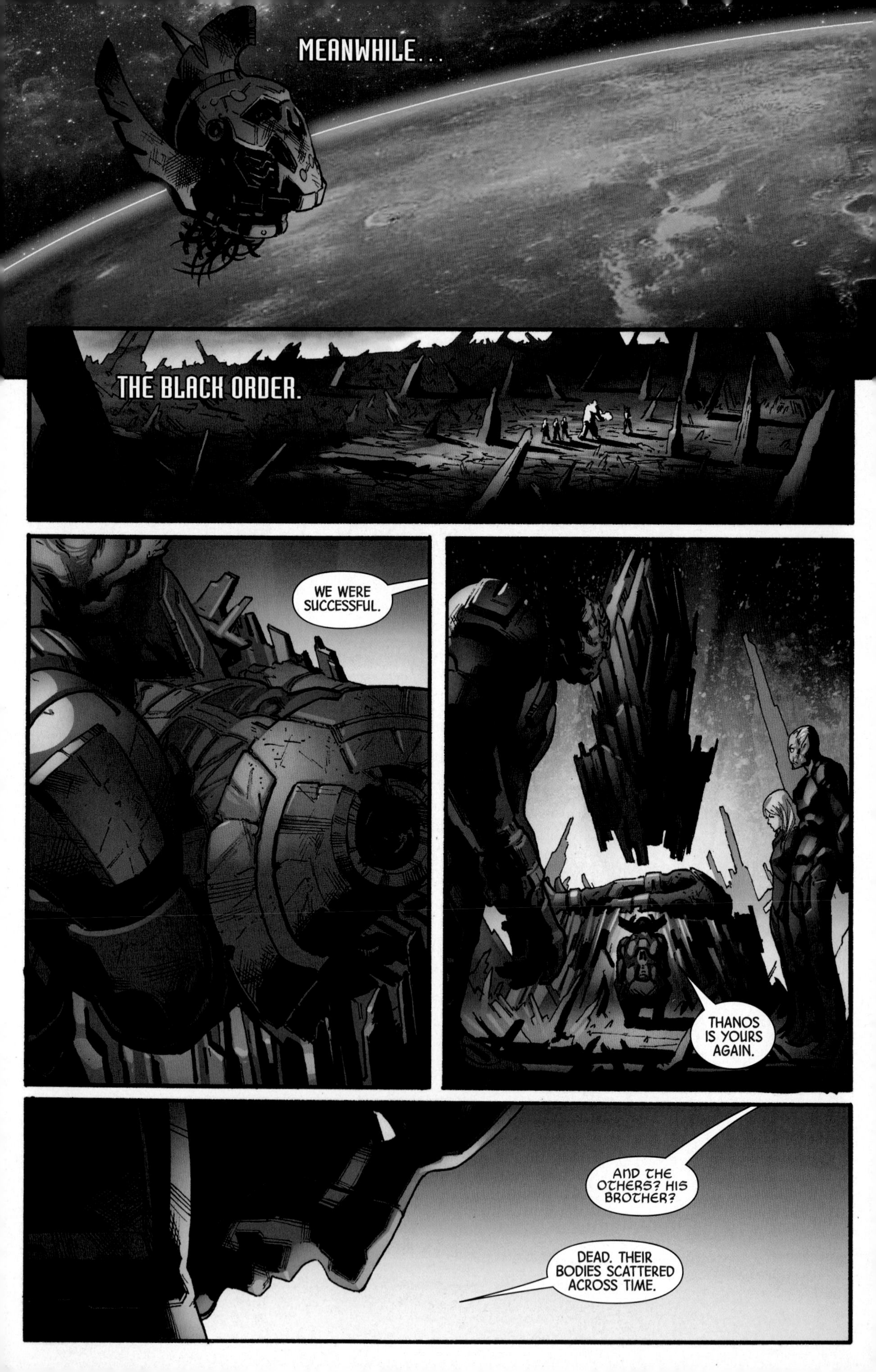
MEANWHILE...
THE BLACK ORDER.
WE WERE SUCCESSFUL.
THANOS IS YOURS AGAIN.
AND THE OTHERS? HIS BROTHER?
DEAD. THEIR BODIES SCATTERED ACROSS TIME.

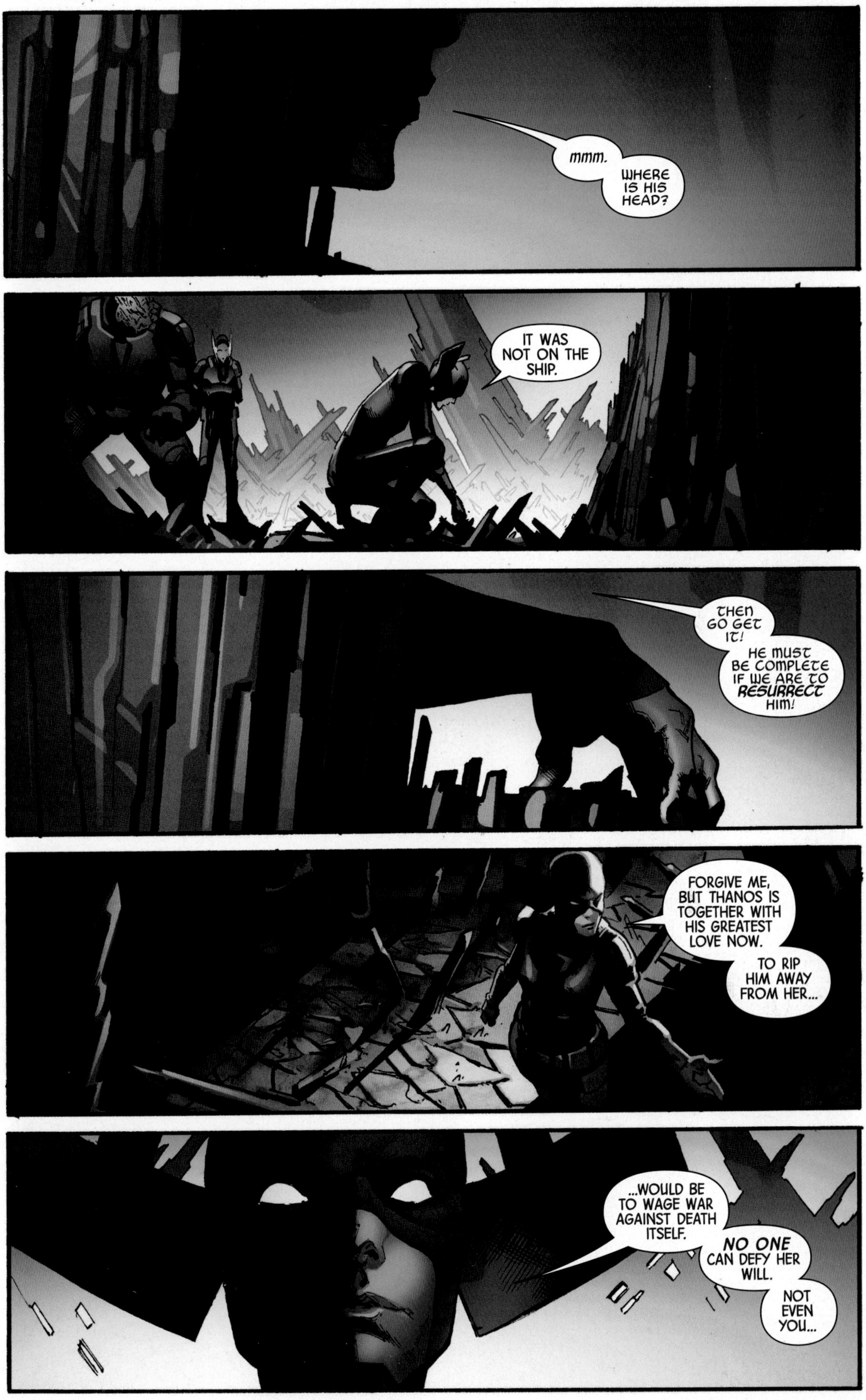
mmm.
WHERE IS HIS HEAD?
IT WAS NOT ON THE SHIP.
THEN GO GET IT!
HE MUST BE COMPLETE IF WE ARE TO RESURRECT HIM!
FORGIVE ME, BUT THANOS IS TOGETHER WITH HIS GREATEST LOVE NOW.
TO RIP HIM AWAY FROM HER...
...WOULD BE TO WAGE WAR AGAINST DEATH ITSELF.
NO ONE CAN DEFY HER WILL.
NOT EVEN YOU...

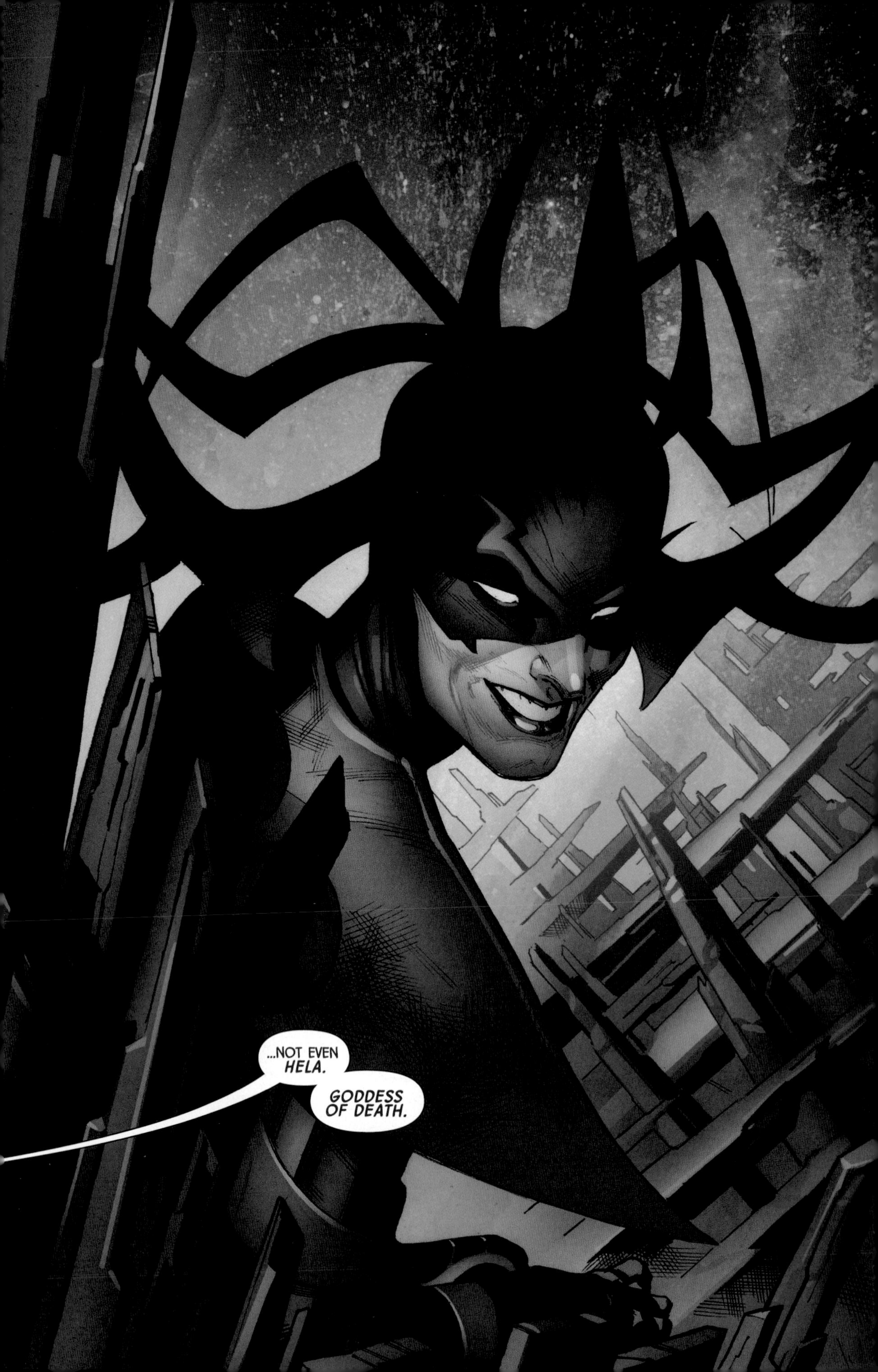
...NOT EVEN HELA.
GODDESS OF DEATH.

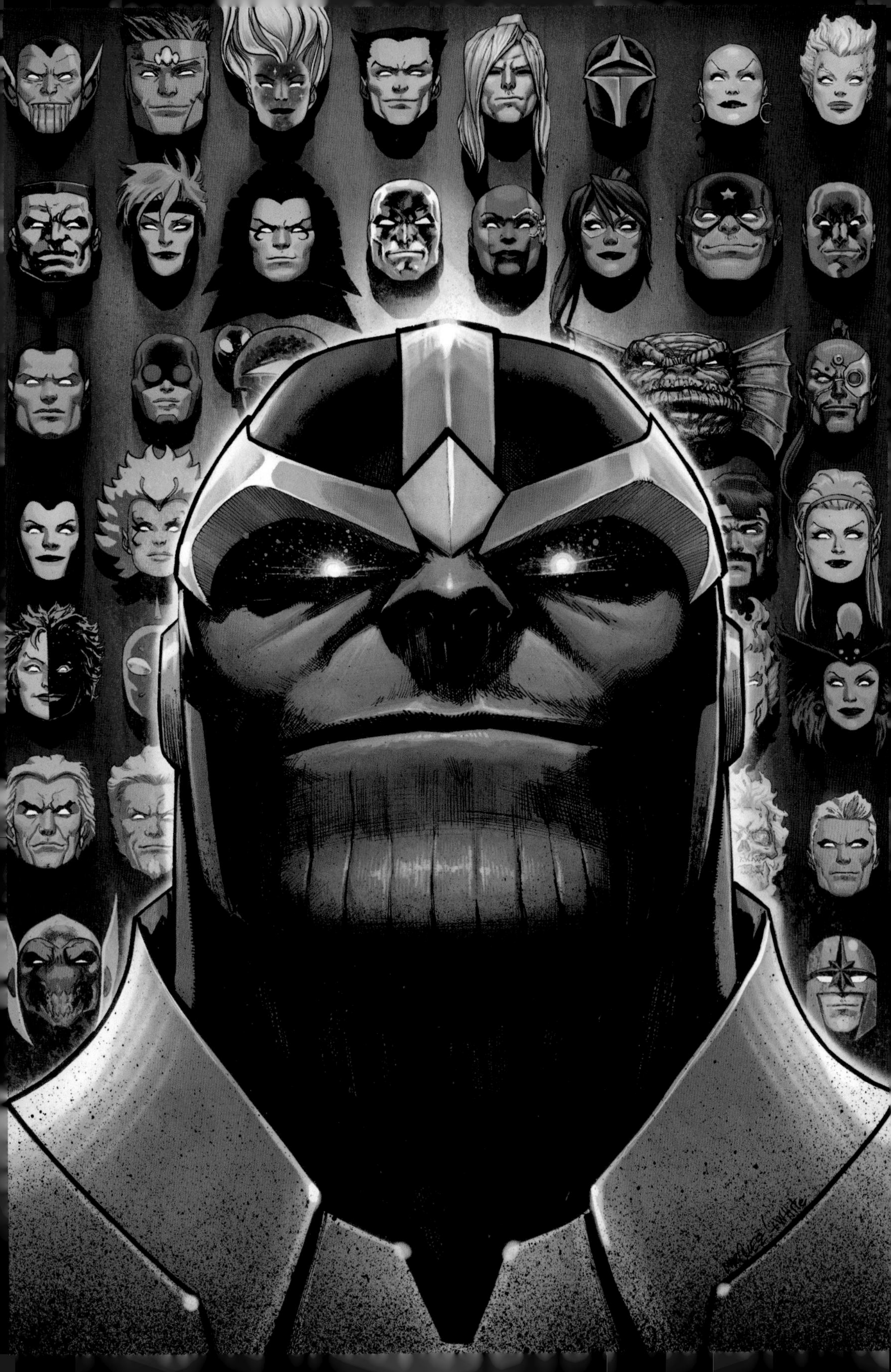

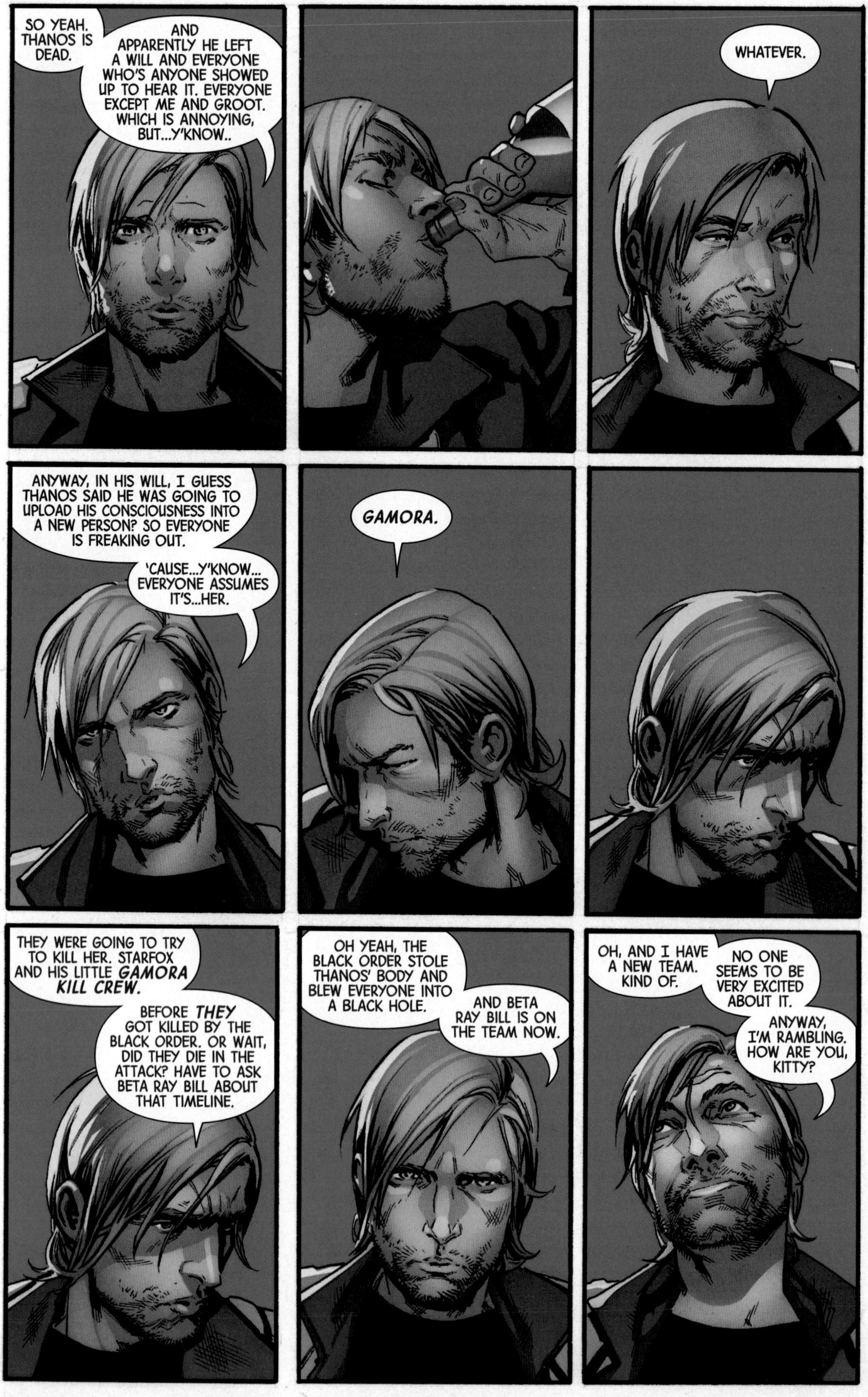
SO YEAH. THANOS IS DEAD.
AND APPARENTLY HE LEFT A WILL AND EVERYONE WHO'S ANYONE SHOWED UP TO HEAR IT. EVERYONE EXCEPT ME AND GROOT. WHICH IS ANNOYING, BUT...Y'KNOW..
WHATEVER.
ANYWAY, IN HIS WILL, I GUESS THANOS SAID HE WAS GOING TO UPLOAD HIS CONSCIOUSNESS INTO A NEW PERSON? SO EVERYONE IS FREAKING OUT.
'CAUSE...Y'KNOW... EVERYONE ASSUMES IT'S...HER.
GAMORA.
THEY WERE GOING TO TRY TO KILL HER. STARFOX AND HIS LITTLE GAMORA KILL CREW.
BEFORE THEY GOT KILLED BY THE BLACK ORDER. OR WAIT, DID THEY DIE IN THE ATTACK? HAVE TO ASK BETA RAY BILL ABOUT THAT TIMELINE.
OH YEAH, THE BLACK ORDER STOLE THANOS' BODY AND BLEW EVERYONE INTO A BLACK HOLE.
AND BETA RAY BILL IS ON THE TEAM NOW.
OH, AND I HAVE A NEW TEAM. KIND OF.
NO ONE SEEMS TO BE VERY EXCITED ABOUT IT.
ANYWAY, I'M RAMBLING. HOW ARE YOU, KITTY?

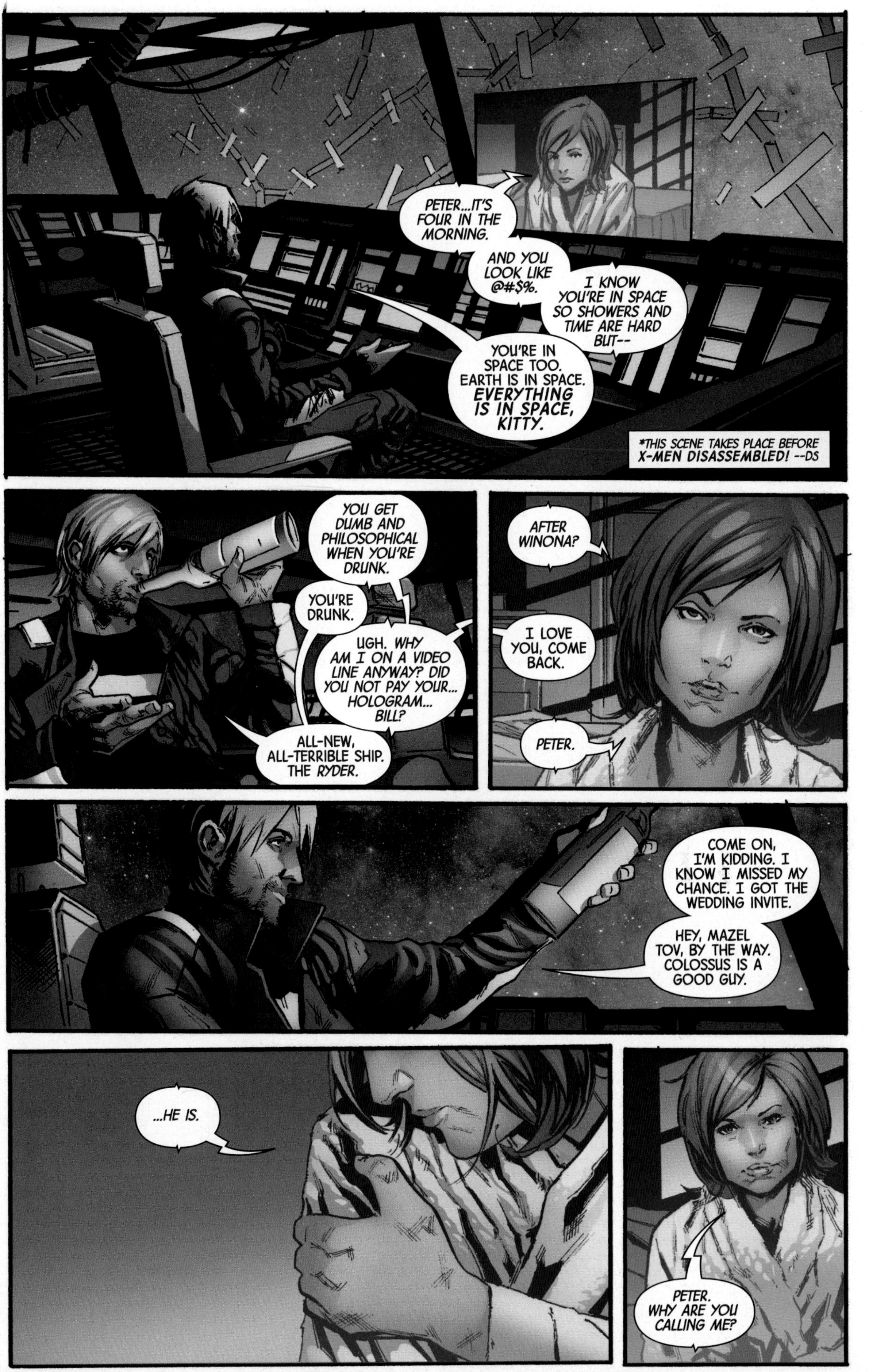
PETER...IT'S FOUR IN THE MORNING.
AND YOU LOOK LIKE @#$%.
I KNOW YOU'RE IN SPACE SO SHOWERS AND TIME ARE HARD BUT--
YOU'RE IN SPACE TOO. EARTH IS IN SPACE. EVERYTHING IS IN SPACE, KITTY.
*THIS SCENE TAKES PLACE BEFORE X-MEN DISASSEMBLED! --DS
YOU GET DUMB AND PHILOSOPHICAL WHEN YOU'RE DRUNK.
YOU'RE DRUNK.
UGH. WHY AM I ON A VIDEO LINE ANYWAY? DID YOU NOT PAY YOUR... HOLOGRAM... BILL?
ALL-NEW, ALL-TERRIBLE SHIP. THE RYDER.
AFTER WINONA?
I LOVE YOU, COME BACK.
PETER.
COME ON, I'M KIDDING. I KNOW I MISSED MY CHANCE. I GOT THE WEDDING INVITE.
HEY, MAZEL TOV, BY THE WAY. COLOSSUS IS A GOOD GUY.
...HE IS.
PETER. WHY ARE YOU CALLING ME?

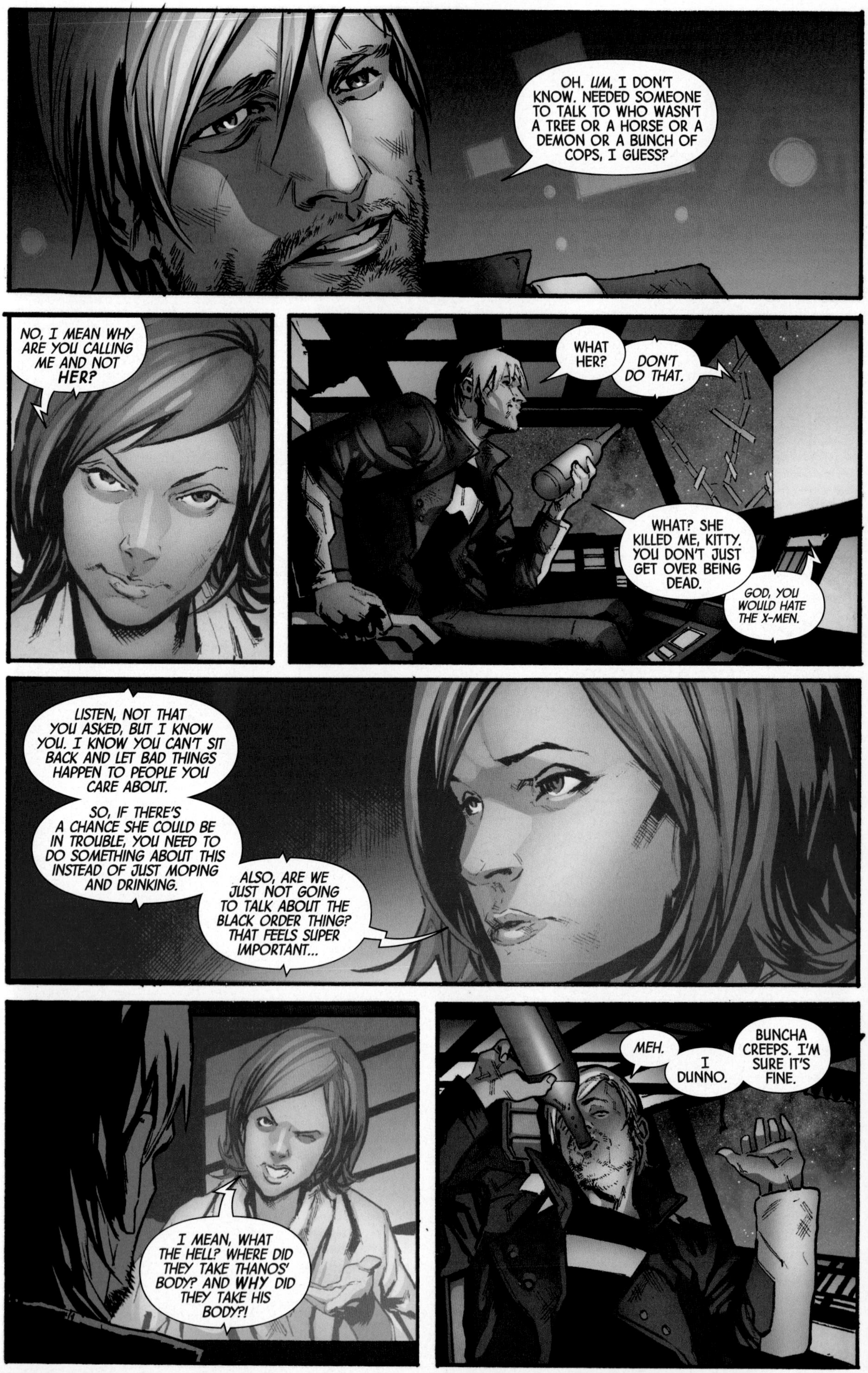
OH. UM, I DON'T KNOW. NEEDED SOMEONE TO TALK TO WHO WASN'T A TREE OR A HORSE OR A DEMON OR A BUNCH OF COPS, I GUESS?
NO, I MEAN WHY ARE YOU CALLING ME AND NOT HER?
WHAT HER?
DON'T DO THAT.
WHAT? SHE KILLED ME, KITTY. YOU DON'T JUST GET OVER BEING DEAD.
GOD, YOU WOULD HATE THE X-MEN.
LISTEN, NOT THAT YOU ASKED, BUT I KNOW YOU. I KNOW YOU CAN'T SIT BACK AND LET BAD THINGS HAPPEN TO PEOPLE YOU CARE ABOUT.
SO, IF THERE'S A CHANCE SHE COULD BE IN TROUBLE, YOU NEED TO DO SOMETHING ABOUT THIS INSTEAD OF JUST MOPING AND DRINKING.
ALSO, ARE WE JUST NOT GOING TO TALK ABOUT THE BLACK ORDER THING? THAT FEELS SUPER IMPORTANT...
I MEAN, WHAT THE HELL? WHERE DID THEY TAKE THANOS' BODY? AND WHY DID THEY TAKE HIS BODY?!
MEH.
I DUNNO.
BUNCHA CREEPS. I'M SURE IT'S FINE.

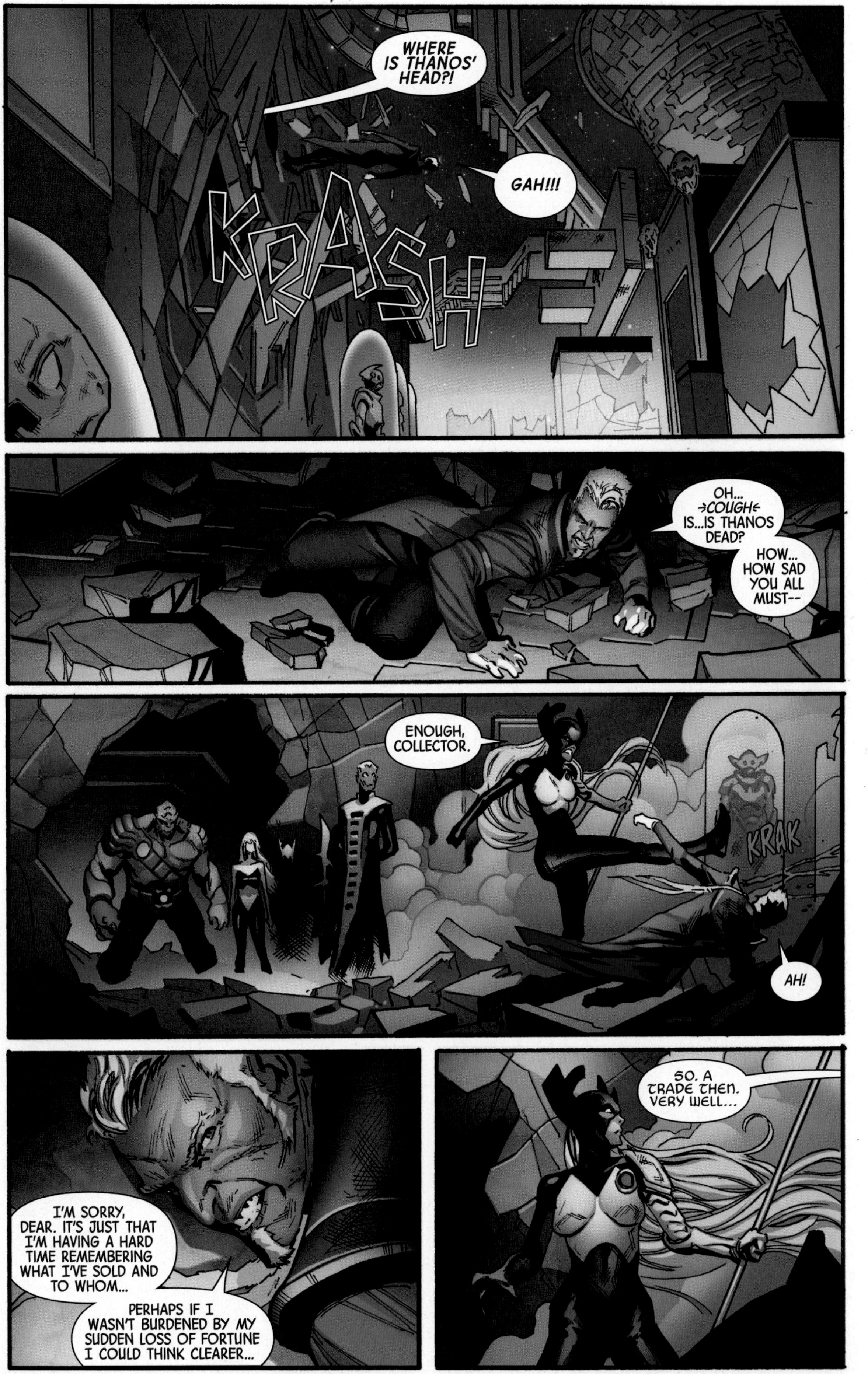
WHERE IS THANOS' HEAD?!
GAH!!!
KRASH
OH... →COUGH← IS...IS THANOS DEAD?
HOW... HOW SAD YOU ALL MUST--
ENOUGH, COLLECTOR.
KRAK
AH!
I'M SORRY, DEAR. IT'S JUST THAT I'M HAVING A HARD TIME REMEMBERING WHAT I'VE SOLD AND TO WHOM...
PERHAPS IF I WASN'T BURDENED BY MY SUDDEN LOSS OF FORTUNE I COULD THINK CLEARER...
SO. A TRADE THEN. VERY WELL...

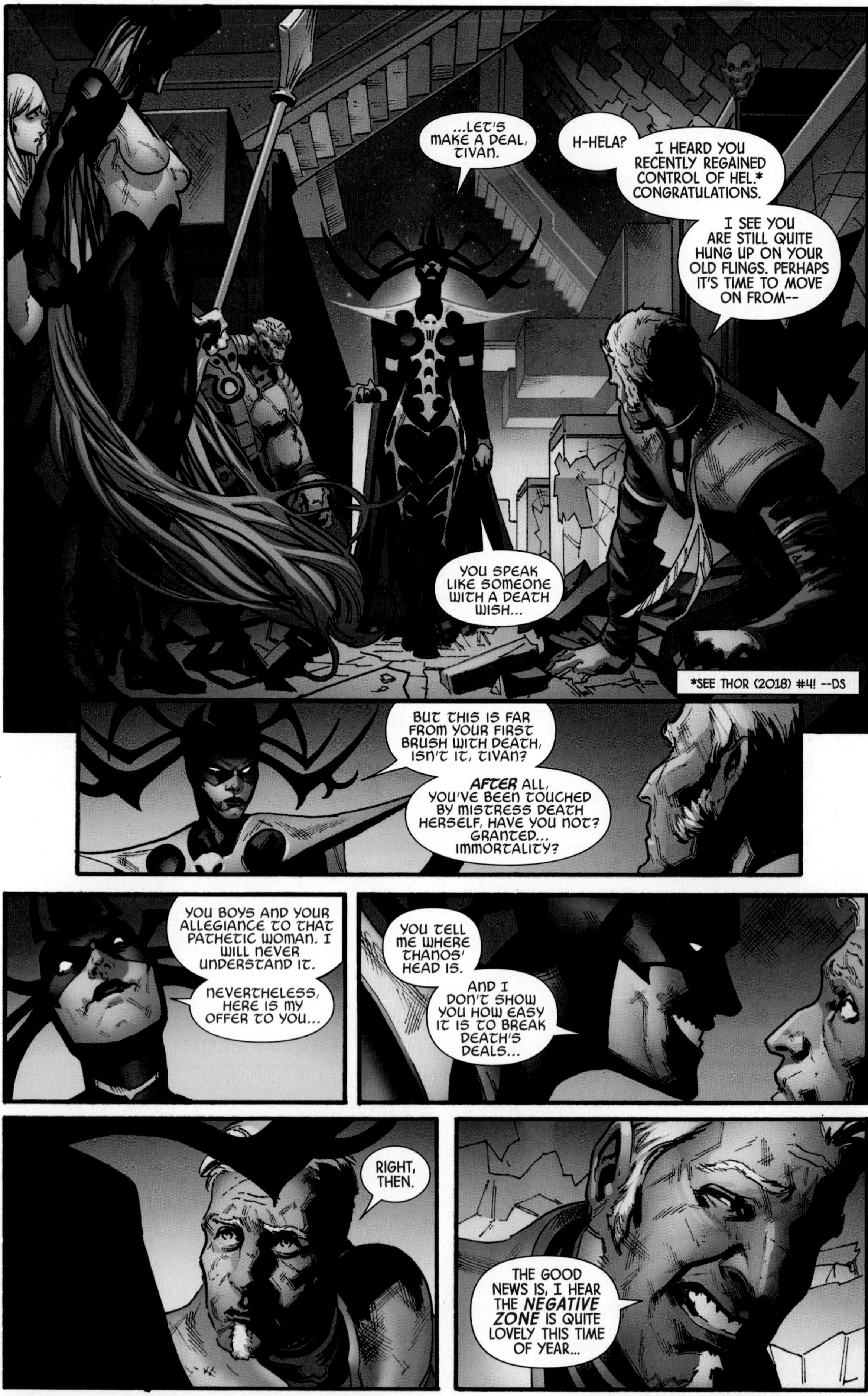
...LET'S MAKE A DEAL, TIVAN.
H-HELA?
I HEARD YOU RECENTLY REGAINED CONTROL OF HEL.* CONGRATULATIONS.
I SEE YOU ARE STILL QUITE HUNG UP ON YOUR OLD FLINGS. PERHAPS IT'S TIME TO MOVE ON FROM--
YOU SPEAK LIKE SOMEONE WITH A DEATH WISH...
*SEE THOR (2018) #4! --DS
BUT THIS IS FAR FROM YOUR FIRST BRUSH WITH DEATH, ISN'T IT, TIVAN?
AFTER ALL, YOU'VE BEEN TOUCHED BY MISTRESS DEATH HERSELF, HAVE YOU NOT? GRANTED... IMMORTALITY?
YOU BOYS AND YOUR ALLEGIANCE TO THAT PATHETIC WOMAN. I WILL NEVER UNDERSTAND IT.
NEVERTHELESS, HERE IS MY OFFER TO YOU...
YOU TELL ME WHERE THANOS' HEAD IS.
AND I DON'T SHOW YOU HOW EASY IT IS TO BREAK DEATH'S DEALS...
RIGHT, THEN.
THE GOOD NEWS IS, I HEAR THE NEGATIVE ZONE IS QUITE LOVELY THIS TIME OF YEAR...

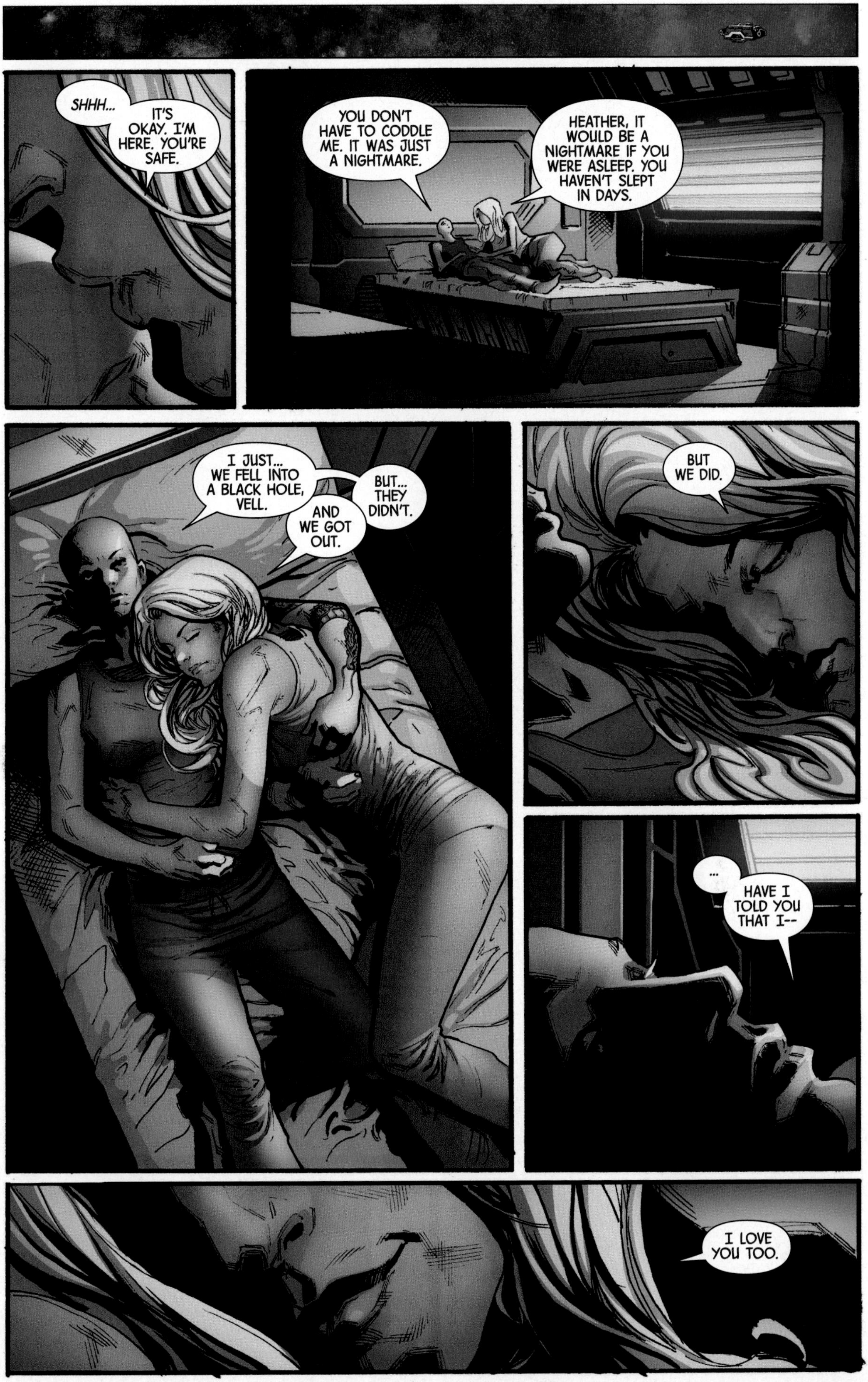
SHHH...
IT'S OKAY. I'M HERE. YOU'RE SAFE.
YOU DON'T HAVE TO CODDLE ME. IT WAS JUST A NIGHTMARE.
HEATHER, IT WOULD BE A NIGHTMARE IF YOU WERE ASLEEP. YOU HAVEN'T SLEPT IN DAYS.
I JUST... WE FELL INTO A BLACK HOLE, VELL.
AND WE GOT OUT.
BUT... THEY DIDN'T.
BUT WE DID.
...
HAVE I TOLD YOU THAT I--
I LOVE YOU TOO.

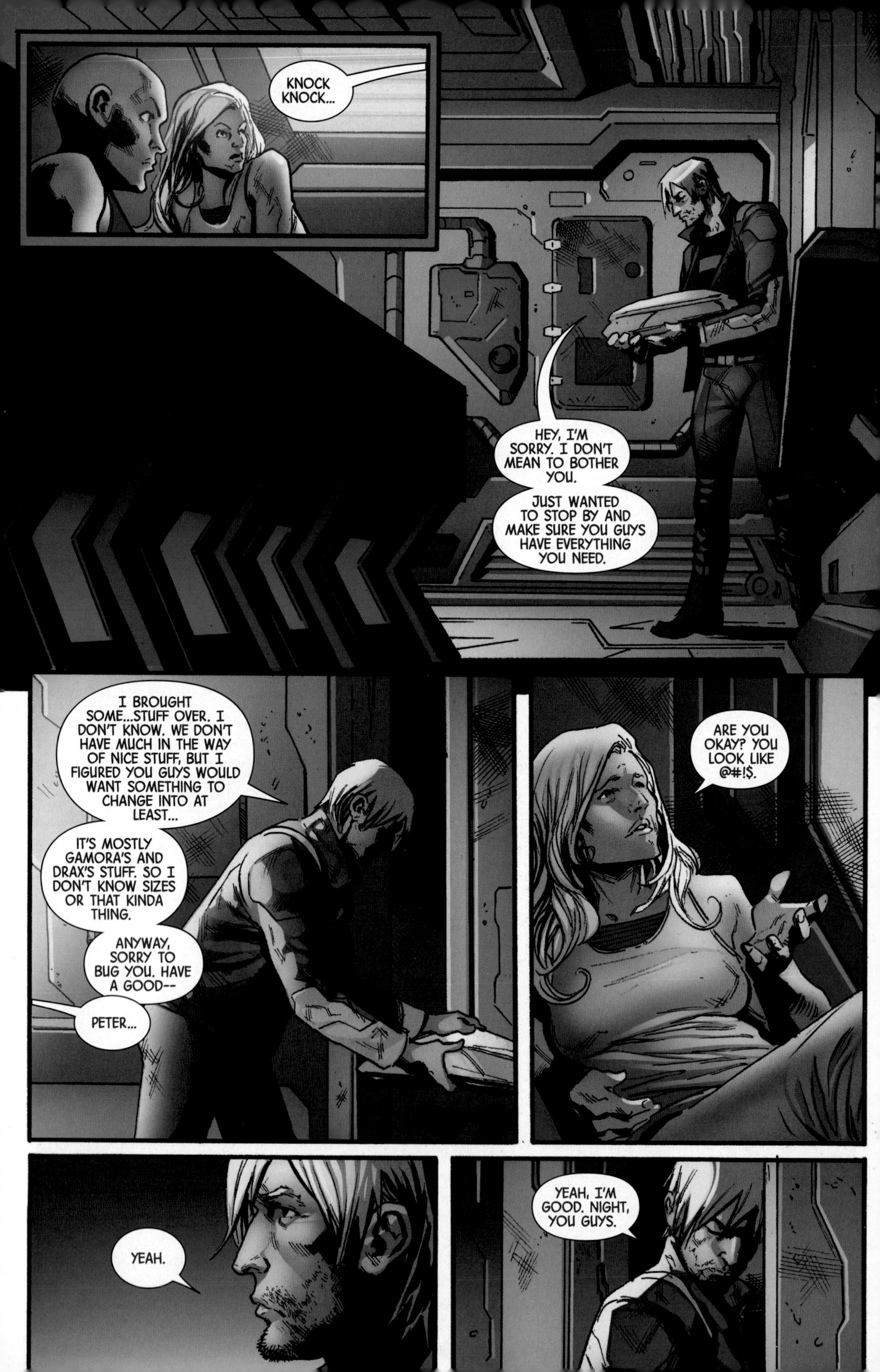
KNOCK KNOCK...
HEY, I'M SORRY. I DON'T MEAN TO BOTHER YOU.
JUST WANTED TO STOP BY AND MAKE SURE YOU GUYS HAVE EVERYTHING YOU NEED.
I BROUGHT SOME...STUFF OVER. I DON'T KNOW. WE DON'T HAVE MUCH IN THE WAY OF NICE STUFF, BUT I FIGURED YOU GUYS WOULD WANT SOMETHING TO CHANGE INTO AT LEAST...
IT'S MOSTLY GAMORA'S AND DRAX'S STUFF. SO I DON'T KNOW SIZES OR THAT KINDA THING.
ANYWAY, SORRY TO BUG YOU. HAVE A GOOD--
PETER...
ARE YOU OKAY? YOU LOOK LIKE @#!$.
YEAH.
YEAH, I'M GOOD. NIGHT, YOU GUYS.

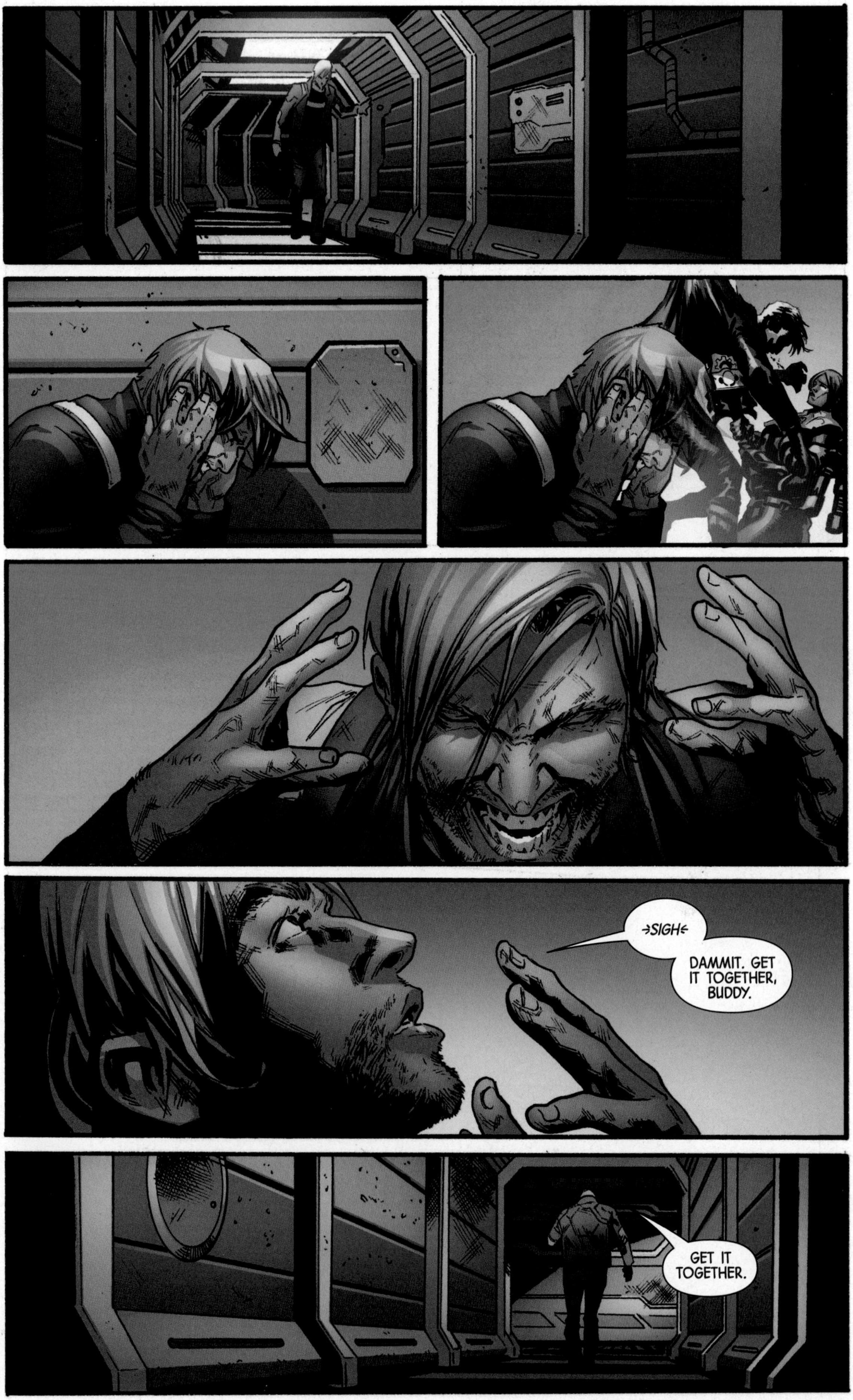

→SIGH←
DAMMIT. GET IT TOGETHER, BUDDY.
GET IT TOGETHER.

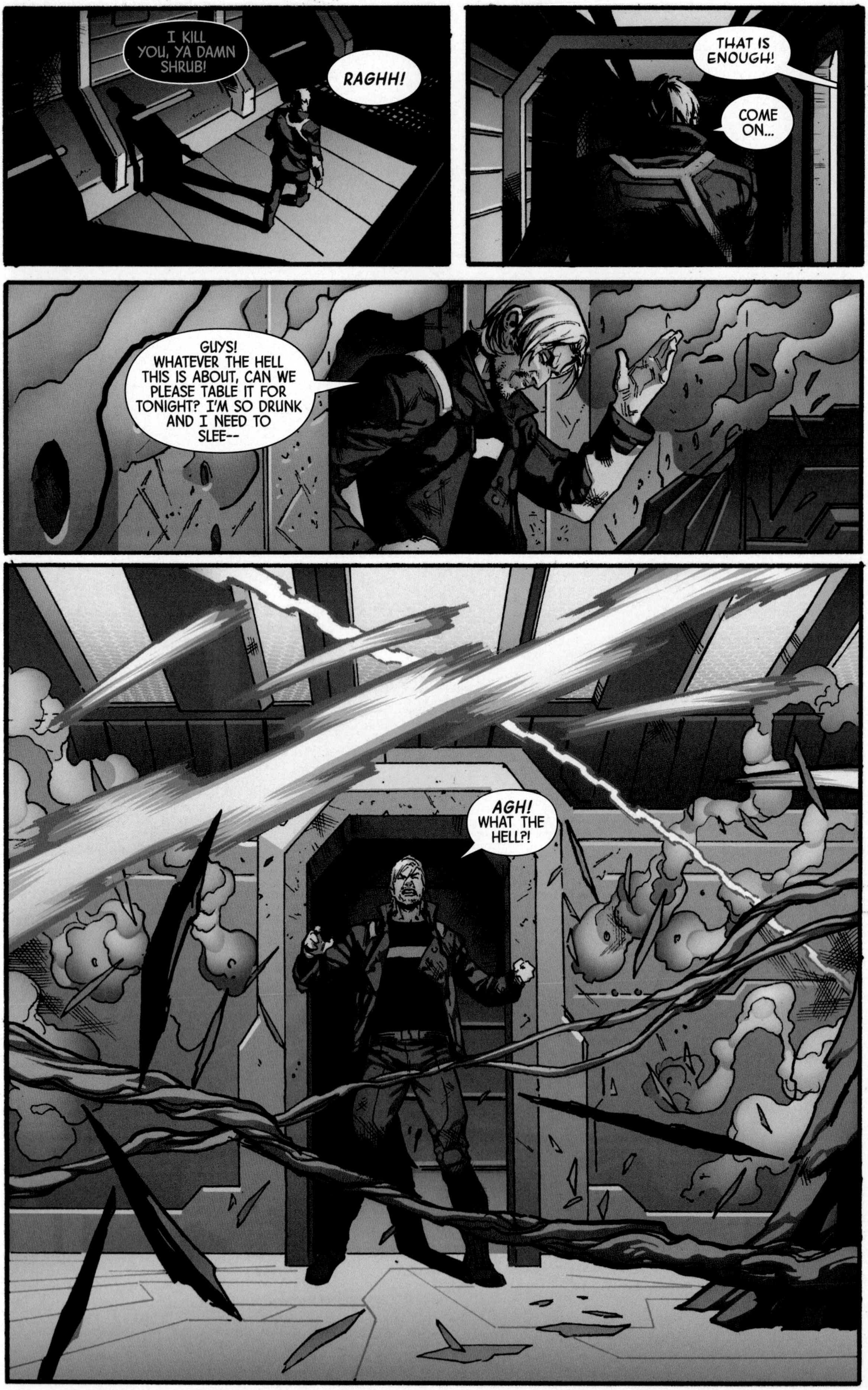
I KILL YOU, YA DAMN SHRUB!
RAGHH!
THAT IS ENOUGH!
COME ON...
GUYS! WHATEVER THE HELL THIS IS ABOUT, CAN WE PLEASE TABLE IT FOR TONIGHT? I'M SO DRUNK AND I NEED TO SLEE--
AGH! WHAT THE HELL?!

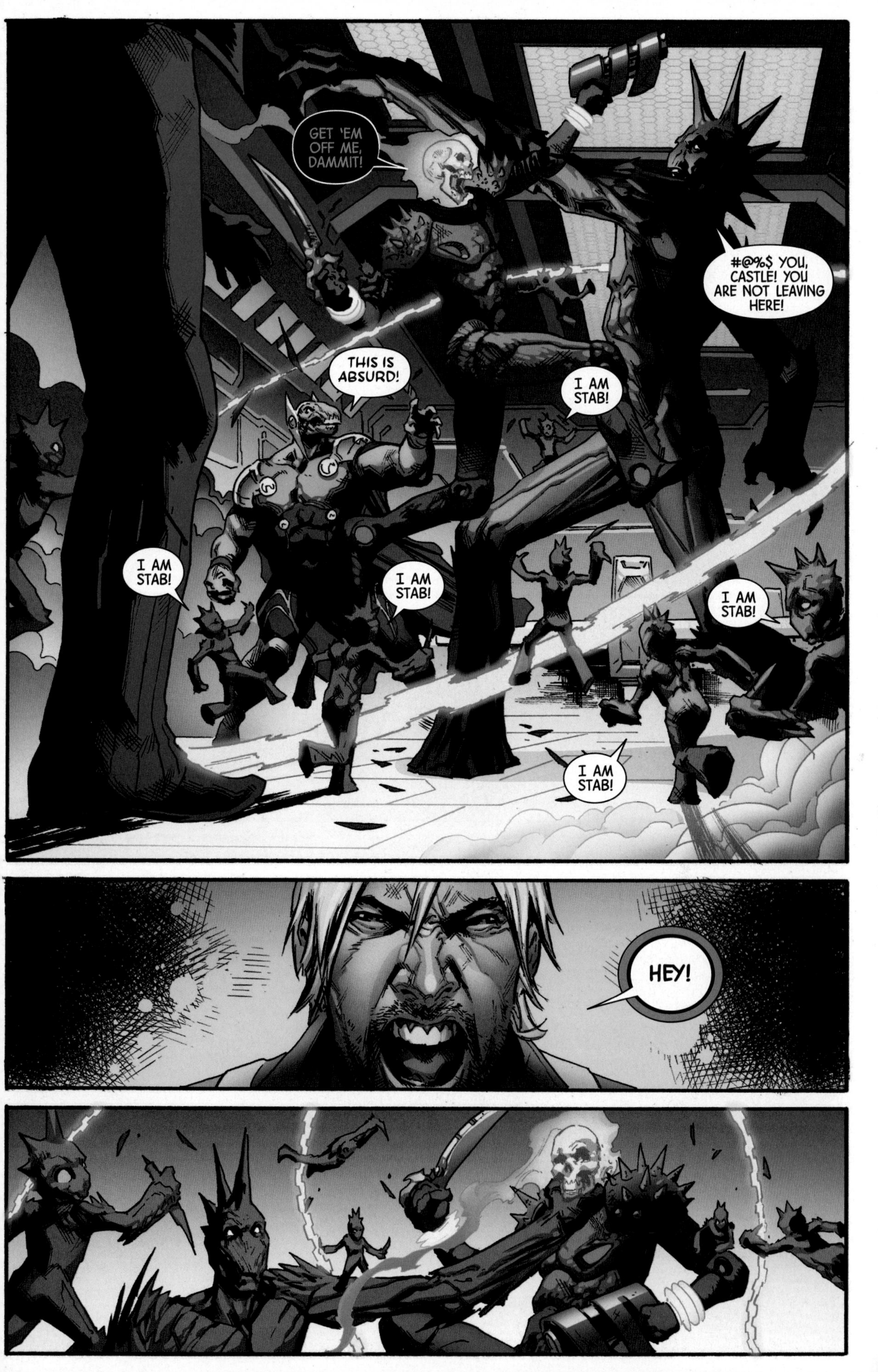
GET 'EM OFF ME, DAMMIT!
#@%$ YOU, CASTLE! YOU ARE NOT LEAVING HERE!
THIS IS ABSURD!
I AM STAB!
I AM STAB!
I AM STAB!
I AM STAB!
I AM STAB!
HEY!

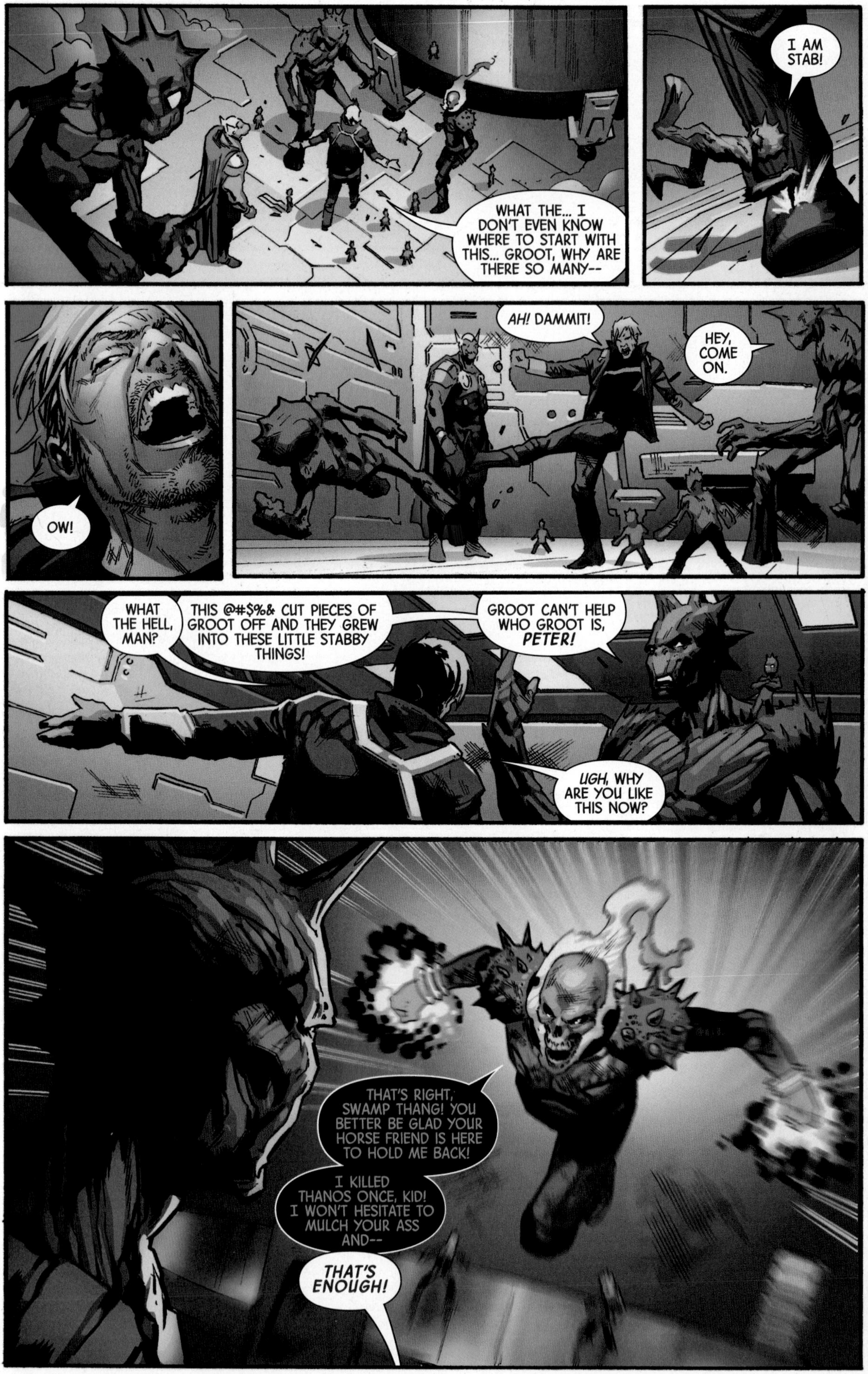
WHAT THE... I DON'T EVEN KNOW WHERE TO START WITH THIS... GROOT, WHY ARE THERE SO MANY--
I AM STAB!
OW!
AH! DAMMIT!
HEY, COME ON.
WHAT THE HELL, MAN?
THIS @#$%& CUT PIECES OF GROOT OFF AND THEY GREW INTO THESE LITTLE STABBY THINGS!
GROOT CAN'T HELP WHO GROOT IS, PETER!
UGH, WHY ARE YOU LIKE THIS NOW?
THAT'S RIGHT, SWAMP THANG! YOU BETTER BE GLAD YOUR HORSE FRIEND IS HERE TO HOLD ME BACK!
I KILLED THANOS ONCE, KID! I WON'T HESITATE TO MULCH YOUR ASS AND--
THAT'S ENOUGH!

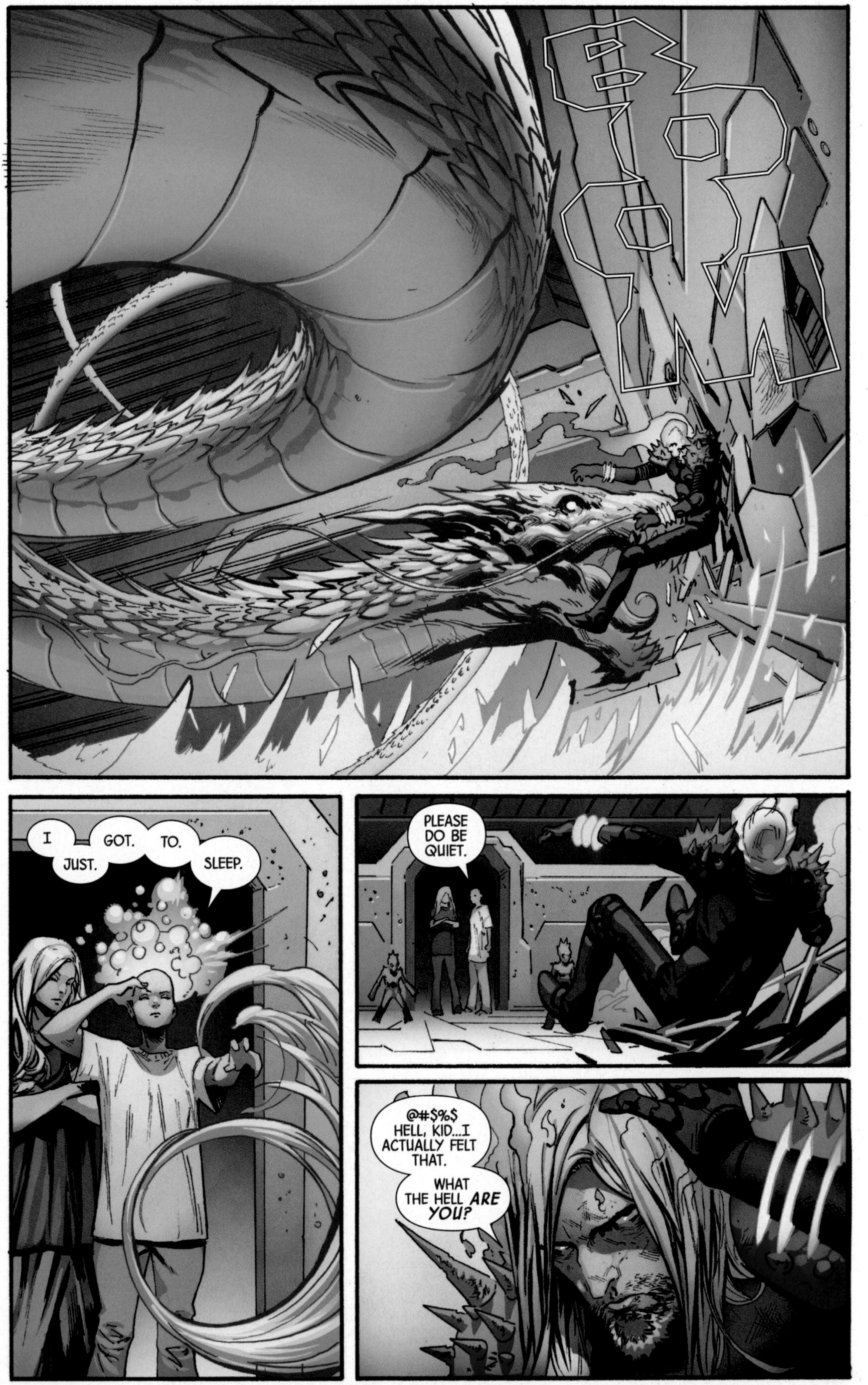
BOOM
I
JUST.
GOT.
TO.
SLEEP.
PLEASE DO BE QUIET.
@#$%$ HELL, KID...I ACTUALLY FELT THAT.
WHAT THE HELL *ARE YOU?*

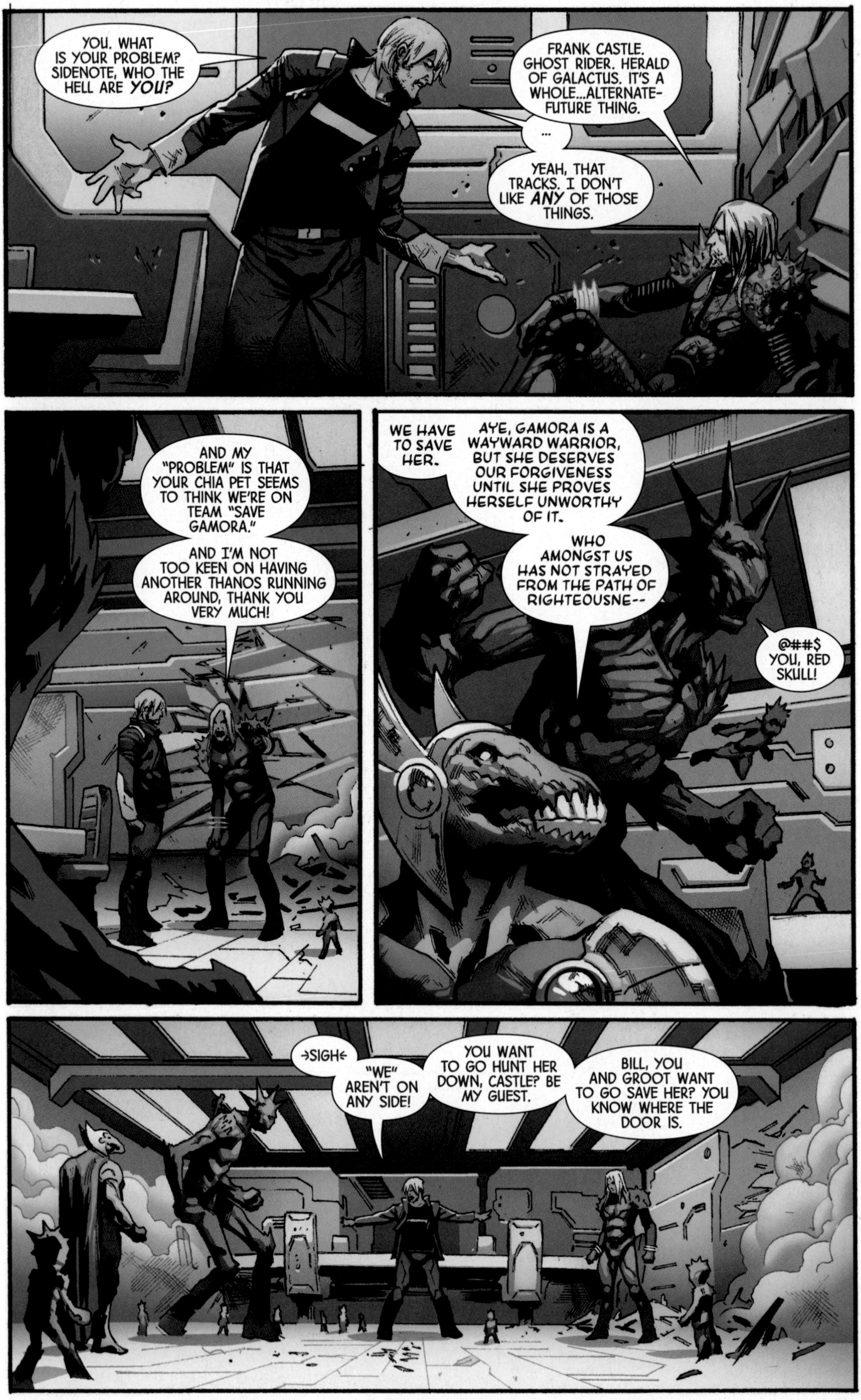
YOU. WHAT IS YOUR PROBLEM? SIDENOTE, WHO THE HELL ARE YOU?
FRANK CASTLE. GHOST RIDER. HERALD OF GALACTUS. IT'S A WHOLE...ALTERNATE-FUTURE THING.
...
YEAH, THAT TRACKS. I DON'T LIKE ANY OF THOSE THINGS.
AND MY "PROBLEM" IS THAT YOUR CHIA PET SEEMS TO THINK WE'RE ON TEAM "SAVE GAMORA."
AND I'M NOT TOO KEEN ON HAVING ANOTHER THANOS RUNNING AROUND, THANK YOU VERY MUCH!
WE HAVE TO SAVE HER.
AYE, GAMORA IS A WAYWARD WARRIOR, BUT SHE DESERVES OUR FORGIVENESS UNTIL SHE PROVES HERSELF UNWORTHY OF IT.
WHO AMONGST US HAS NOT STRAYED FROM THE PATH OF RIGHTEOUSNE--
@##$ YOU, RED SKULL!
SIGH
"WE" AREN'T ON ANY SIDE!
YOU WANT TO GO HUNT HER DOWN, CASTLE? BE MY GUEST.
BILL, YOU AND GROOT WANT TO GO SAVE HER? YOU KNOW WHERE THE DOOR IS.

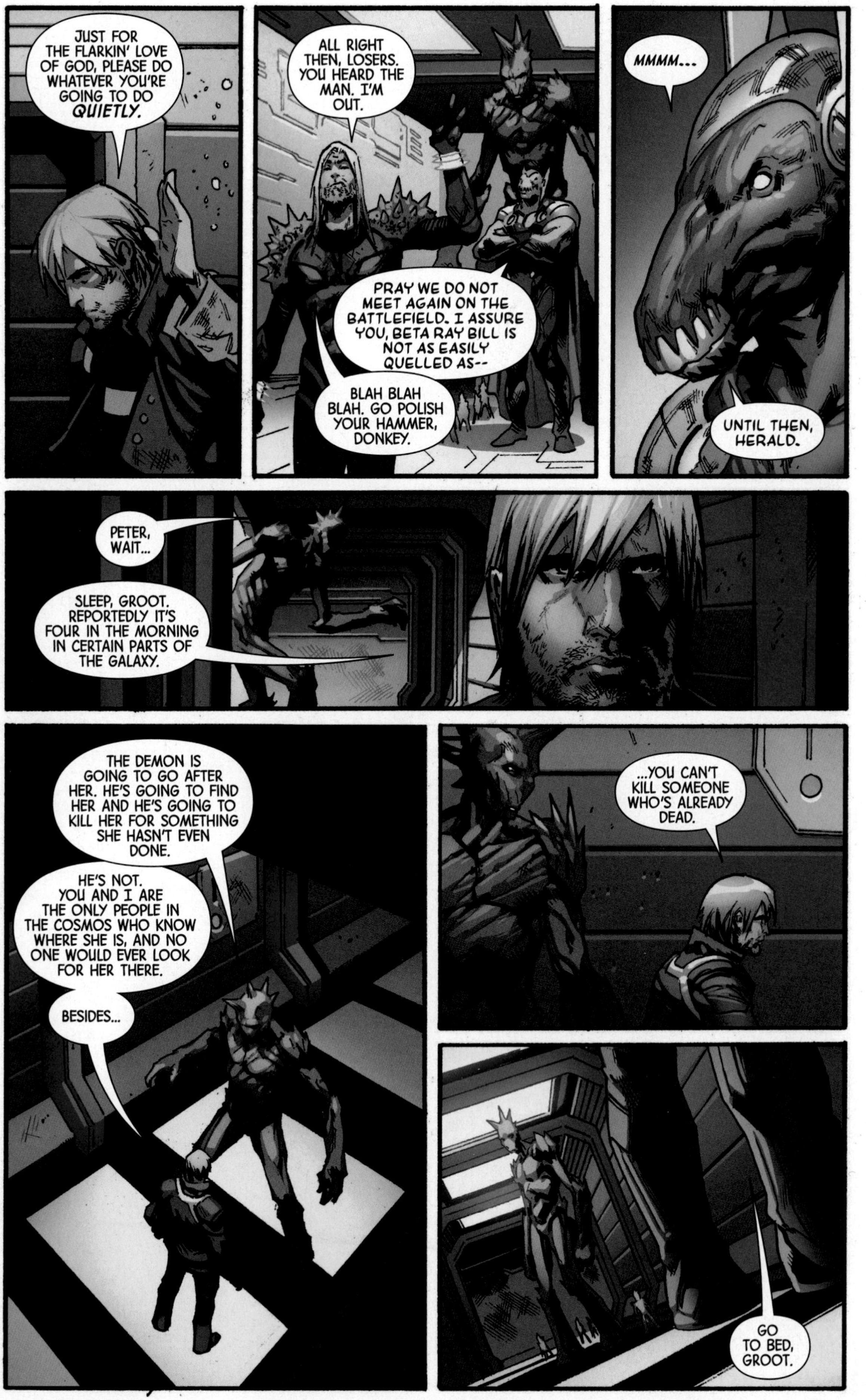
JUST FOR THE FLARKIN' LOVE OF GOD, PLEASE DO WHATEVER YOU'RE GOING TO DO QUIETLY.
ALL RIGHT THEN, LOSERS. YOU HEARD THE MAN. I'M OUT.
PRAY WE DO NOT MEET AGAIN ON THE BATTLEFIELD. I ASSURE YOU, BETA RAY BILL IS NOT AS EASILY QUELLED AS--
BLAH BLAH BLAH. GO POLISH YOUR HAMMER, DONKEY.
MMMM...
UNTIL THEN, HERALD.
PETER, WAIT...
SLEEP, GROOT. REPORTEDLY IT'S FOUR IN THE MORNING IN CERTAIN PARTS OF THE GALAXY.
THE DEMON IS GOING TO GO AFTER HER. HE'S GOING TO FIND HER AND HE'S GOING TO KILL HER FOR SOMETHING SHE HASN'T EVEN DONE.
HE'S NOT. YOU AND I ARE THE ONLY PEOPLE IN THE COSMOS WHO KNOW WHERE SHE IS, AND NO ONE WOULD EVER LOOK FOR HER THERE.
BESIDES...
...YOU CAN'T KILL SOMEONE WHO'S ALREADY DEAD.
GO TO BED, GROOT.

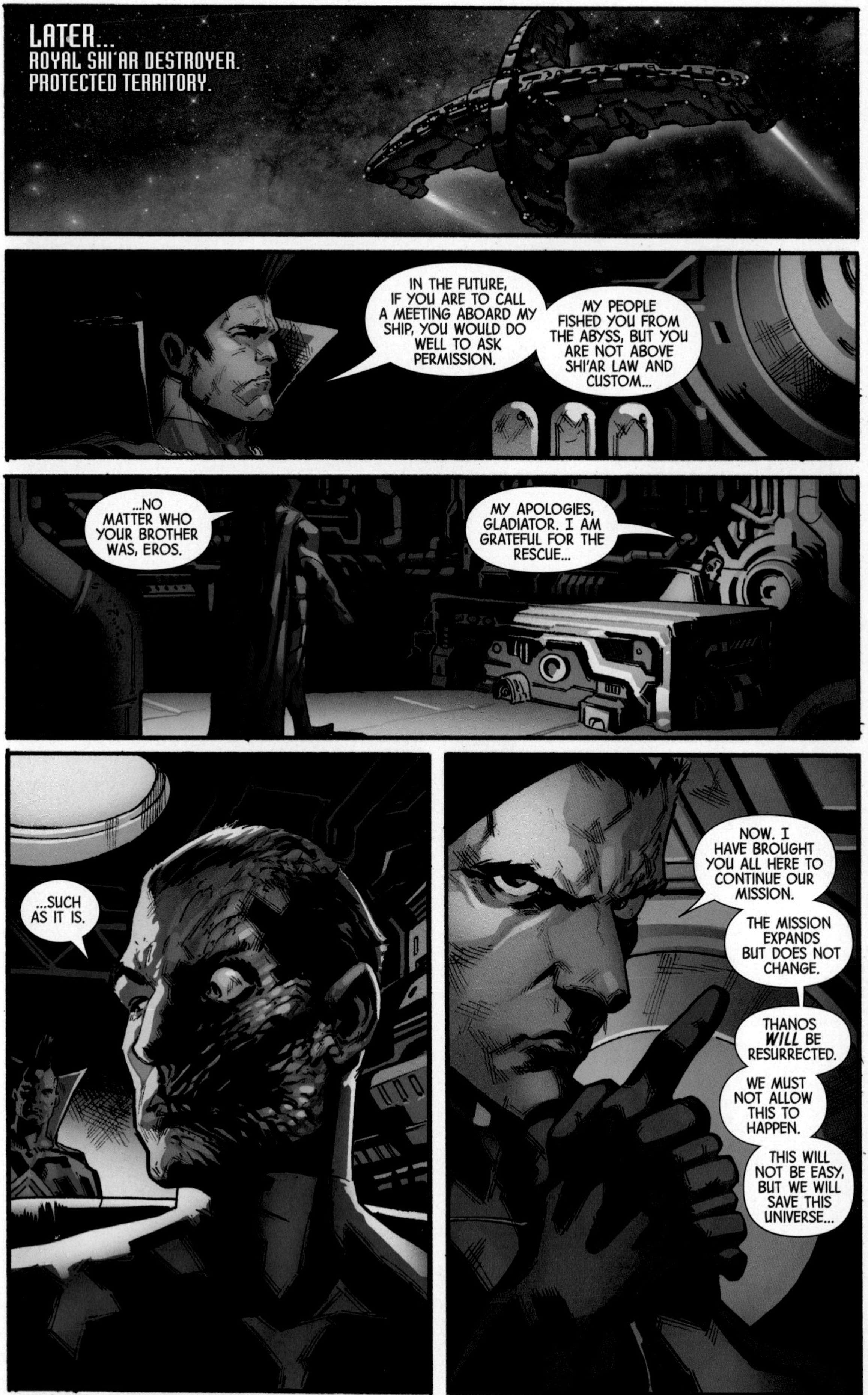
LATER...
ROYAL SHI'AR DESTROYER.
PROTECTED TERRITORY.
IN THE FUTURE, IF YOU ARE TO CALL A MEETING ABOARD MY SHIP, YOU WOULD DO WELL TO ASK PERMISSION.
MY PEOPLE FISHED YOU FROM THE ABYSS, BUT YOU ARE NOT ABOVE SHI'AR LAW AND CUSTOM...
...NO MATTER WHO YOUR BROTHER WAS, EROS.
MY APOLOGIES, GLADIATOR. I AM GRATEFUL FOR THE RESCUE...
...SUCH AS IT IS.
NOW. I HAVE BROUGHT YOU ALL HERE TO CONTINUE OUR MISSION.
THE MISSION EXPANDS BUT DOES NOT CHANGE.
THANOS *WILL* BE RESURRECTED.
WE MUST NOT ALLOW THIS TO HAPPEN.
THIS WILL NOT BE EASY, BUT WE WILL SAVE THIS UNIVERSE...

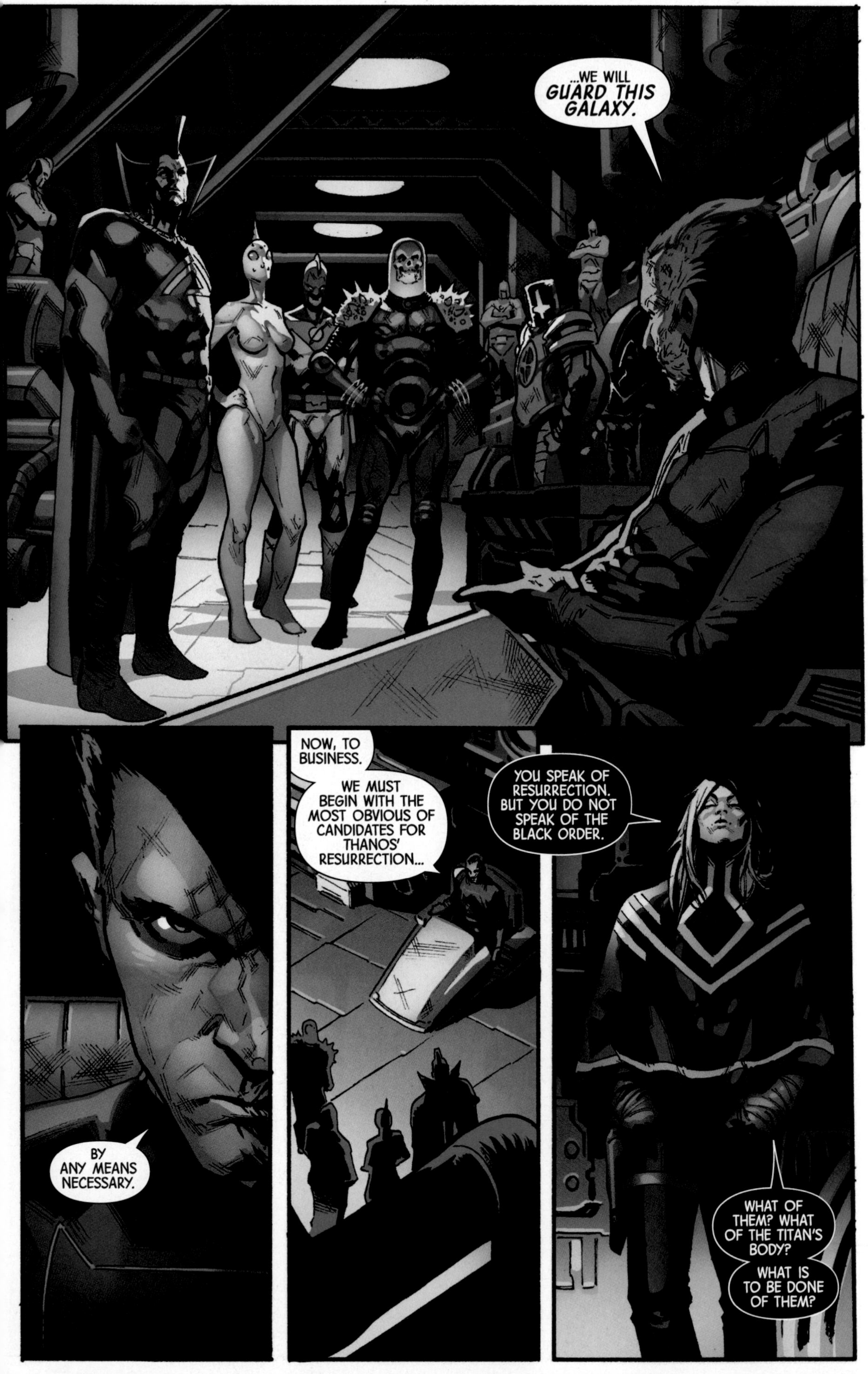
...WE WILL GUARD THIS GALAXY.
BY ANY MEANS NECESSARY.
NOW, TO BUSINESS.
WE MUST BEGIN WITH THE MOST OBVIOUS OF CANDIDATES FOR THANOS' RESURRECTION...
YOU SPEAK OF RESURRECTION. BUT YOU DO NOT SPEAK OF THE BLACK ORDER.
WHAT OF THEM? WHAT OF THE TITAN'S BODY?
WHAT IS TO BE DONE OF THEM?

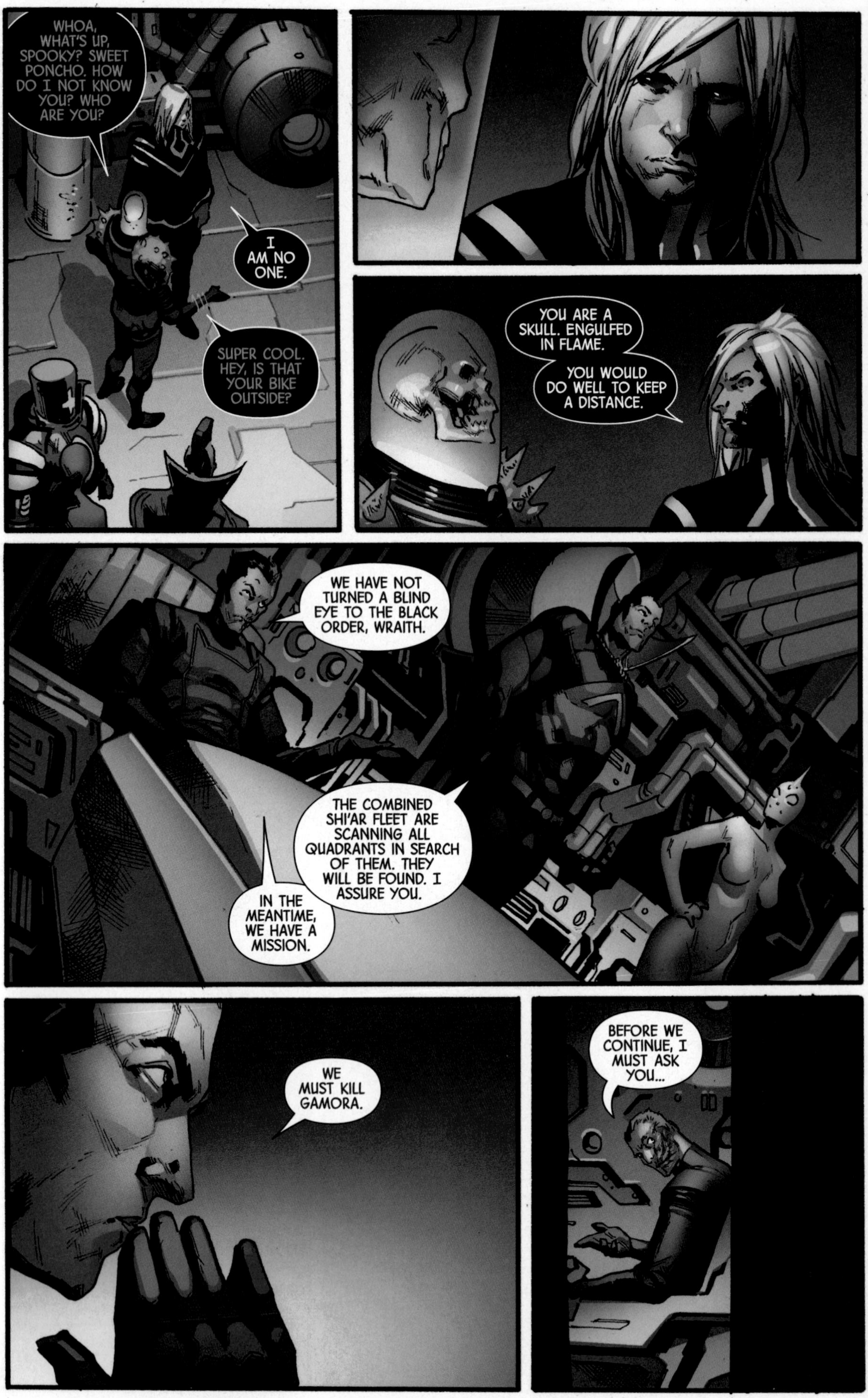
WHOA, WHAT'S UP, SPOOKY? SWEET PONCHO. HOW DO I NOT KNOW YOU? WHO ARE YOU?
I AM NO ONE.
SUPER COOL. HEY, IS THAT YOUR BIKE OUTSIDE?
YOU ARE A SKULL. ENGULFED IN FLAME.
YOU WOULD DO WELL TO KEEP A DISTANCE.
WE HAVE NOT TURNED A BLIND EYE TO THE BLACK ORDER, WRAITH.
THE COMBINED SHI'AR FLEET ARE SCANNING ALL QUADRANTS IN SEARCH OF THEM. THEY WILL BE FOUND. I ASSURE YOU.
IN THE MEANTIME, WE HAVE A MISSION.
WE MUST KILL GAMORA.
BEFORE WE CONTINUE, I MUST ASK YOU...

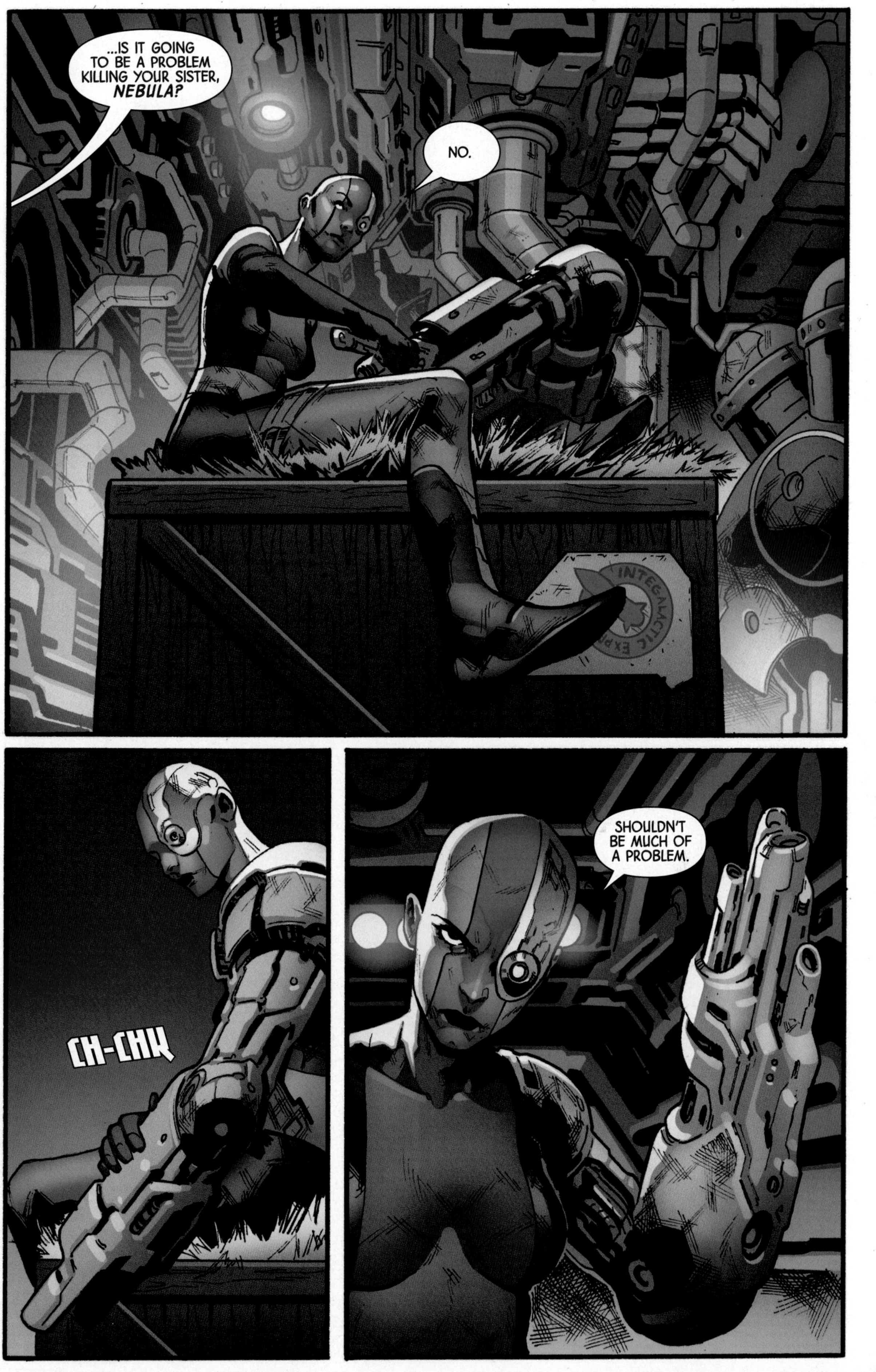
...IS IT GOING TO BE A PROBLEM KILLING YOUR SISTER, *NEBULA?*
NO.
CH-CHK
SHOULDN'T BE MUCH OF A PROBLEM.

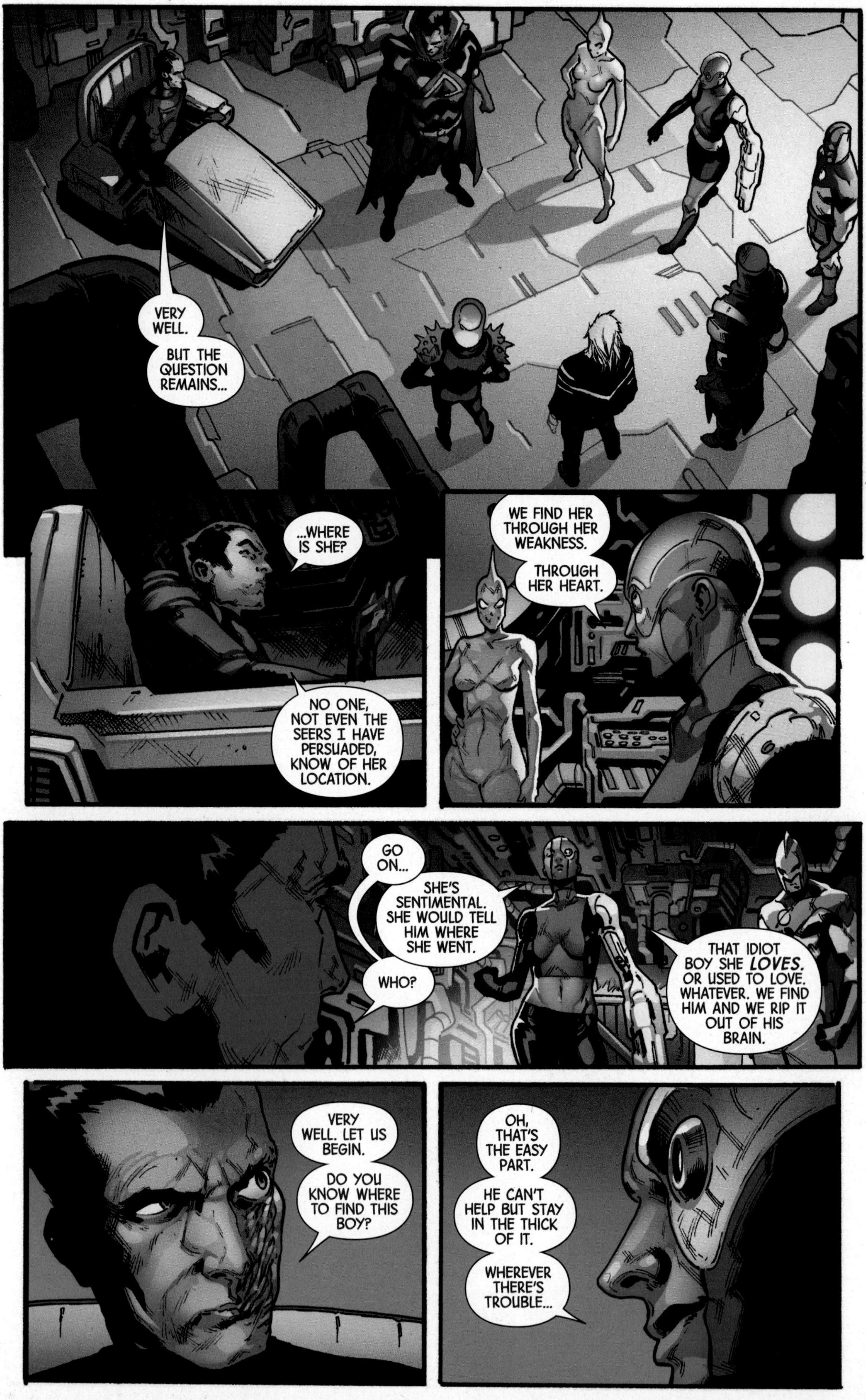
VERY WELL.
BUT THE QUESTION REMAINS...
...WHERE IS SHE?
NO ONE, NOT EVEN THE SEERS I HAVE PERSUADED, KNOW OF HER LOCATION.
WE FIND HER THROUGH HER WEAKNESS.
THROUGH HER HEART.
GO ON...
SHE'S SENTIMENTAL. SHE WOULD TELL HIM WHERE SHE WENT.
WHO?
THAT IDIOT BOY SHE *LOVES.* OR USED TO LOVE. WHATEVER. WE FIND HIM AND WE RIP IT OUT OF HIS BRAIN.
VERY WELL. LET US BEGIN.
DO YOU KNOW WHERE TO FIND THIS BOY?
OH, THAT'S THE EASY PART.
HE CAN'T HELP BUT STAY IN THE THICK OF IT.
WHEREVER THERE'S TROUBLE...

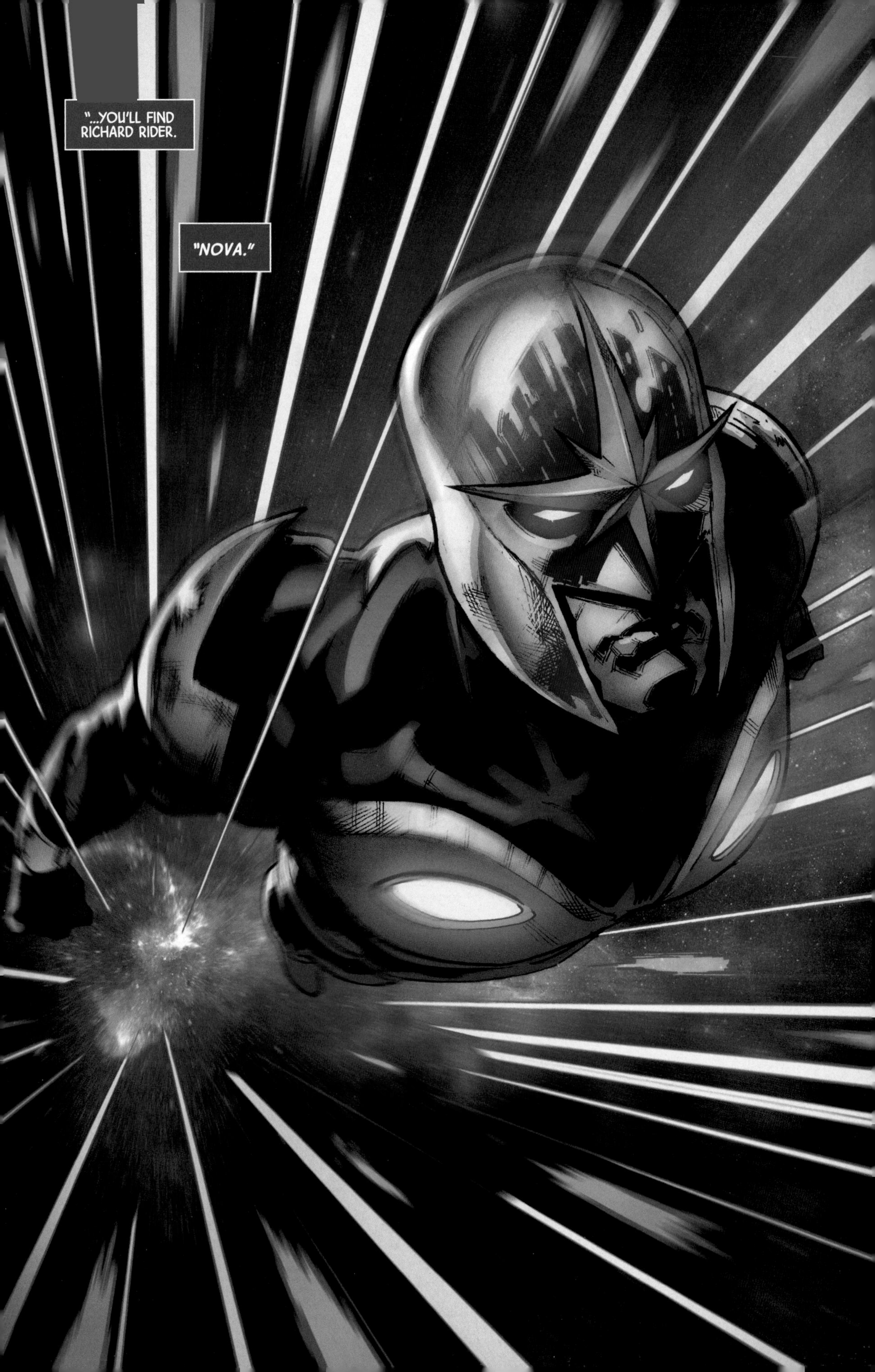
"...YOU'LL FIND RICHARD RIDER.
"NOVA."

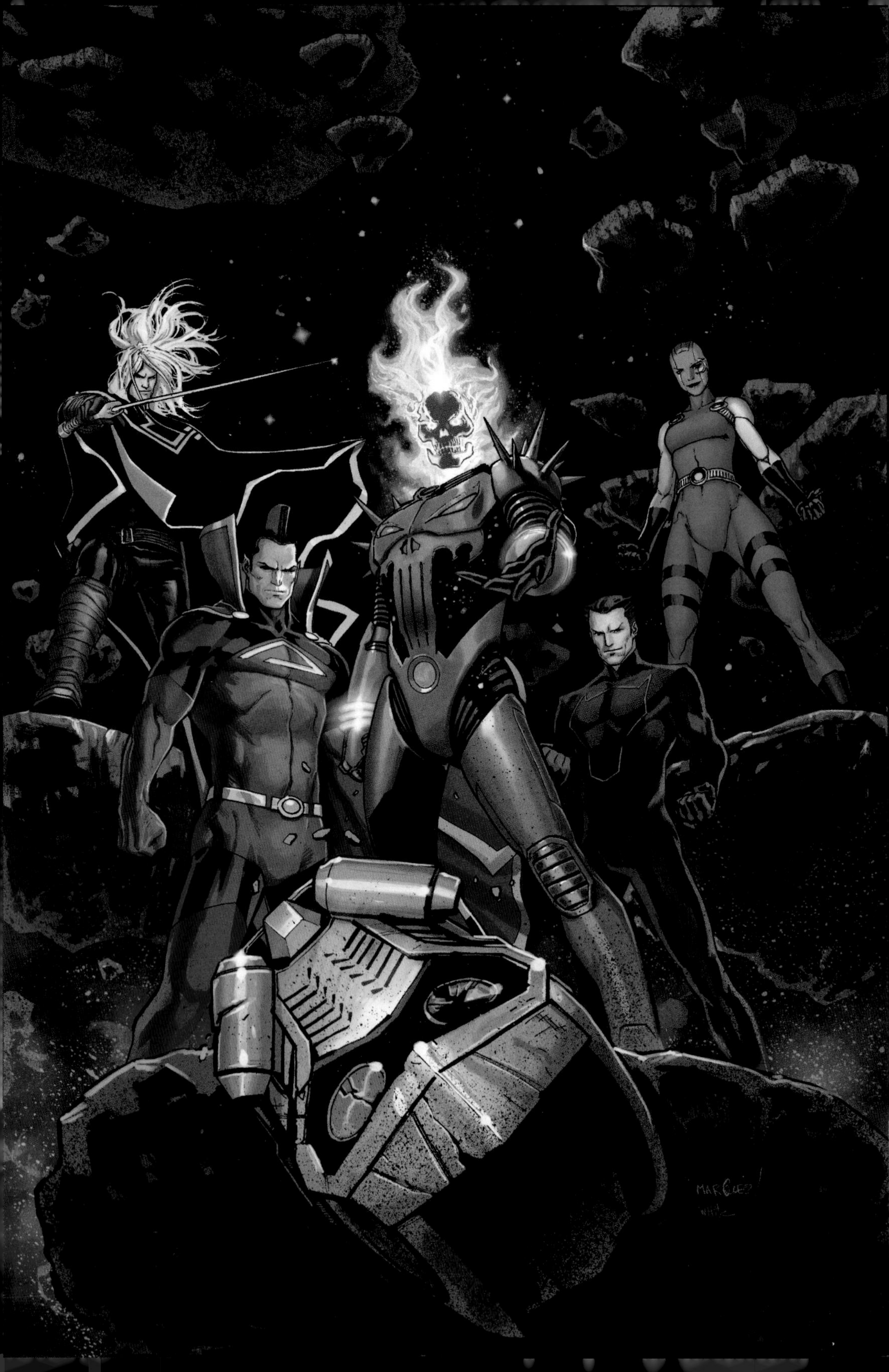

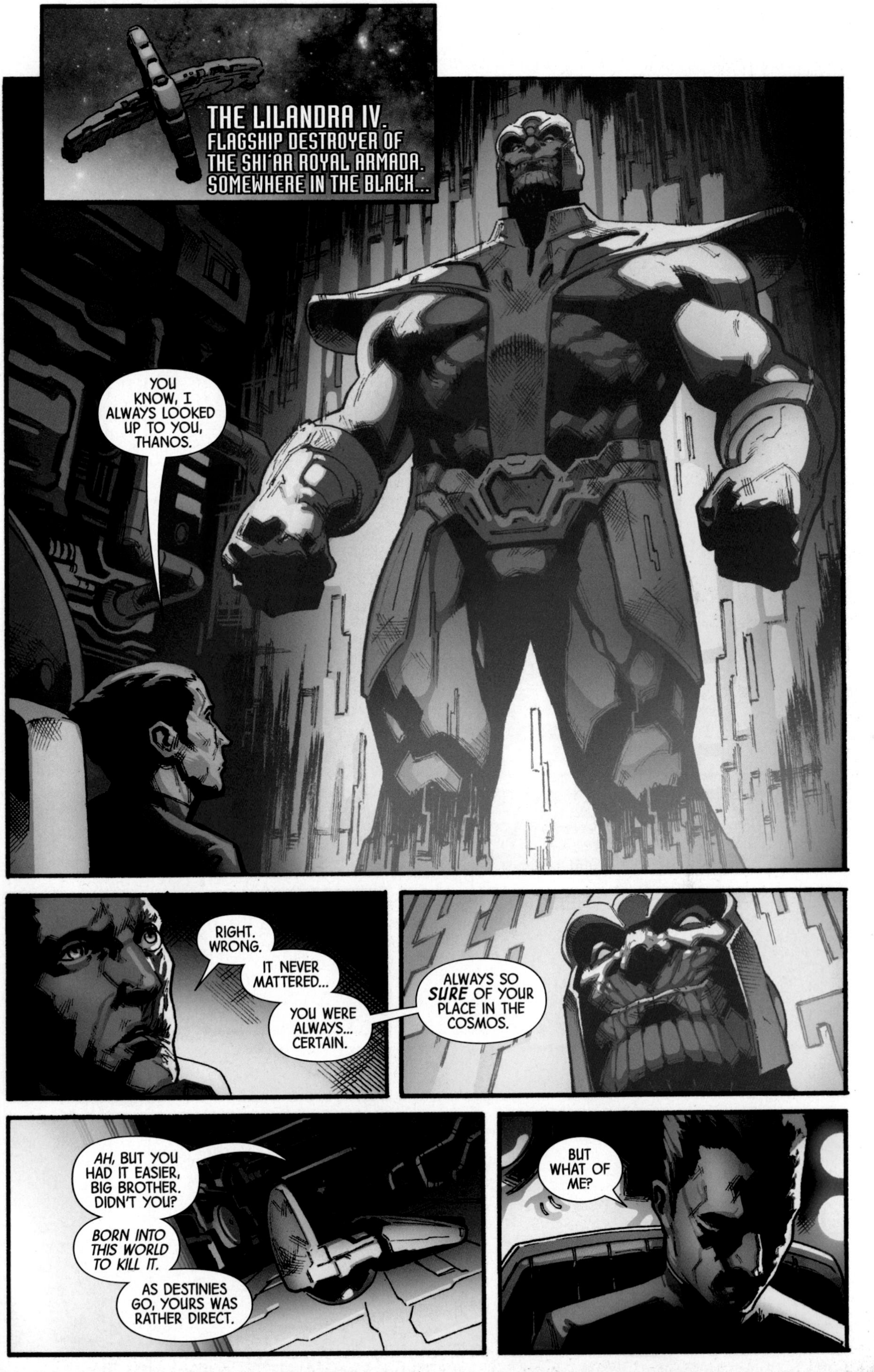
THE LILANDRA IV. FLAGSHIP DESTROYER OF THE SHI'AR ROYAL ARMADA. SOMEWHERE IN THE BLACK...
YOU KNOW, I ALWAYS LOOKED UP TO YOU, THANOS.
RIGHT. WRONG.
IT NEVER MATTERED...
YOU WERE ALWAYS... CERTAIN.
ALWAYS SO *SURE* OF YOUR PLACE IN THE COSMOS.
AH, BUT YOU HAD IT EASIER, BIG BROTHER. DIDN'T YOU?
BORN INTO THIS WORLD TO KILL IT.
AS DESTINIES GO, YOURS WAS RATHER DIRECT.
BUT WHAT OF ME?

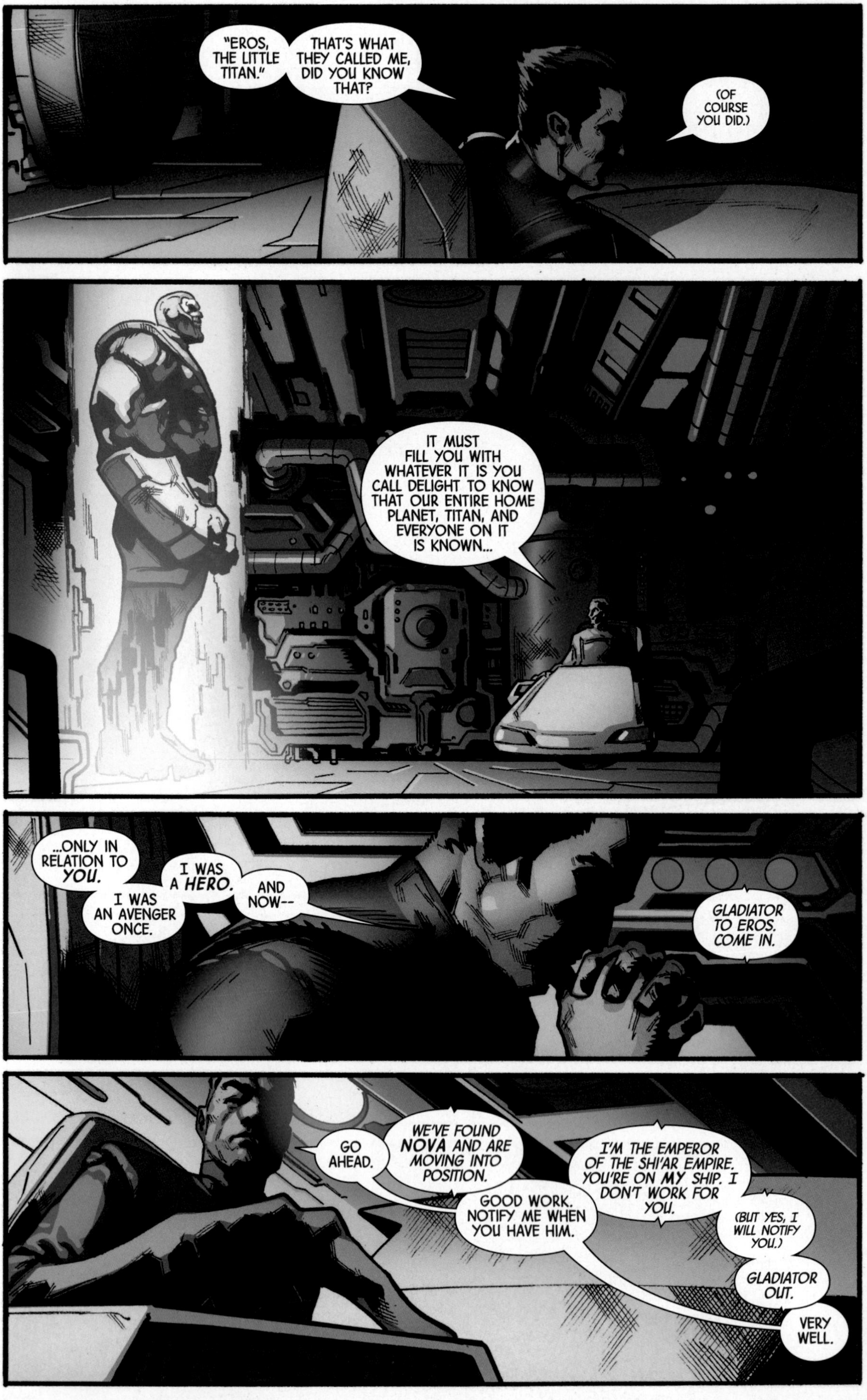
"EROS, THE LITTLE TITAN."
THAT'S WHAT THEY CALLED ME, DID YOU KNOW THAT?
(OF COURSE YOU DID.)
IT MUST FILL YOU WITH WHATEVER IT IS YOU CALL DELIGHT TO KNOW THAT OUR ENTIRE HOME PLANET, TITAN, AND EVERYONE ON IT IS KNOWN...
...ONLY IN RELATION TO *YOU.*
I WAS AN AVENGER ONCE.
I WAS A *HERO.*
AND NOW--
GLADIATOR TO EROS. COME IN.
GO AHEAD.
*WE'VE FOUND **NOVA** AND ARE MOVING INTO POSITION.*
GOOD WORK. NOTIFY ME WHEN YOU HAVE HIM.
*I'M THE EMPEROR OF THE SHI'AR EMPIRE. YOU'RE ON **MY** SHIP. I DON'T WORK FOR YOU.*
(BUT YES, I WILL NOTIFY YOU.)
GLADIATOR OUT.
VERY WELL.

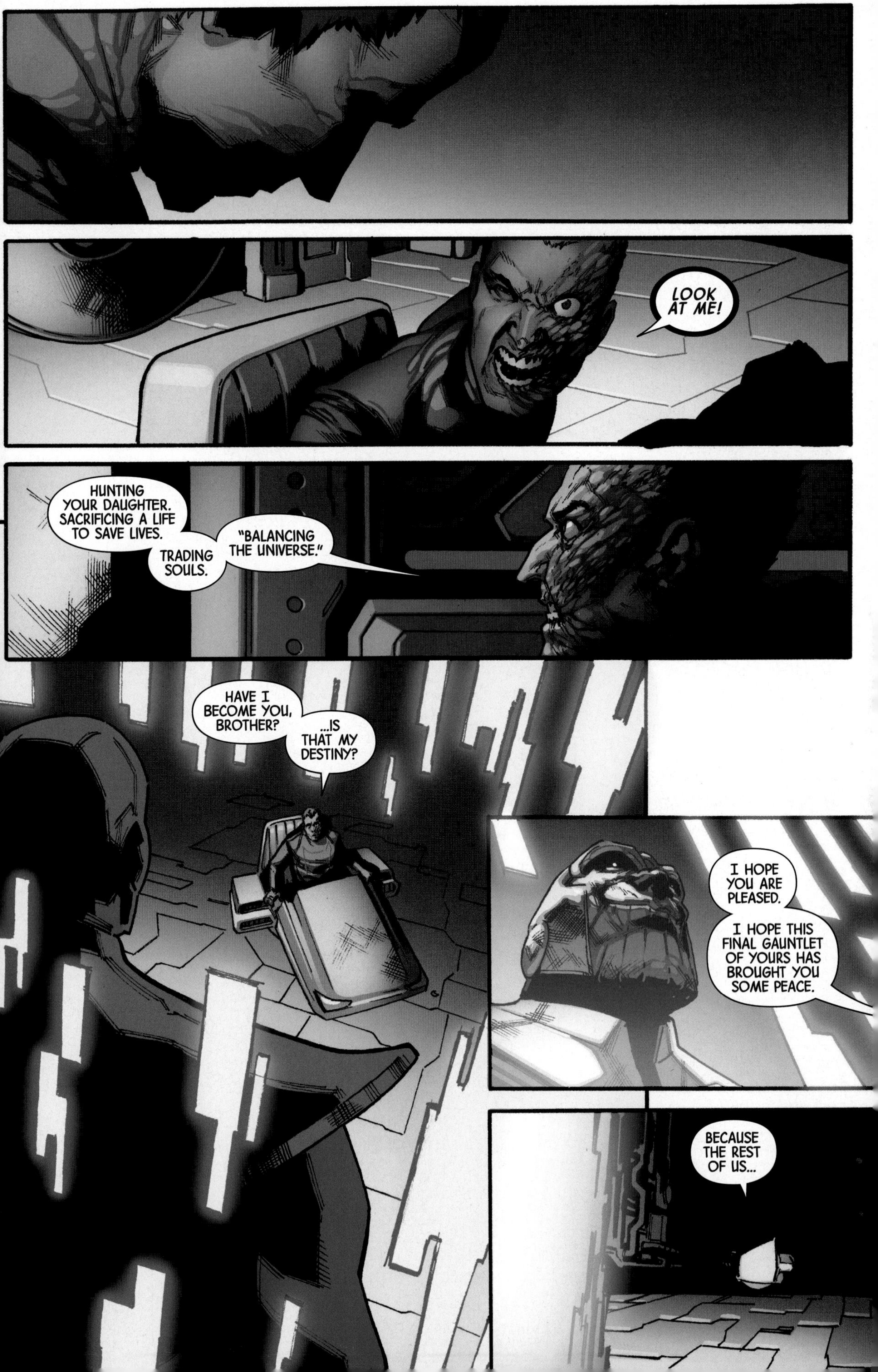
LOOK AT ME!
HUNTING YOUR DAUGHTER. SACRIFICING A LIFE TO SAVE LIVES.
TRADING SOULS.
"BALANCING THE UNIVERSE."
HAVE I BECOME YOU, BROTHER?
...IS THAT MY DESTINY?
I HOPE YOU ARE PLEASED.
I HOPE THIS FINAL GAUNTLET OF YOURS HAS BROUGHT YOU SOME PEACE.
BECAUSE THE REST OF US...

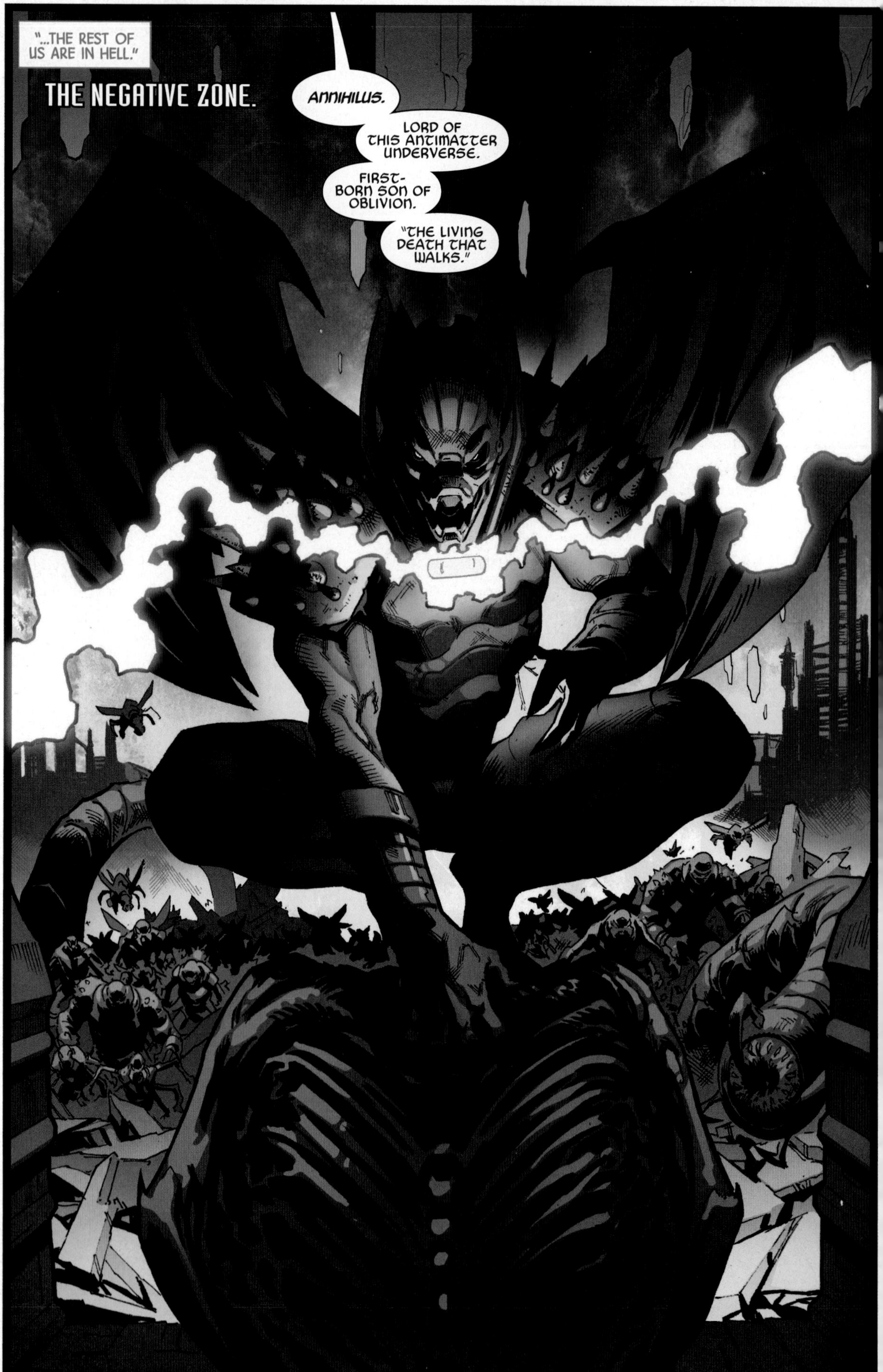
"...THE REST OF US ARE IN HELL."
THE NEGATIVE ZONE.
ANNIHILUS.
LORD OF THIS ANTIMATTER UNDERVERSE.
FIRST-BORN SON OF OBLIVION.
"THE LIVING DEATH THAT WALKS."

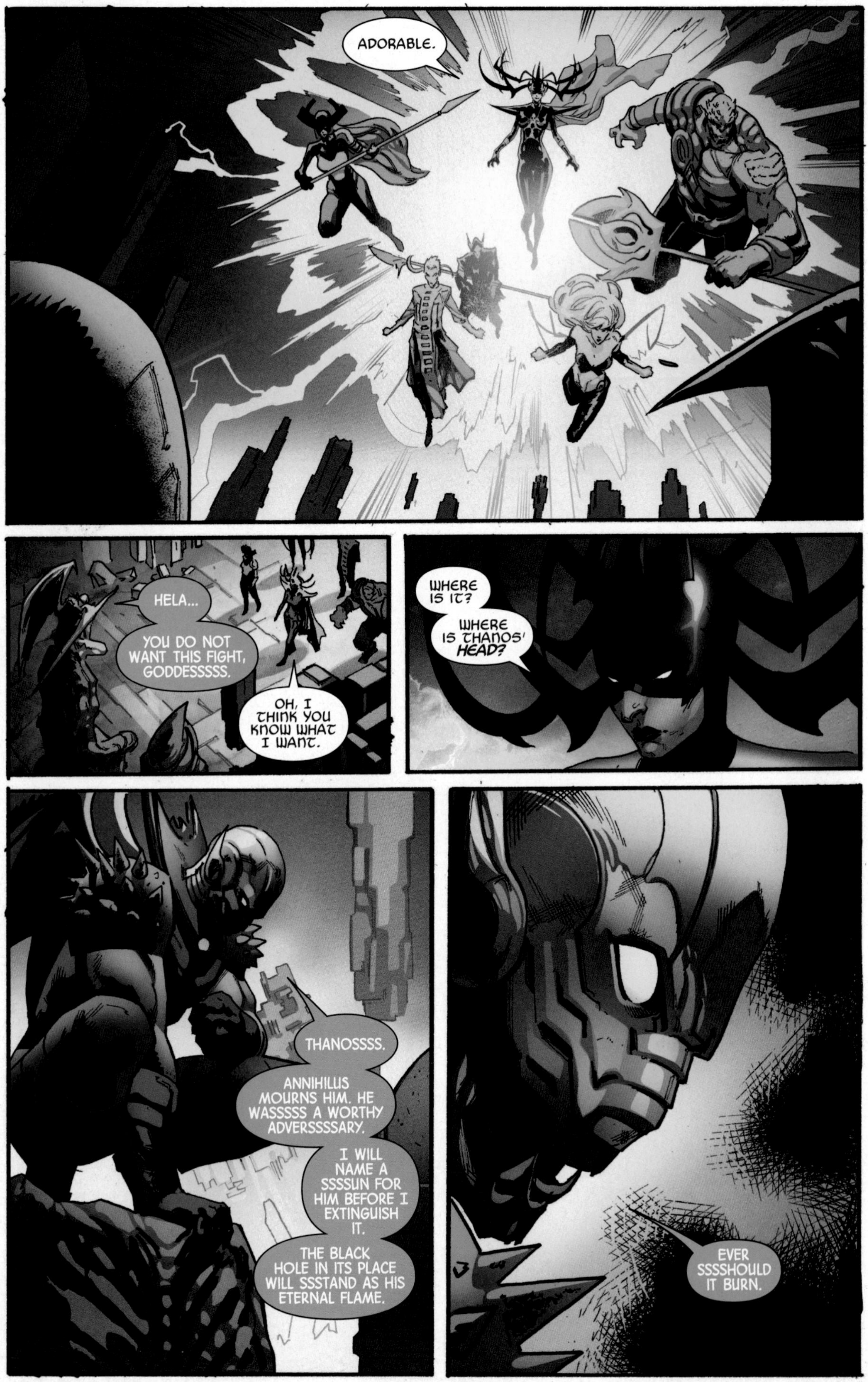
ADORABLE.
HELA...
YOU DO NOT WANT THIS FIGHT, GODDESSSSS.
OH, I THINK YOU KNOW WHAT I WANT.
WHERE IS IT?
WHERE IS THANOS' HEAD?
THANOSSSS.
ANNIHILUS MOURNS HIM. HE WASSSSS A WORTHY ADVERSSSSARY.
I WILL NAME A SSSSUN FOR HIM BEFORE I EXTINGUISH IT.
THE BLACK HOLE IN ITS PLACE WILL SSSTAND AS HIS ETERNAL FLAME.
EVER SSSSHOULD IT BURN.

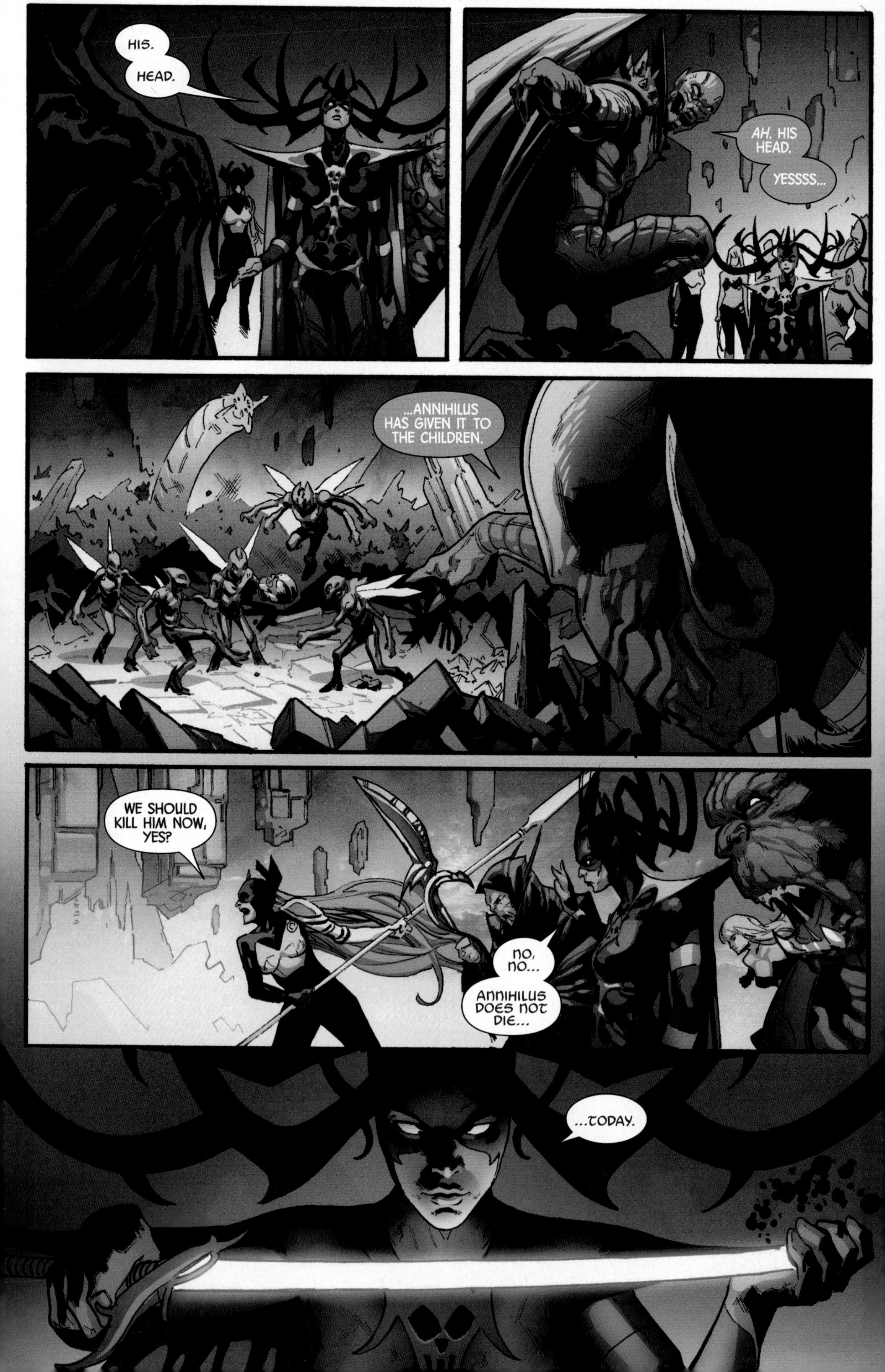
HIS.
HEAD.
AH. HIS HEAD.
YESSSS...
...ANNIHILUS HAS GIVEN IT TO THE CHILDREN.
WE SHOULD KILL HIM NOW, YES?
no, no...
ANNIHILUS DOES NOT DIE...
...TODAY.

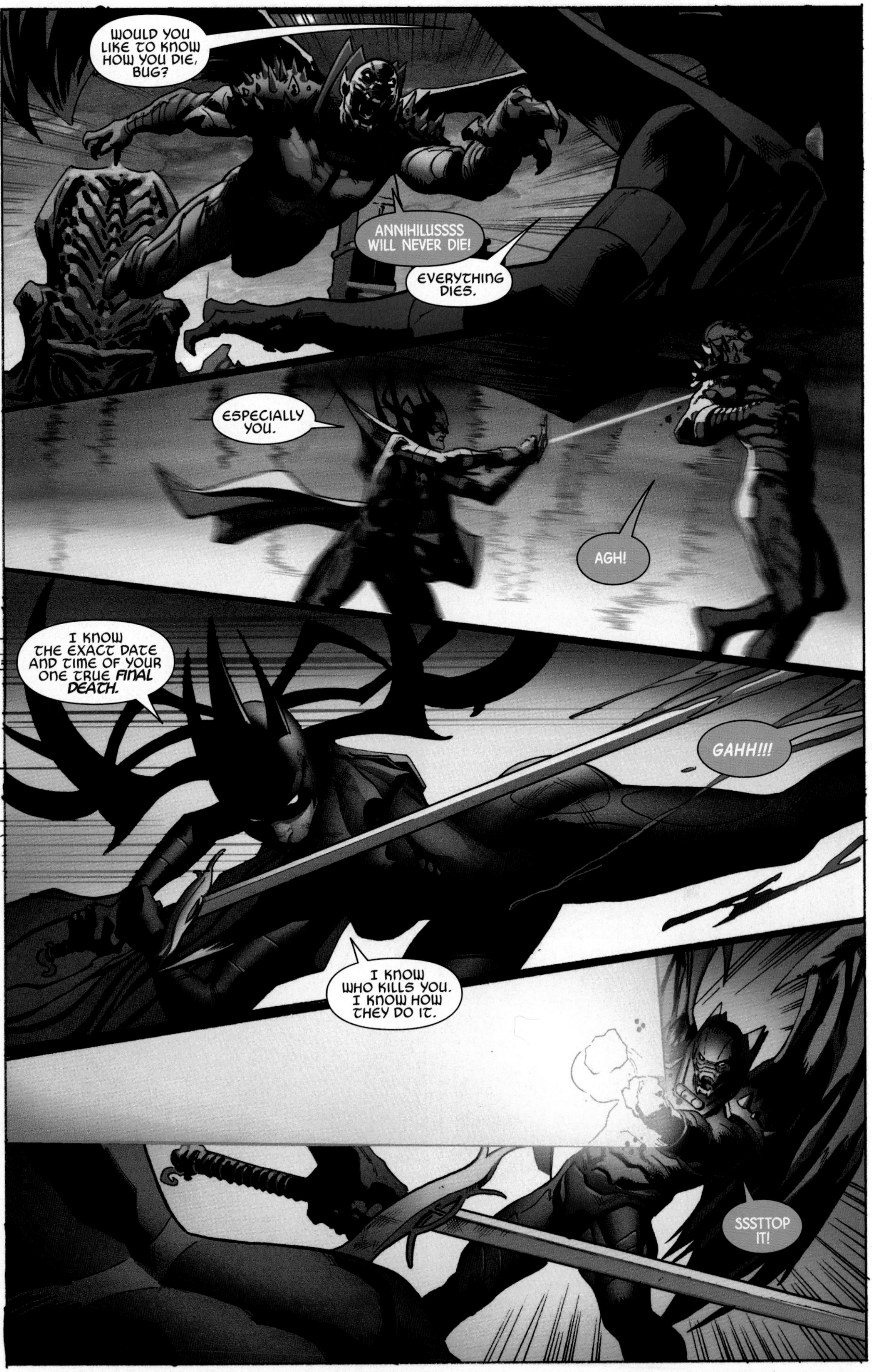
WOULD YOU LIKE TO KNOW HOW YOU DIE, BUG?
ANNIHILUSSSS WILL NEVER DIE!
EVERYTHING DIES.
ESPECIALLY YOU.
AGH!
I KNOW THE EXACT DATE AND TIME OF YOUR ONE TRUE FINAL DEATH.
GAHH!!!
I KNOW WHO KILLS YOU. I KNOW HOW THEY DO IT.
SSSTTOP IT!

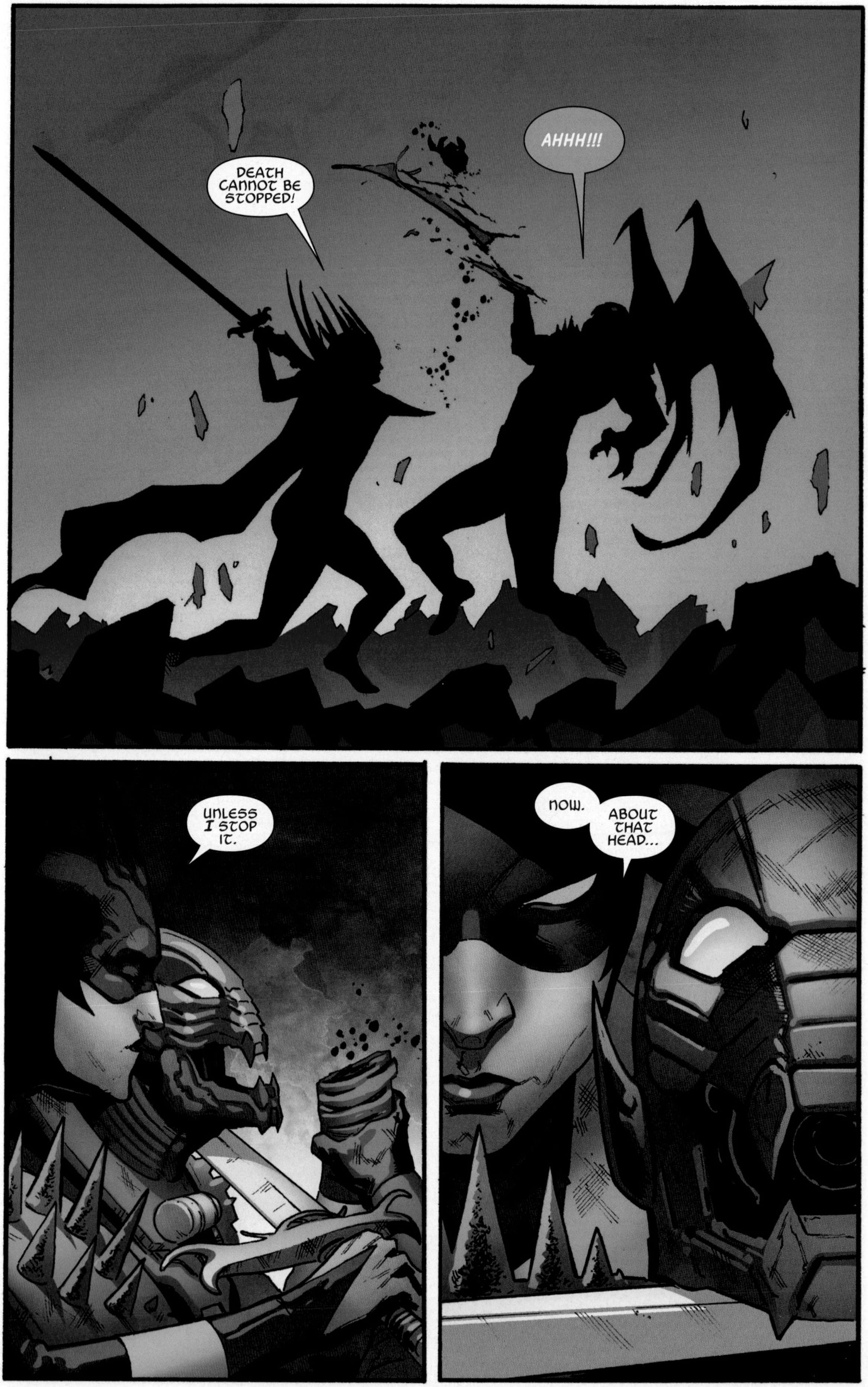
DEATH CANNOT BE STOPPED!
AHHH!!!
UNLESS I STOP IT.
NOW.
ABOUT THAT HEAD...

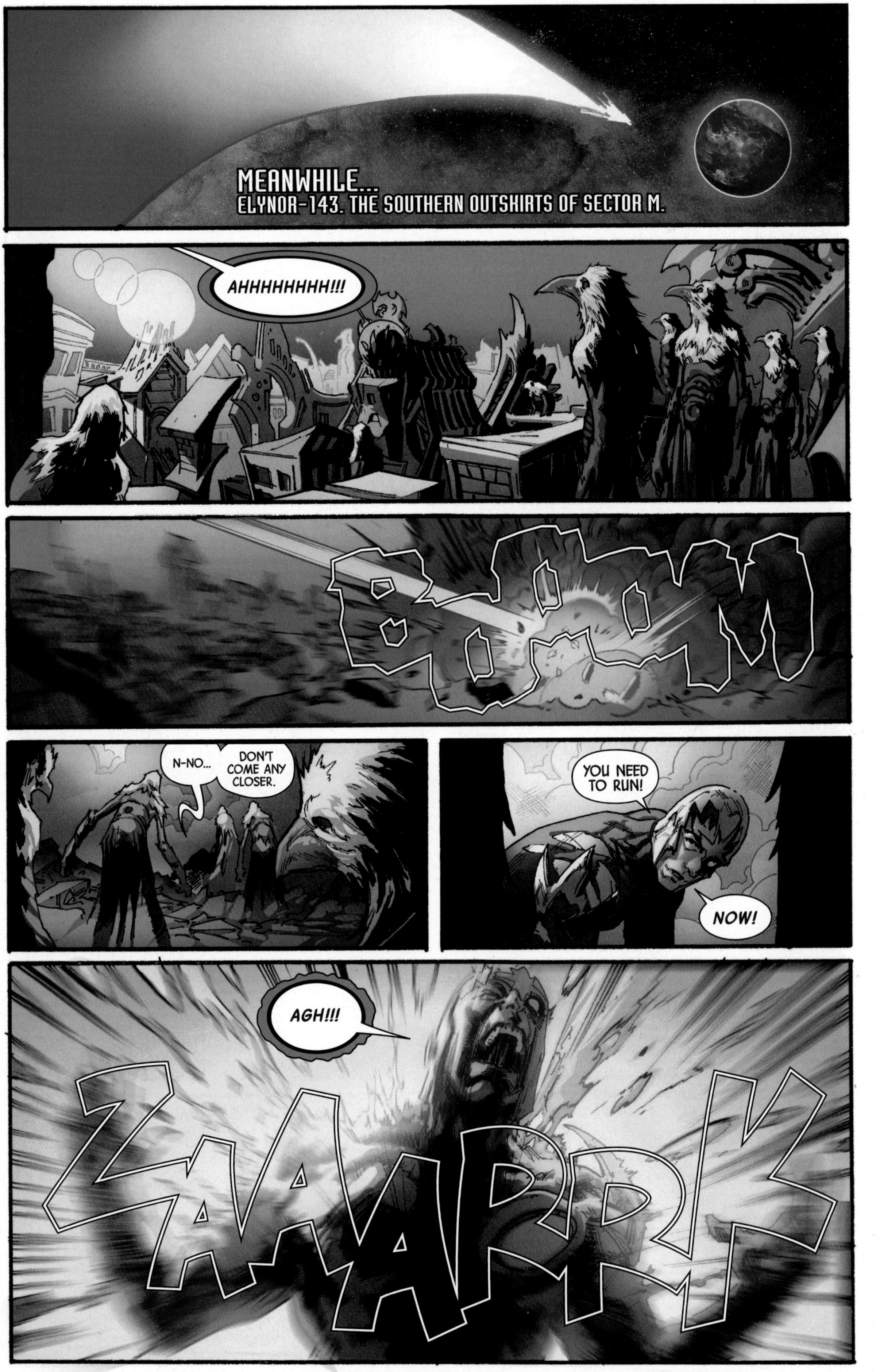
MEANWHILE...
ELYNOR-143. THE SOUTHERN OUTSKIRTS OF SECTOR M.
AHHHHHHHH!!!
BOOOM
N-NO...
DON'T COME ANY CLOSER.
YOU NEED TO RUN!
NOW!
AGH!!!
ZAARRK

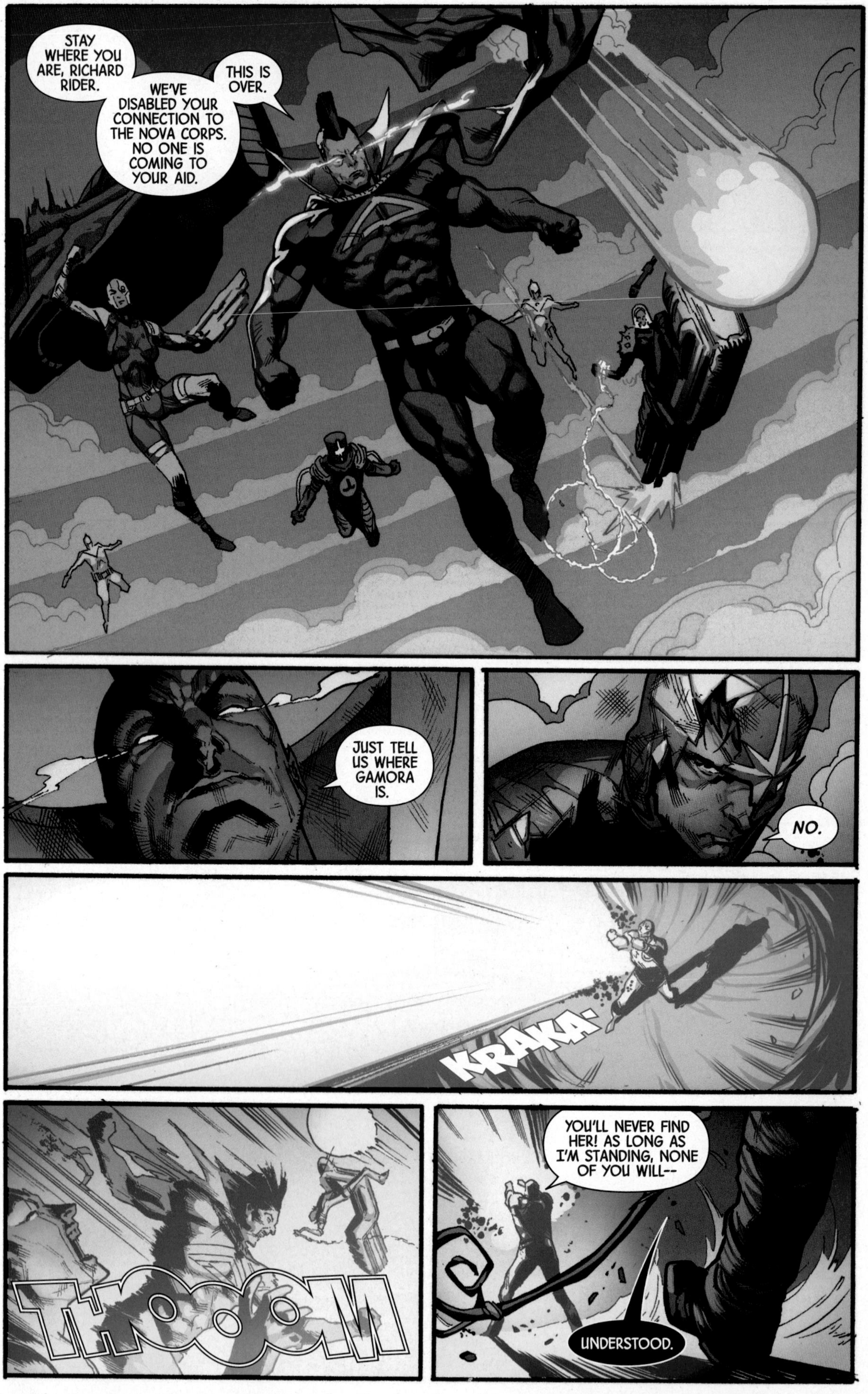
STAY WHERE YOU ARE, RICHARD RIDER.
THIS IS OVER.
WE'VE DISABLED YOUR CONNECTION TO THE NOVA CORPS. NO ONE IS COMING TO YOUR AID.
JUST TELL US WHERE GAMORA IS.
NO.
KRAKA-
THOOOOM
YOU'LL NEVER FIND HER! AS LONG AS I'M STANDING, NONE OF YOU WILL--
UNDERSTOOD.

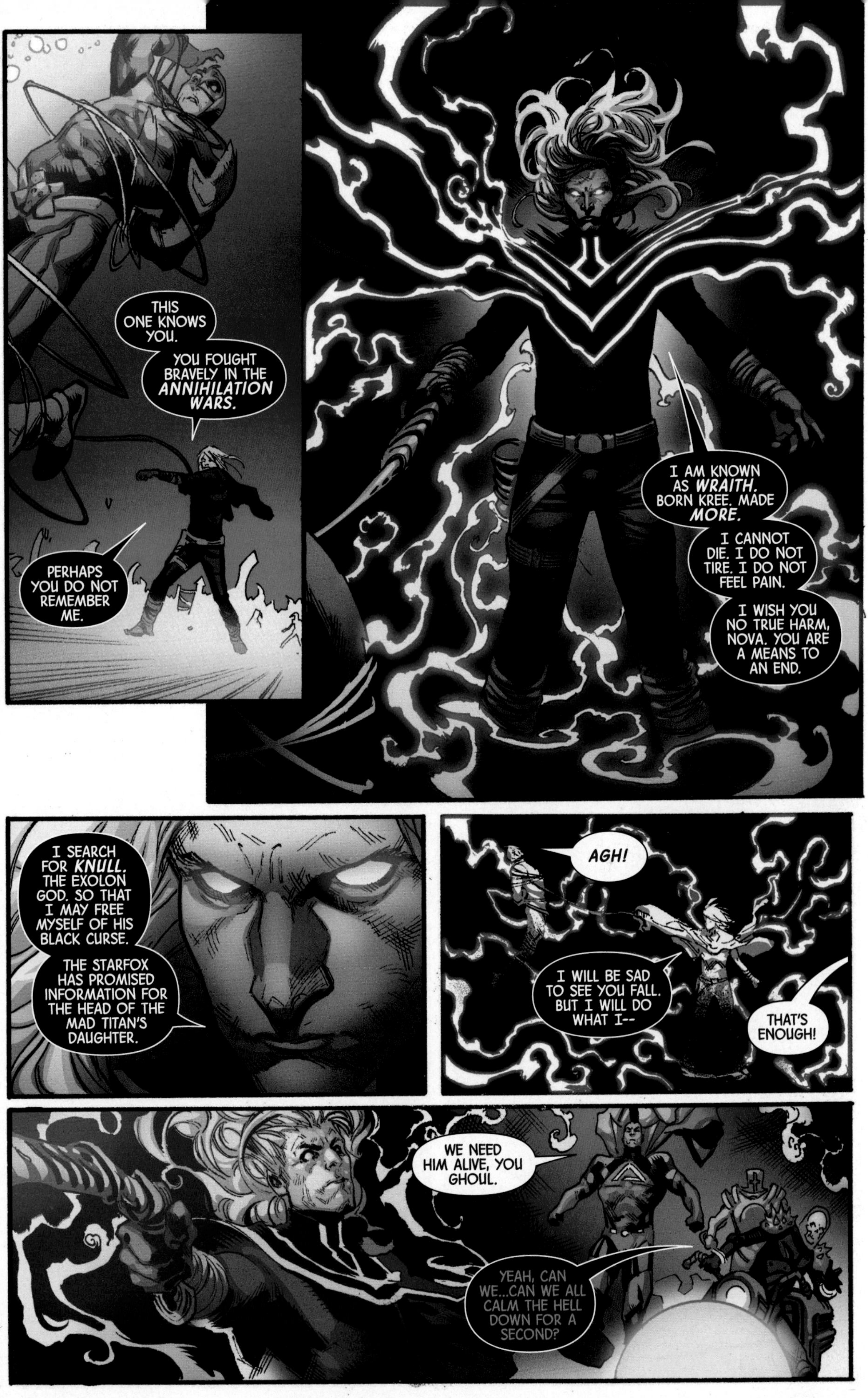
THIS ONE KNOWS YOU.
YOU FOUGHT BRAVELY IN THE ANNIHILATION WARS.
PERHAPS YOU DO NOT REMEMBER ME.
I AM KNOWN AS WRAITH. BORN KREE. MADE MORE.
I CANNOT DIE. I DO NOT TIRE. I DO NOT FEEL PAIN.
I WISH YOU NO TRUE HARM, NOVA. YOU ARE A MEANS TO AN END.
I SEARCH FOR KNULL. THE EXOLON GOD. SO THAT I MAY FREE MYSELF OF HIS BLACK CURSE.
THE STARFOX HAS PROMISED INFORMATION FOR THE HEAD OF THE MAD TITAN'S DAUGHTER.
AGH!
I WILL BE SAD TO SEE YOU FALL. BUT I WILL DO WHAT I--
THAT'S ENOUGH!
WE NEED HIM ALIVE, YOU GHOUL.
YEAH, CAN WE...CAN WE ALL CALM THE HELL DOWN FOR A SECOND?

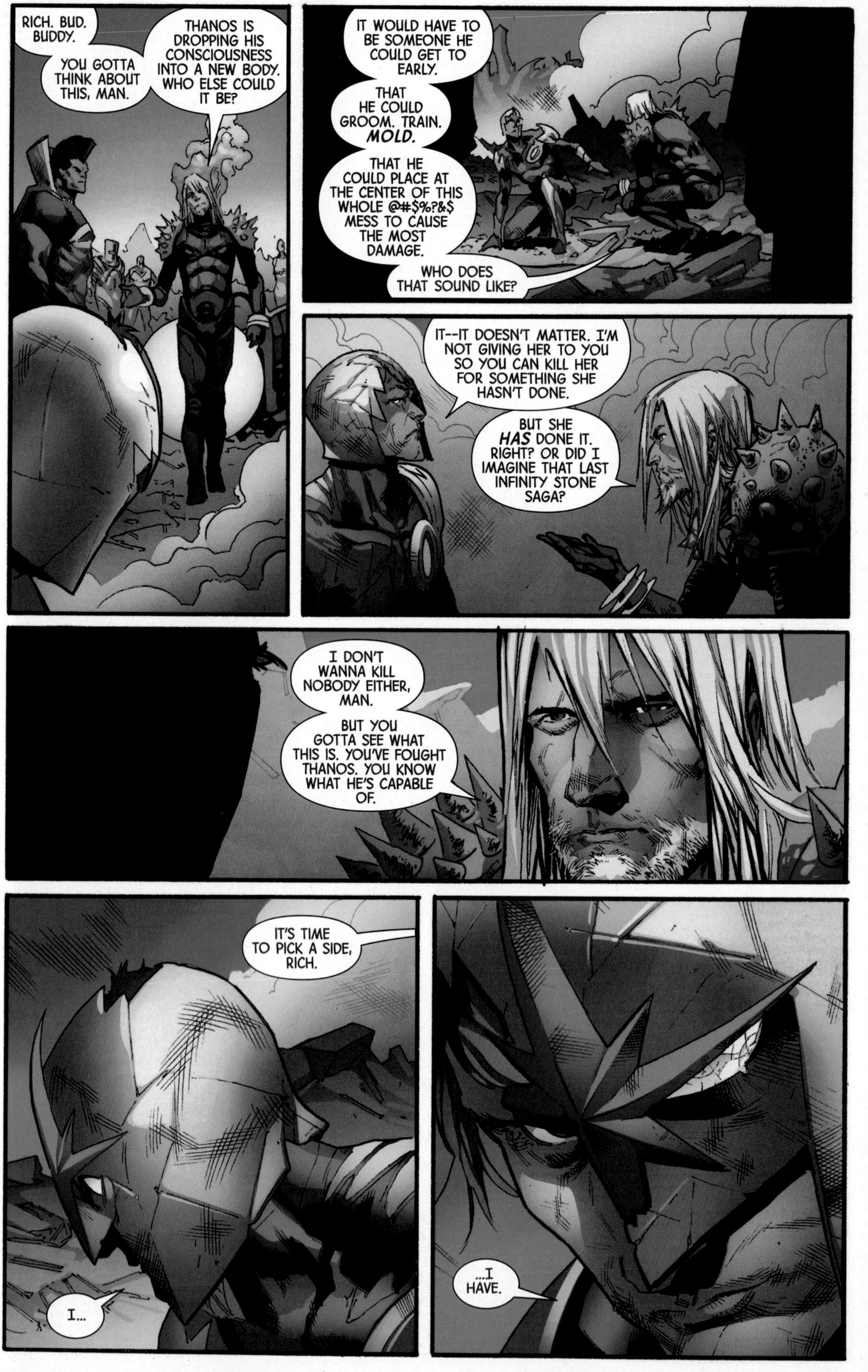
RICH. BUD. BUDDY.
YOU GOTTA THINK ABOUT THIS, MAN.
THANOS IS DROPPING HIS CONSCIOUSNESS INTO A NEW BODY. WHO ELSE COULD IT BE?
IT WOULD HAVE TO BE SOMEONE HE COULD GET TO EARLY.
THAT HE COULD GROOM. TRAIN. MOLD.
THAT HE COULD PLACE AT THE CENTER OF THIS WHOLE @#$%?&$ MESS TO CAUSE THE MOST DAMAGE.
WHO DOES THAT SOUND LIKE?
IT--IT DOESN'T MATTER. I'M NOT GIVING HER TO YOU SO YOU CAN KILL HER FOR SOMETHING SHE HASN'T DONE.
BUT SHE HAS DONE IT. RIGHT? OR DID I IMAGINE THAT LAST INFINITY STONE SAGA?
I DON'T WANNA KILL NOBODY EITHER, MAN.
BUT YOU GOTTA SEE WHAT THIS IS. YOU'VE FOUGHT THANOS. YOU KNOW WHAT HE'S CAPABLE OF.
IT'S TIME TO PICK A SIDE, RICH.
I...
...I HAVE.

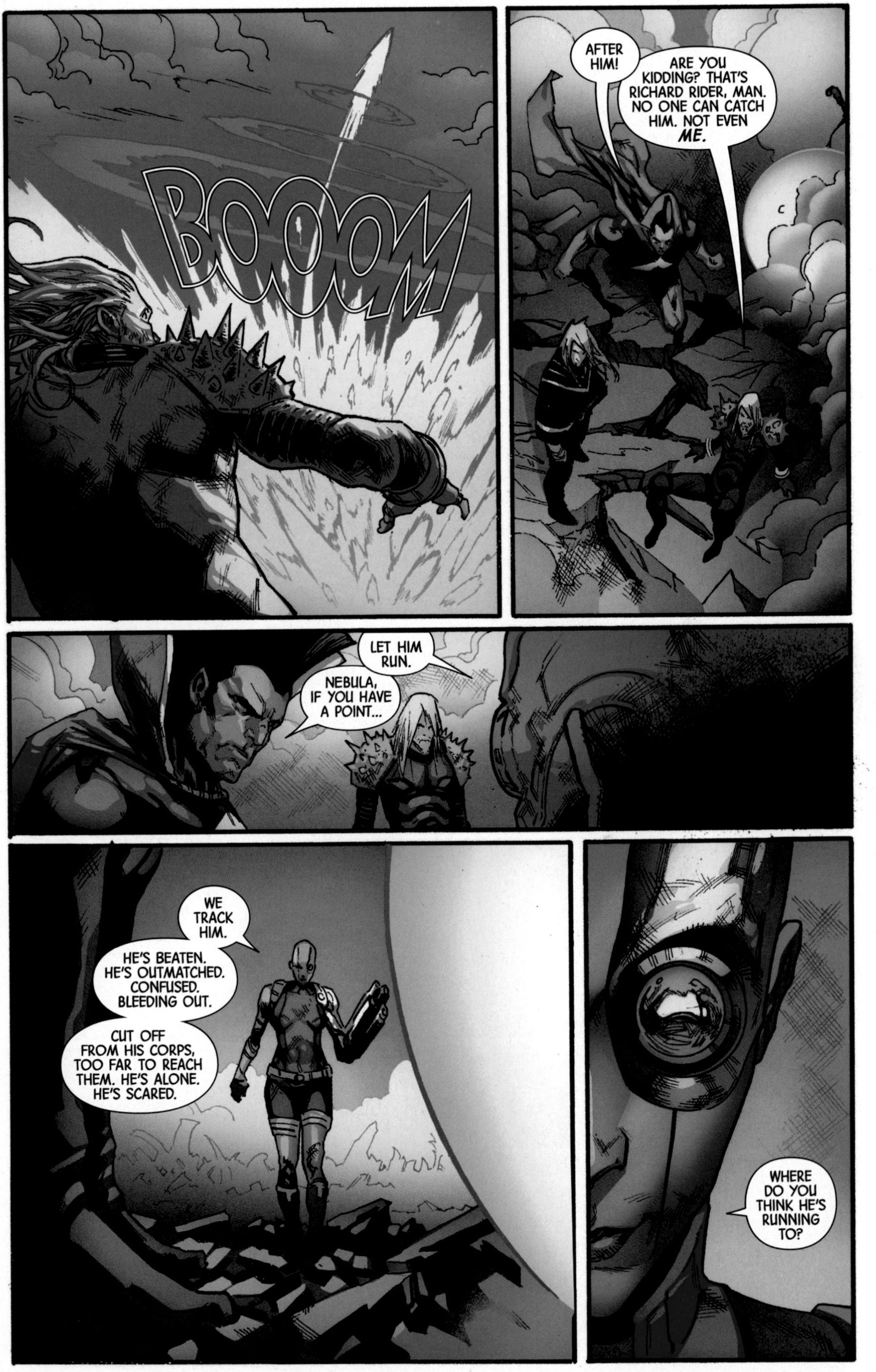
BOOOM
AFTER HIM!
ARE YOU KIDDING? THAT'S RICHARD RIDER, MAN. NO ONE CAN CATCH HIM. NOT EVEN ME.
LET HIM RUN.
NEBULA, IF YOU HAVE A POINT...
WE TRACK HIM.
HE'S BEATEN. HE'S OUTMATCHED. CONFUSED. BLEEDING OUT.
CUT OFF FROM HIS CORPS, TOO FAR TO REACH THEM. HE'S ALONE. HE'S SCARED.
WHERE DO YOU THINK HE'S RUNNING TO?

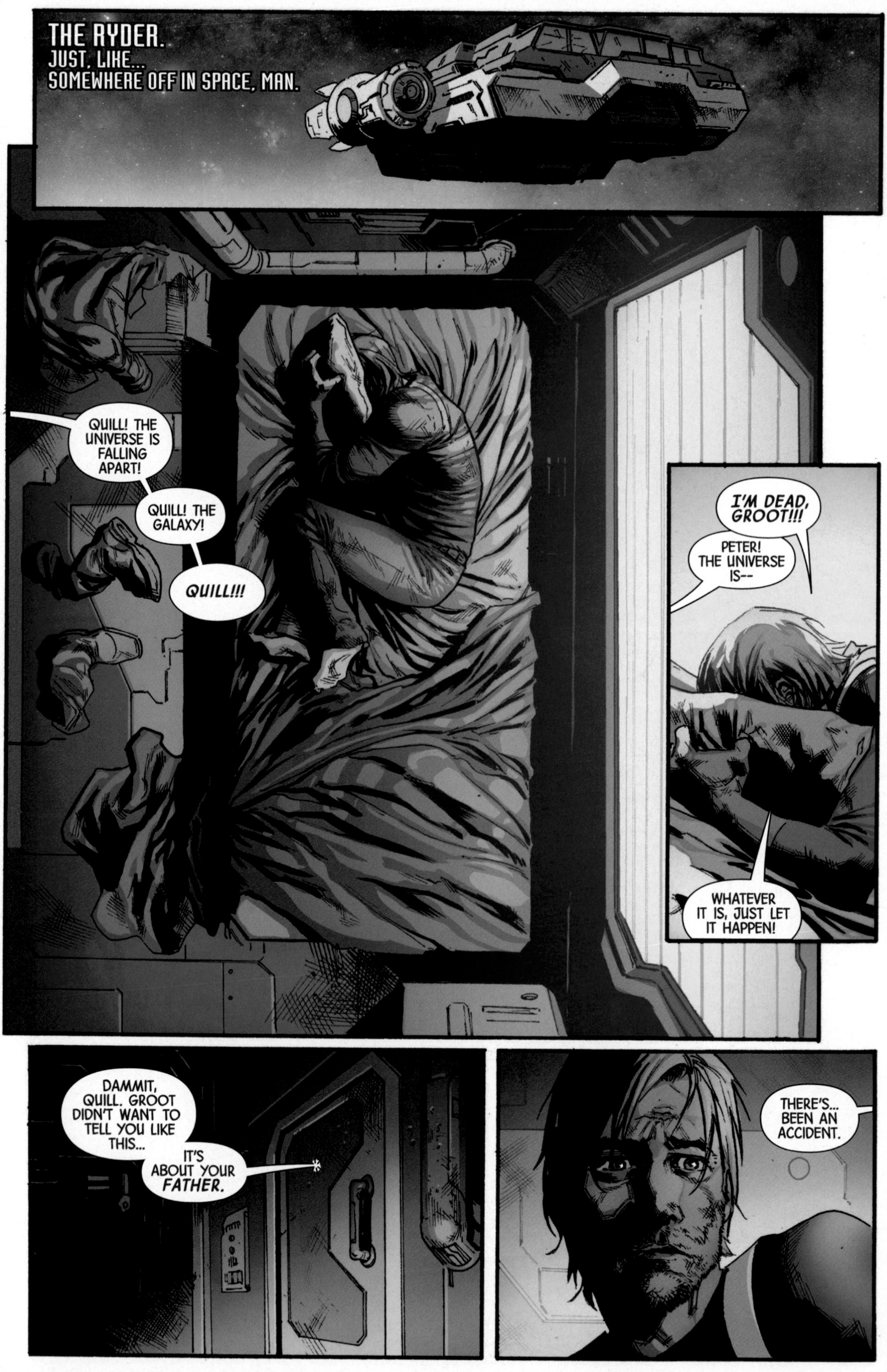
THE RYDER.
JUST, LIKE...
SOMEWHERE OFF IN SPACE, MAN.
QUILL! THE UNIVERSE IS FALLING APART!
QUILL! THE GALAXY!
QUILL!!!
I'M DEAD, GROOT!!!
PETER! THE UNIVERSE IS--
WHATEVER IT IS, JUST LET IT HAPPEN!
DAMMIT, QUILL. GROOT DIDN'T WANT TO TELL YOU LIKE THIS...
IT'S ABOUT YOUR FATHER.
THERE'S... BEEN AN ACCIDENT.

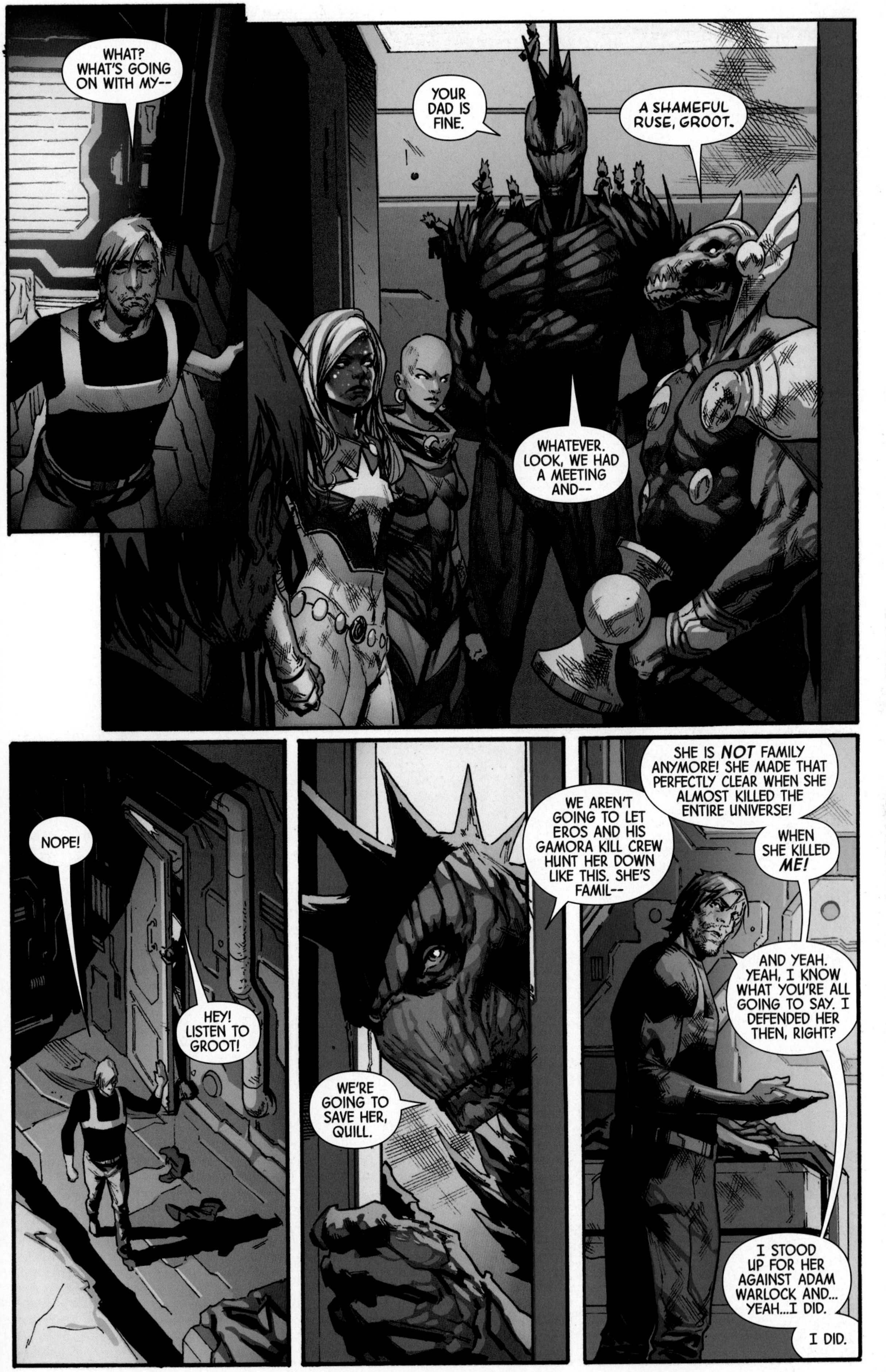
WHAT? WHAT'S GOING ON WITH MY--
YOUR DAD IS FINE.
A SHAMEFUL RUSE, GROOT.
WHATEVER. LOOK, WE HAD A MEETING AND--
NOPE!
HEY! LISTEN TO GROOT!
WE AREN'T GOING TO LET EROS AND HIS GAMORA KILL CREW HUNT HER DOWN LIKE THIS. SHE'S FAMIL--
WE'RE GOING TO SAVE HER, QUILL.
SHE IS NOT FAMILY ANYMORE! SHE MADE THAT PERFECTLY CLEAR WHEN SHE ALMOST KILLED THE ENTIRE UNIVERSE!
WHEN SHE KILLED ME!
AND YEAH. YEAH, I KNOW WHAT YOU'RE ALL GOING TO SAY. I DEFENDED HER THEN, RIGHT?
I STOOD UP FOR HER AGAINST ADAM WARLOCK AND... YEAH...I DID.
I DID.

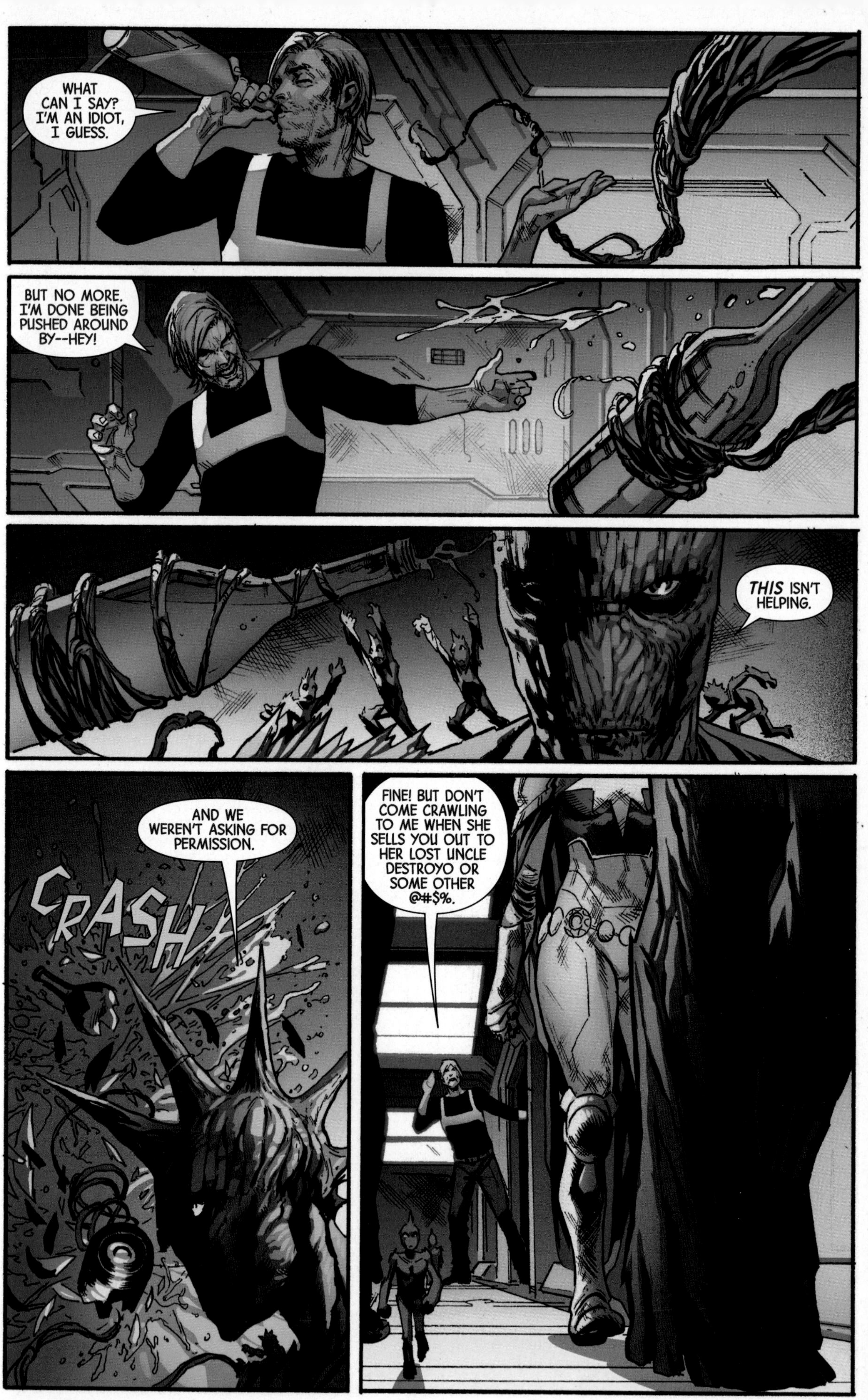
WHAT CAN I SAY? I'M AN IDIOT, I GUESS.
BUT NO MORE. I'M DONE BEING PUSHED AROUND BY--HEY!
THIS ISN'T HELPING.
AND WE WEREN'T ASKING FOR PERMISSION.
CRASH
FINE! BUT DON'T COME CRAWLING TO ME WHEN SHE SELLS YOU OUT TO HER LOST UNCLE DESTROYO OR SOME OTHER @#$%.

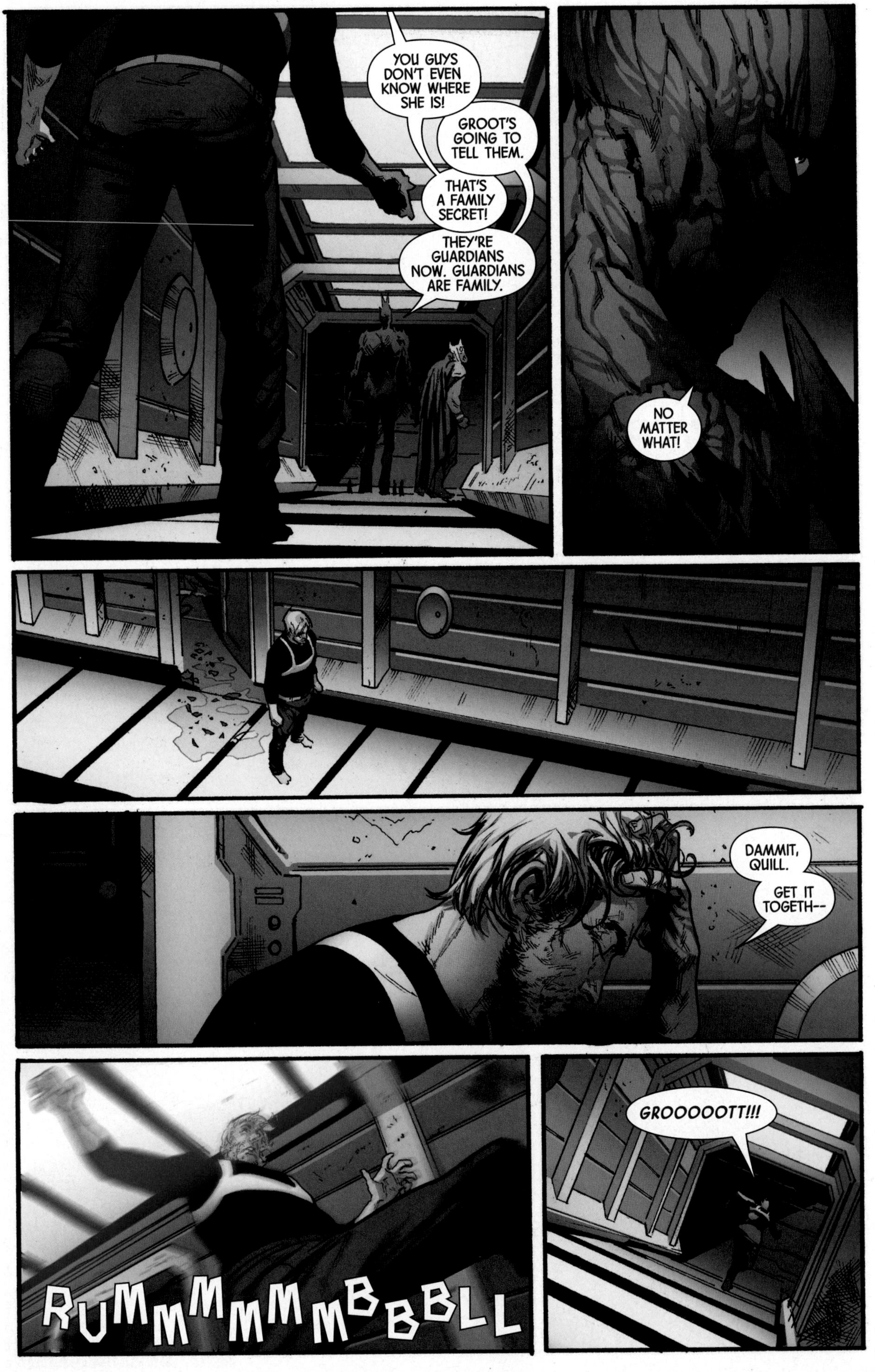
YOU GUYS DON'T EVEN KNOW WHERE SHE IS!
GROOT'S GOING TO TELL THEM.
THAT'S A FAMILY SECRET!
THEY'RE GUARDIANS NOW. GUARDIANS ARE FAMILY.
NO MATTER WHAT!
DAMMIT, QUILL.
GET IT TOGETH--
RUMMMMMMBBBLL
GROOOOOTT!!!

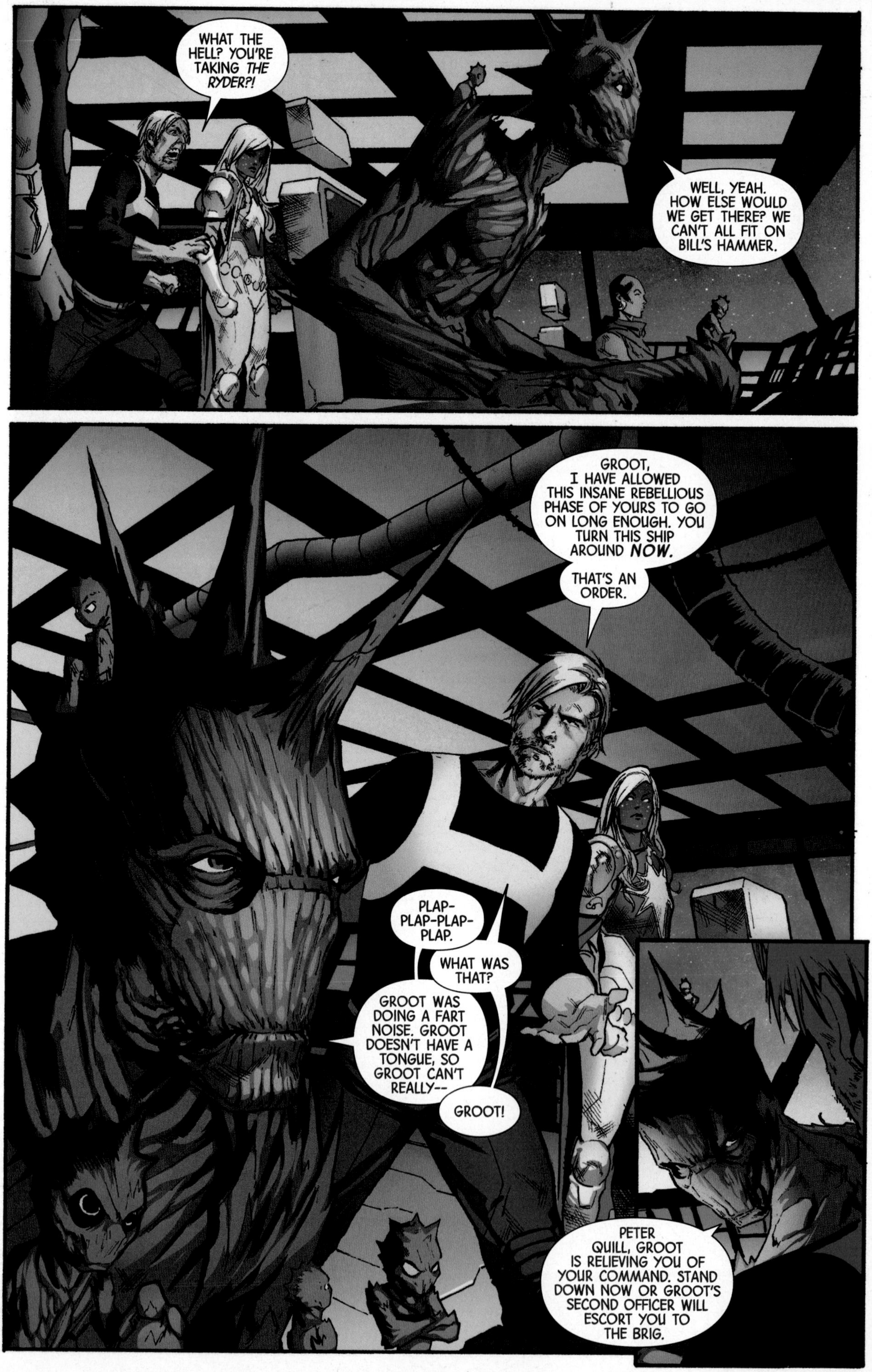
WHAT THE HELL? YOU'RE TAKING *THE RYDER?!*
WELL, YEAH. HOW ELSE WOULD WE GET THERE? WE CAN'T ALL FIT ON BILL'S HAMMER.
GROOT, I HAVE ALLOWED THIS INSANE REBELLIOUS PHASE OF YOURS TO GO ON LONG ENOUGH. YOU TURN THIS SHIP AROUND **NOW.**
THAT'S AN ORDER.
PLAP-PLAP-PLAP-PLAP.
WHAT WAS THAT?
GROOT WAS DOING A FART NOISE. GROOT DOESN'T HAVE A TONGUE, SO GROOT CAN'T REALLY--
GROOT!
PETER QUILL, GROOT IS RELIEVING YOU OF YOUR COMMAND. STAND DOWN NOW OR GROOT'S SECOND OFFICER WILL ESCORT YOU TO THE BRIG.

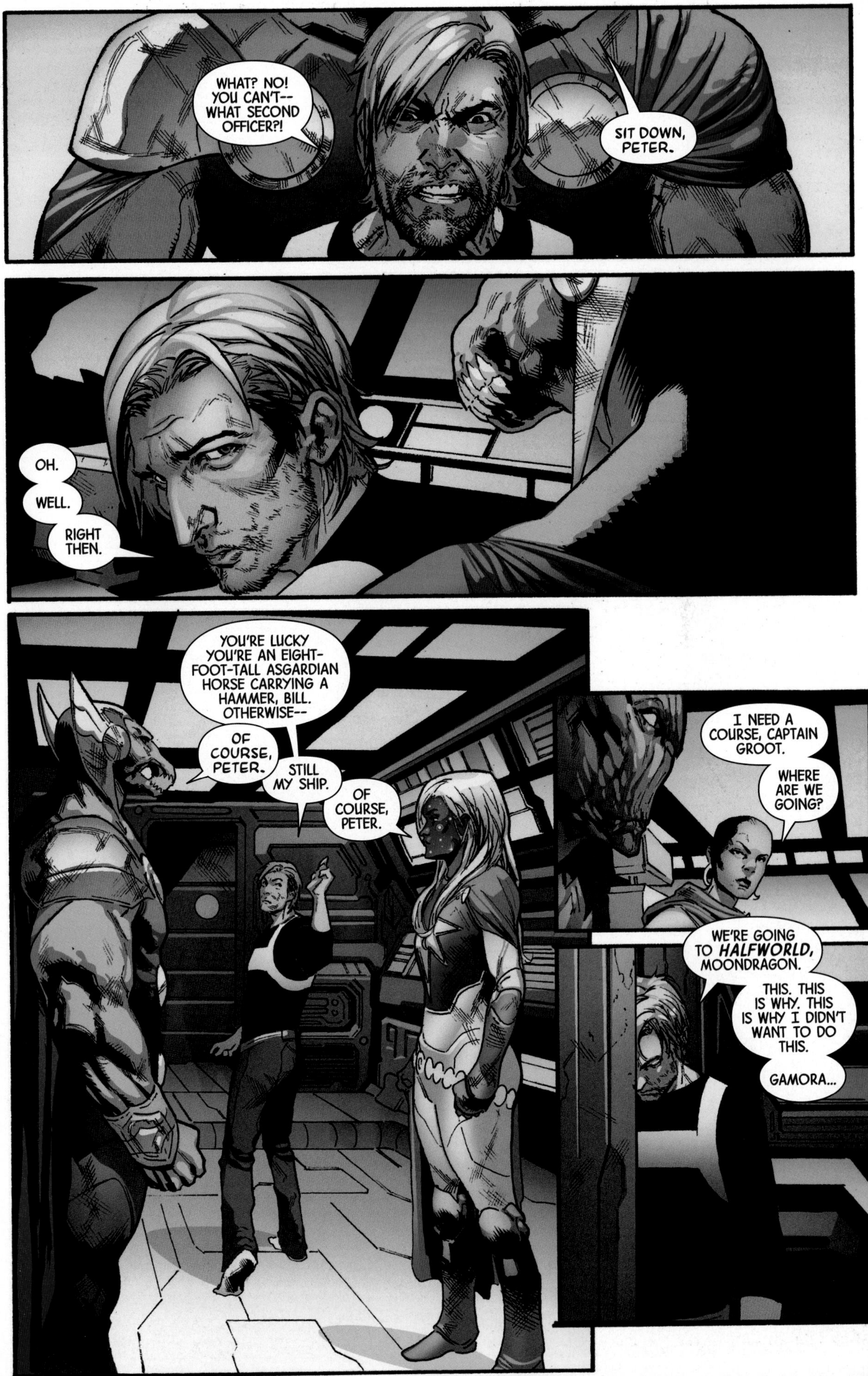
WHAT? NO! YOU CAN'T-- WHAT SECOND OFFICER?!
SIT DOWN, PETER.
OH.
WELL.
RIGHT THEN.
YOU'RE LUCKY YOU'RE AN EIGHT-FOOT-TALL ASGARDIAN HORSE CARRYING A HAMMER, BILL. OTHERWISE--
OF COURSE, PETER.
STILL MY SHIP.
OF COURSE, PETER.
I NEED A COURSE, CAPTAIN GROOT.
WHERE ARE WE GOING?
WE'RE GOING TO HALFWORLD, MOONDRAGON.
THIS. THIS IS WHY. THIS IS WHY I DIDN'T WANT TO DO THIS.
GAMORA...

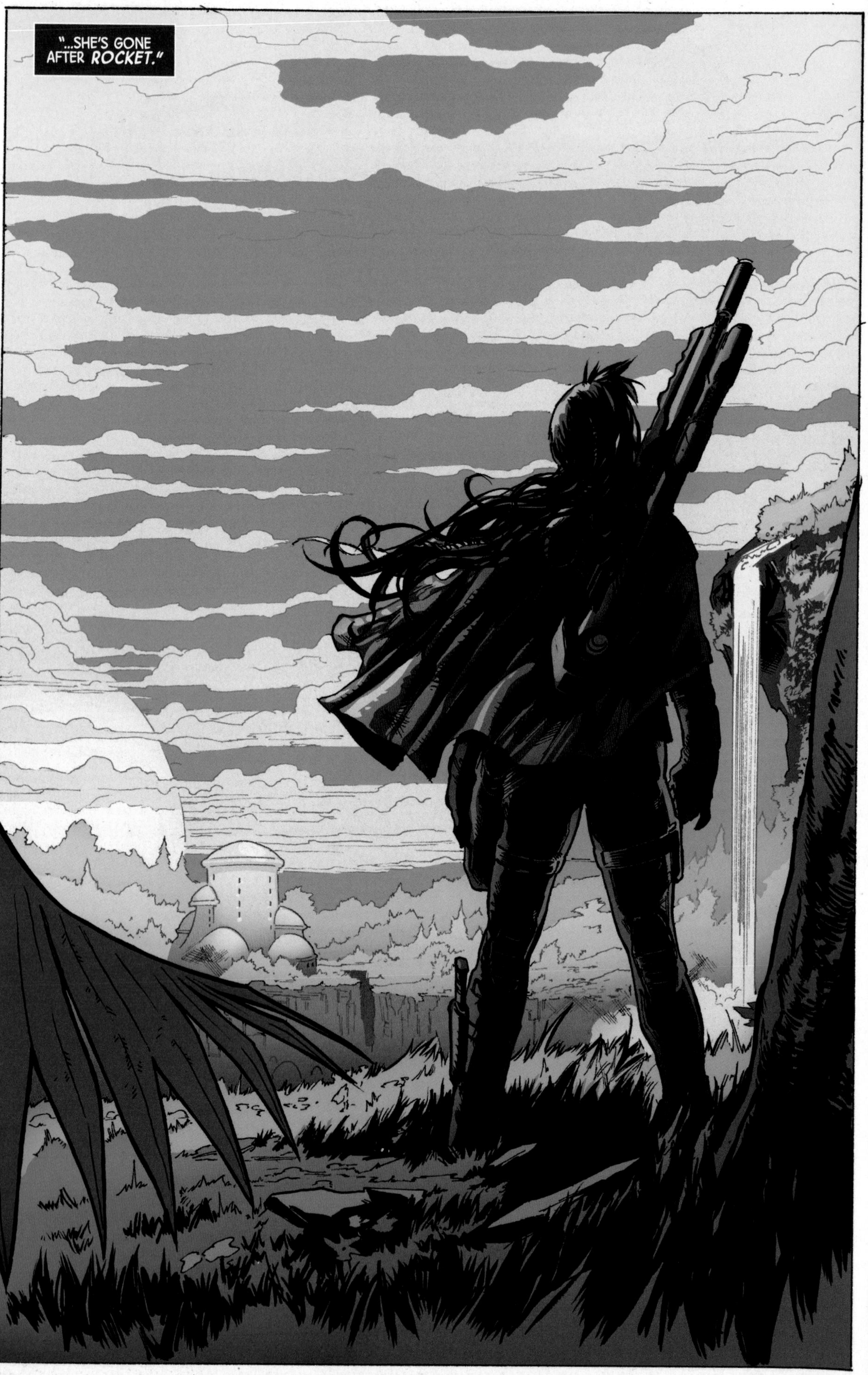
"...SHE'S GONE AFTER ROCKET."

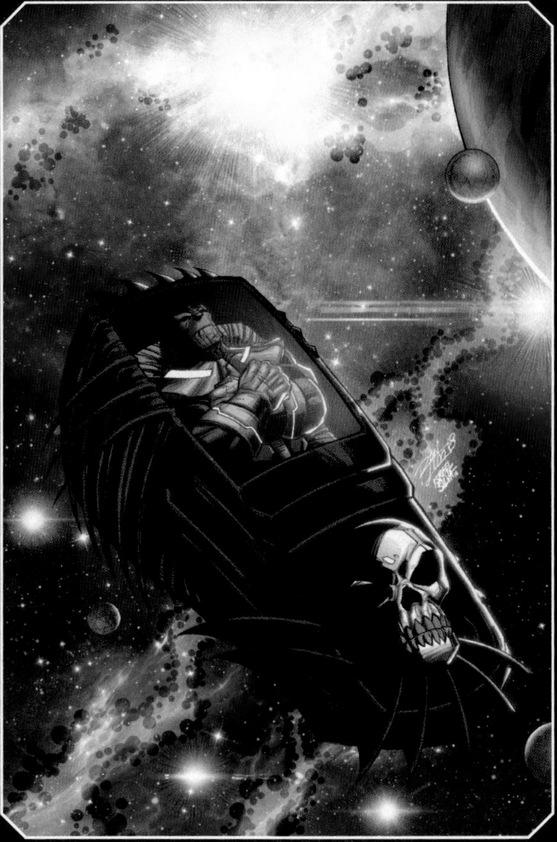

RON LIM & ISRAEL SILVA
#1 variant

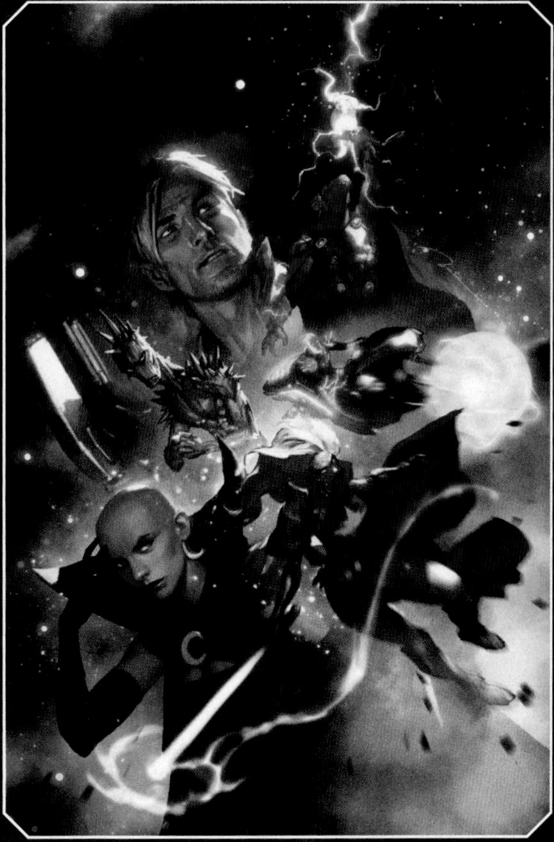

GERALD PAREL
#1 variant

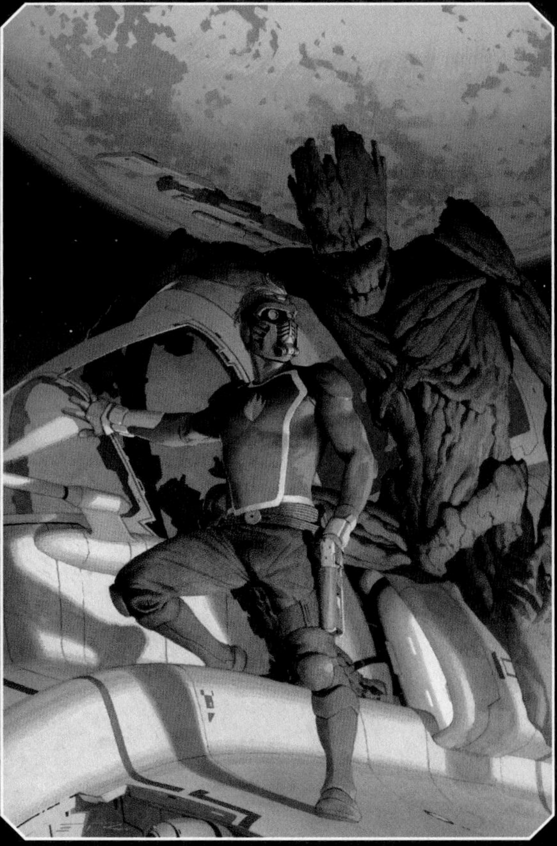

ESAD RIBIĆ
#1 variant

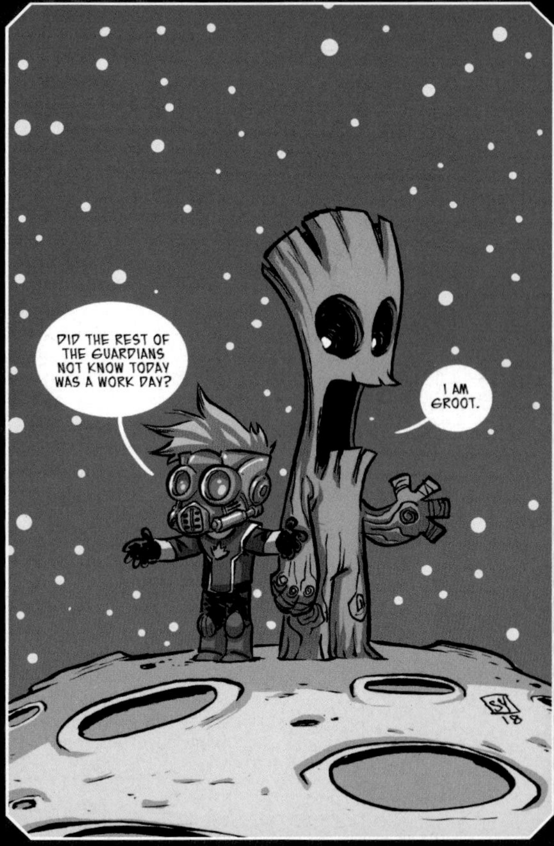
DID THE REST OF THE GUARDIANS NOT KNOW TODAY WAS A WORK DAY?
I AM GROOT.

SKOTTIE YOUNG
#1 variant

FOUR

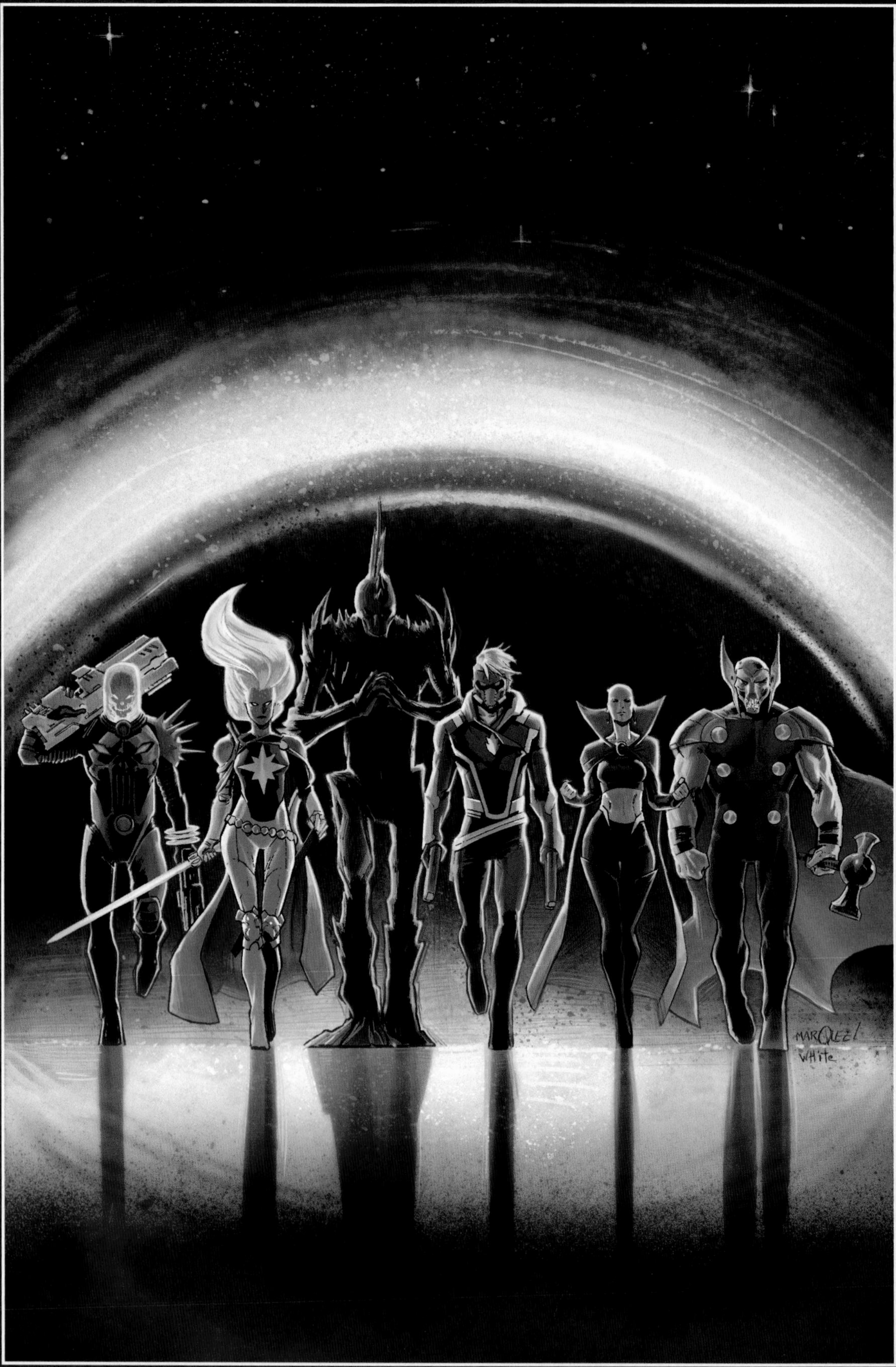
MARQUEZ/
WHITE

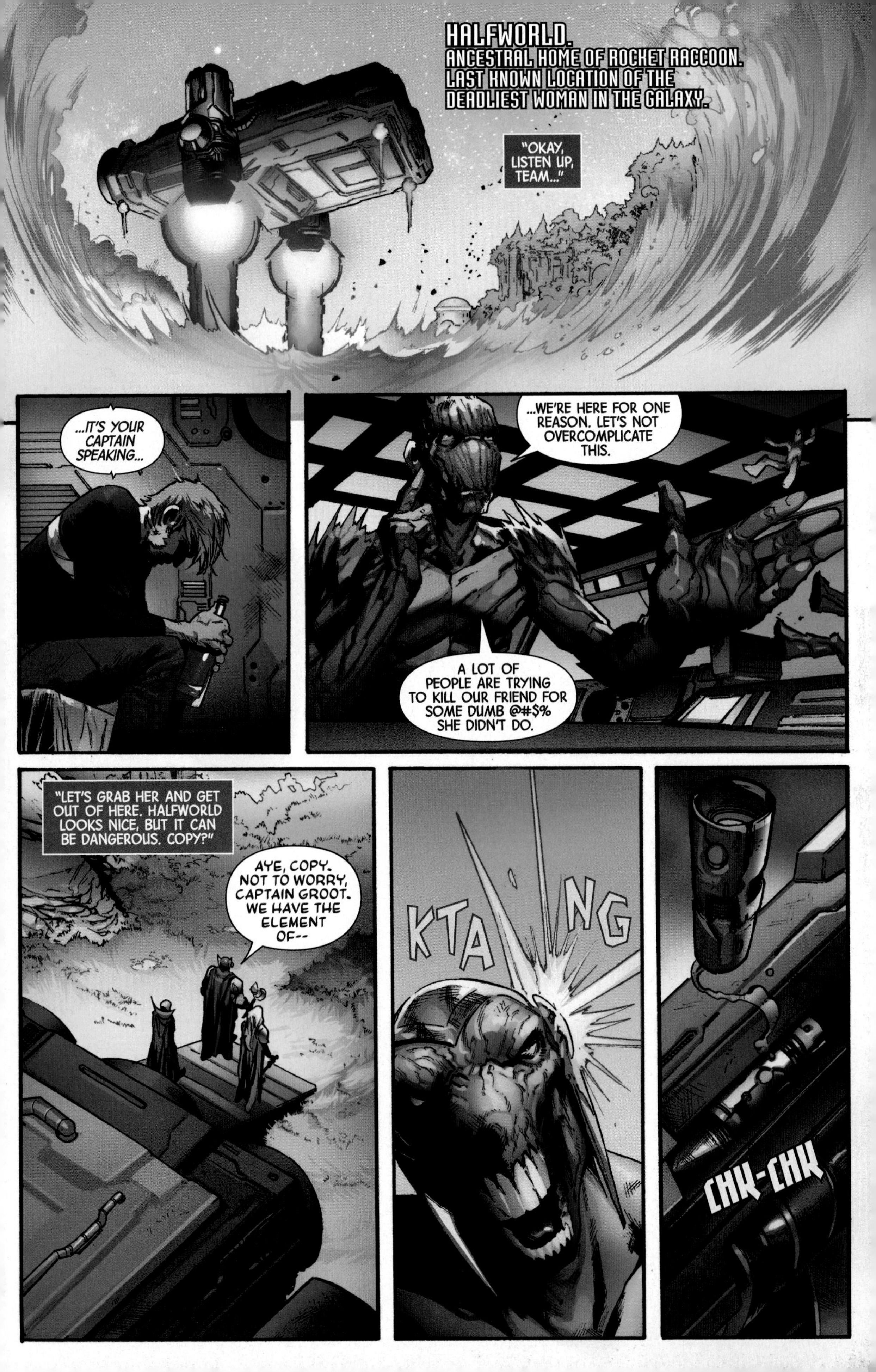
HALFWORLD.
ANCESTRAL HOME OF ROCKET RACCOON. LAST KNOWN LOCATION OF THE DEADLIEST WOMAN IN THE GALAXY.
"OKAY, LISTEN UP, TEAM..."
...IT'S YOUR CAPTAIN SPEAKING...
...WE'RE HERE FOR ONE REASON. LET'S NOT OVERCOMPLICATE THIS.
A LOT OF PEOPLE ARE TRYING TO KILL OUR FRIEND FOR SOME DUMB @#$% SHE DIDN'T DO.
"LET'S GRAB HER AND GET OUT OF HERE. HALFWORLD LOOKS NICE, BUT IT CAN BE DANGEROUS. COPY?"
AYE, COPY. NOT TO WORRY, CAPTAIN GROOT. WE HAVE THE ELEMENT OF--
KTANG
CHK-CHK

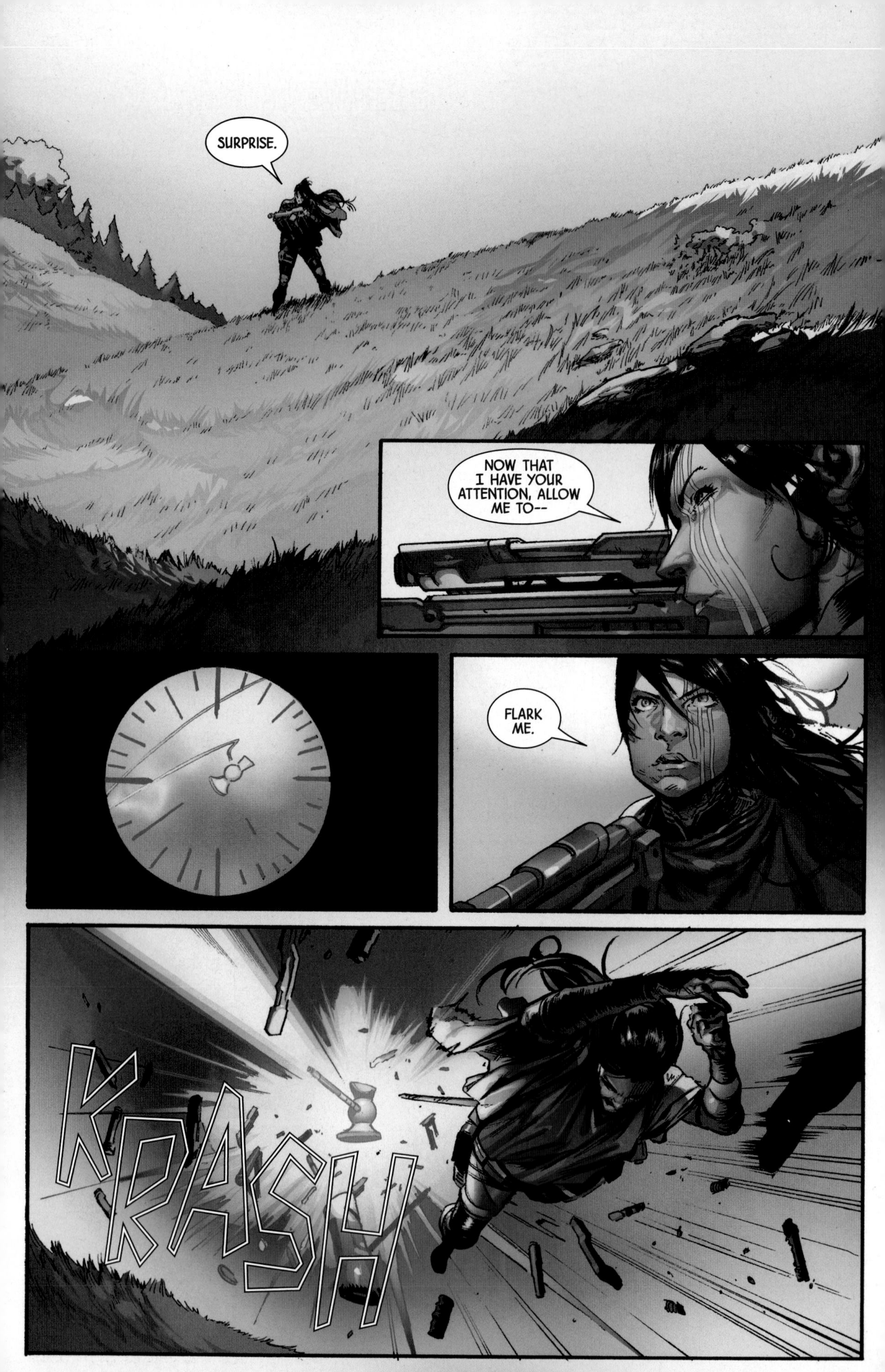
SURPRISE.
NOW THAT I HAVE YOUR ATTENTION, ALLOW ME TO--
FLARK ME.
KRASH

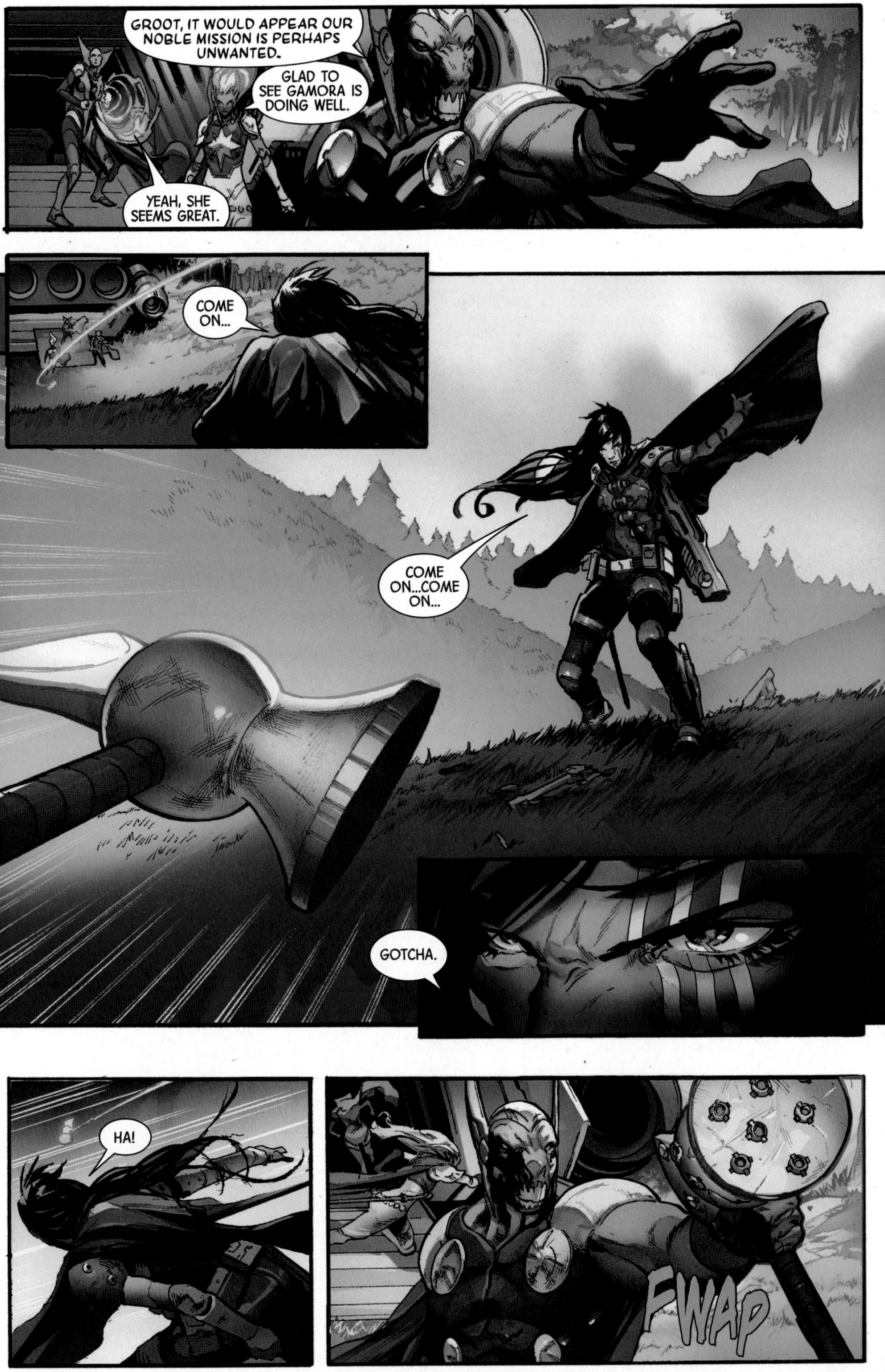
GROOT, IT WOULD APPEAR OUR NOBLE MISSION IS PERHAPS UNWANTED.
GLAD TO SEE GAMORA IS DOING WELL.
YEAH, SHE SEEMS GREAT.
COME ON...
COME ON...COME ON...
GOTCHA.
HA!
FWAP

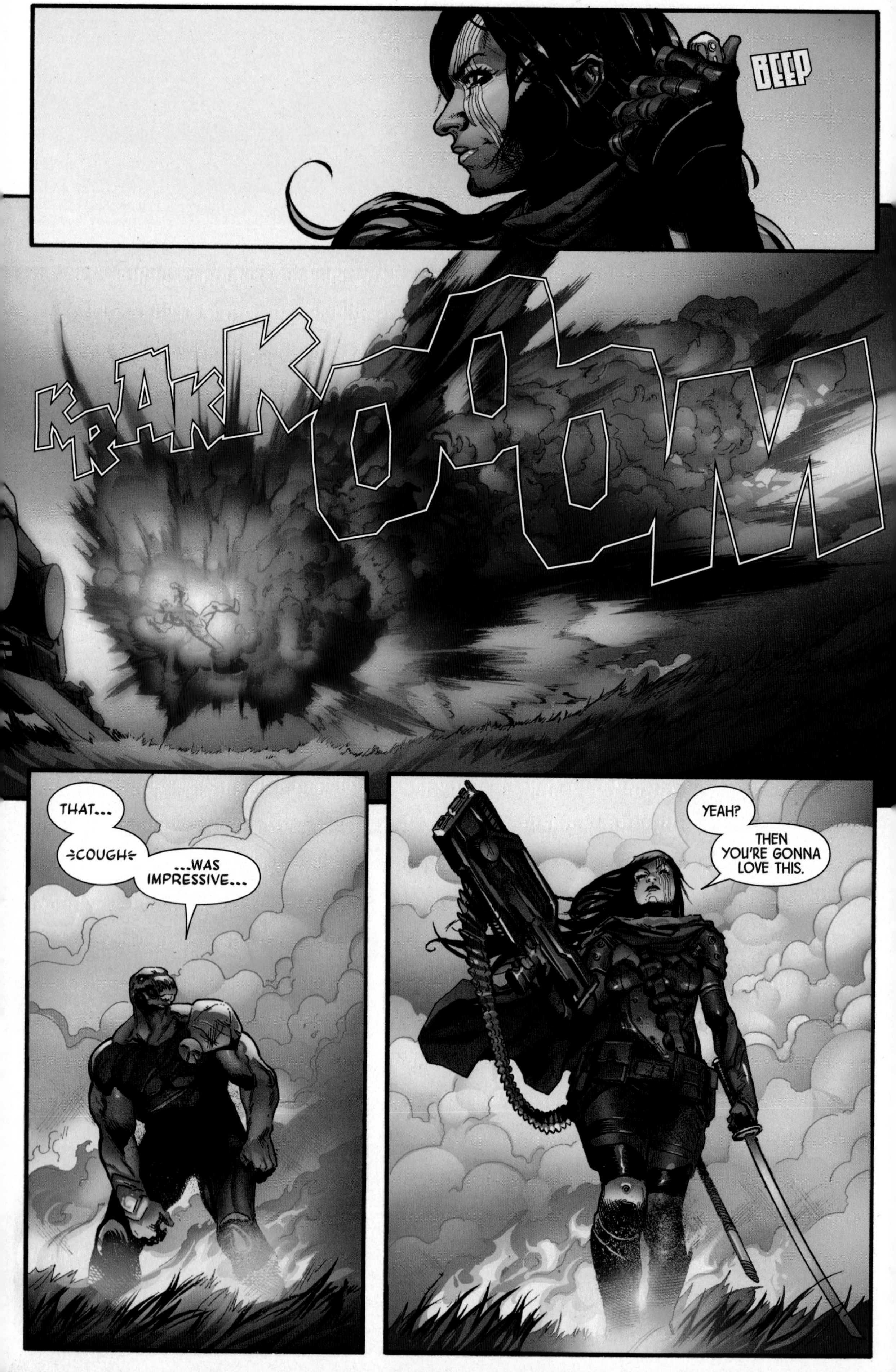

BEEP
KRAK KOOOM
THAT...
≈COUGH≈
...WAS IMPRESSIVE...
YEAH?
THEN YOU'RE GONNA LOVE THIS.

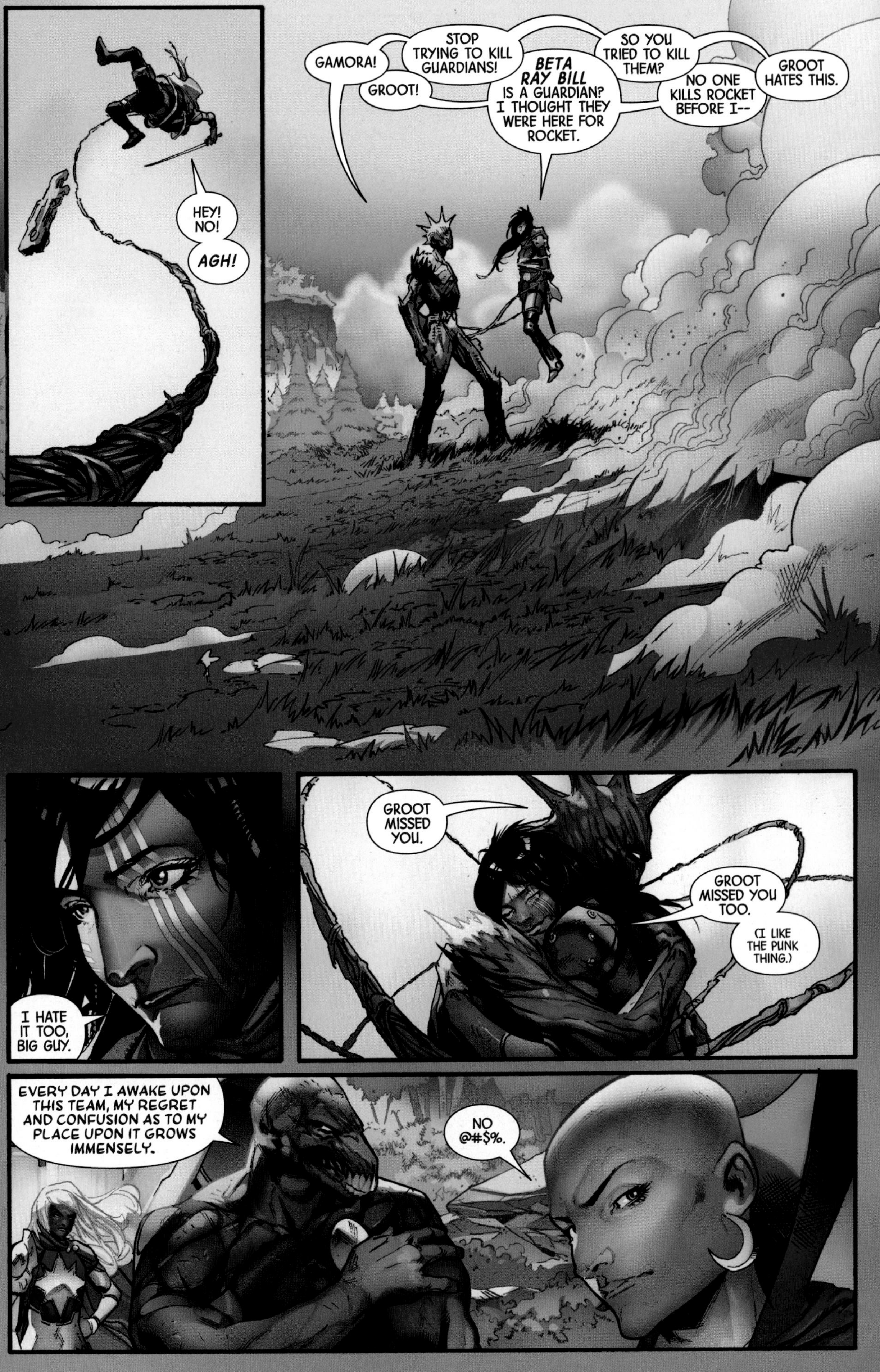
HEY! NO!
AGH!
GAMORA!
GROOT!
STOP TRYING TO KILL GUARDIANS!
BETA RAY BILL IS A GUARDIAN? I THOUGHT THEY WERE HERE FOR ROCKET.
SO YOU TRIED TO KILL THEM?
NO ONE KILLS ROCKET BEFORE I--
GROOT HATES THIS.
I HATE IT TOO, BIG GUY.
GROOT MISSED YOU.
GROOT MISSED YOU TOO.
(I LIKE THE PUNK THING.)
EVERY DAY I AWAKE UPON THIS TEAM, MY REGRET AND CONFUSION AS TO MY PLACE UPON IT GROWS IMMENSELY.
NO @#$%.

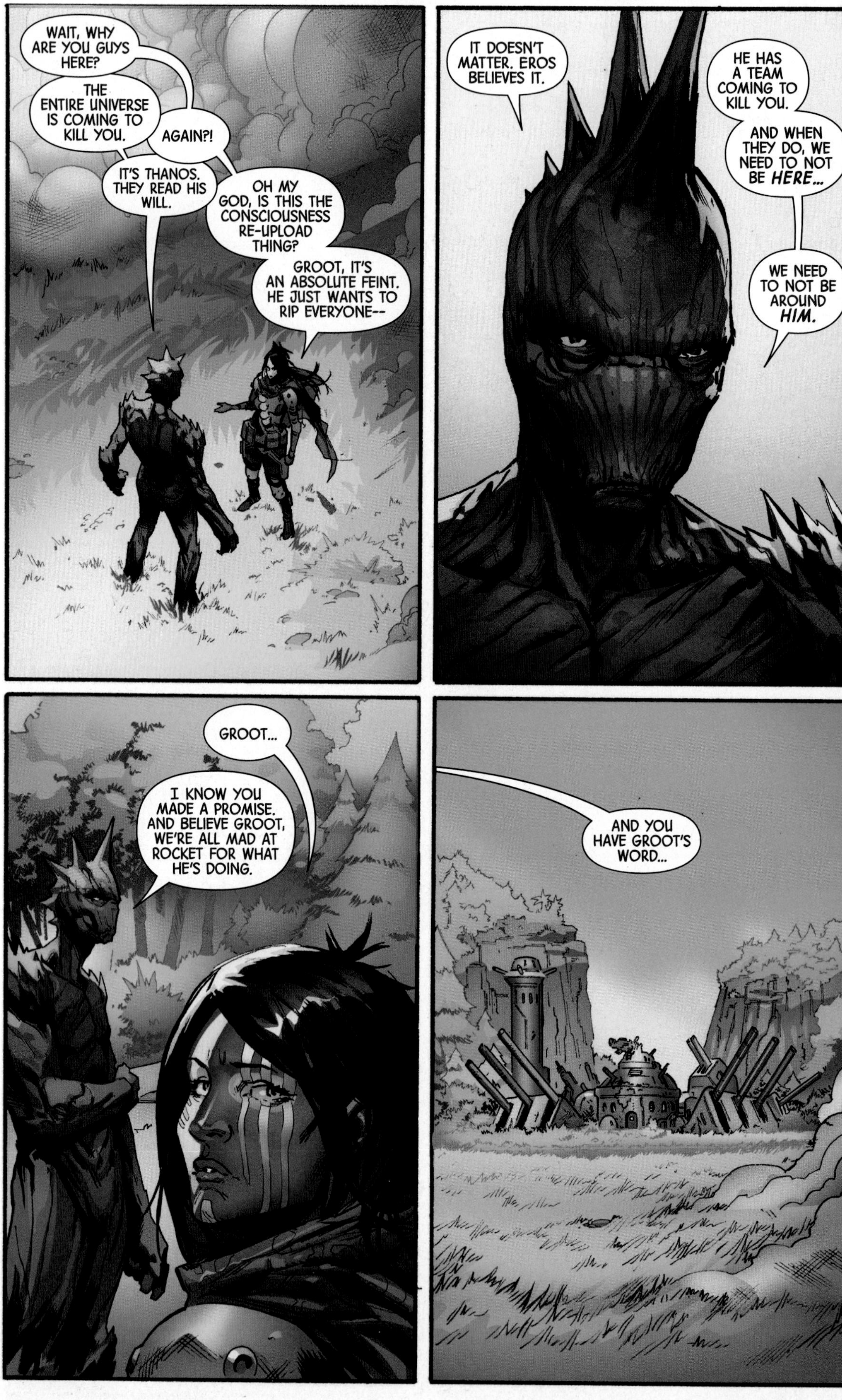
WAIT, WHY ARE YOU GUYS HERE?
THE ENTIRE UNIVERSE IS COMING TO KILL YOU.
AGAIN?!
IT'S THANOS. THEY READ HIS WILL.
OH MY GOD, IS THIS THE CONSCIOUSNESS RE-UPLOAD THING?
GROOT, IT'S AN ABSOLUTE FEINT. HE JUST WANTS TO RIP EVERYONE--
IT DOESN'T MATTER. EROS BELIEVES IT.
HE HAS A TEAM COMING TO KILL YOU.
AND WHEN THEY DO, WE NEED TO NOT BE *HERE*...
WE NEED TO NOT BE AROUND *HIM.*
GROOT...
I KNOW YOU MADE A PROMISE. AND BELIEVE GROOT, WE'RE ALL MAD AT ROCKET FOR WHAT HE'S DOING.
AND YOU HAVE GROOT'S WORD...

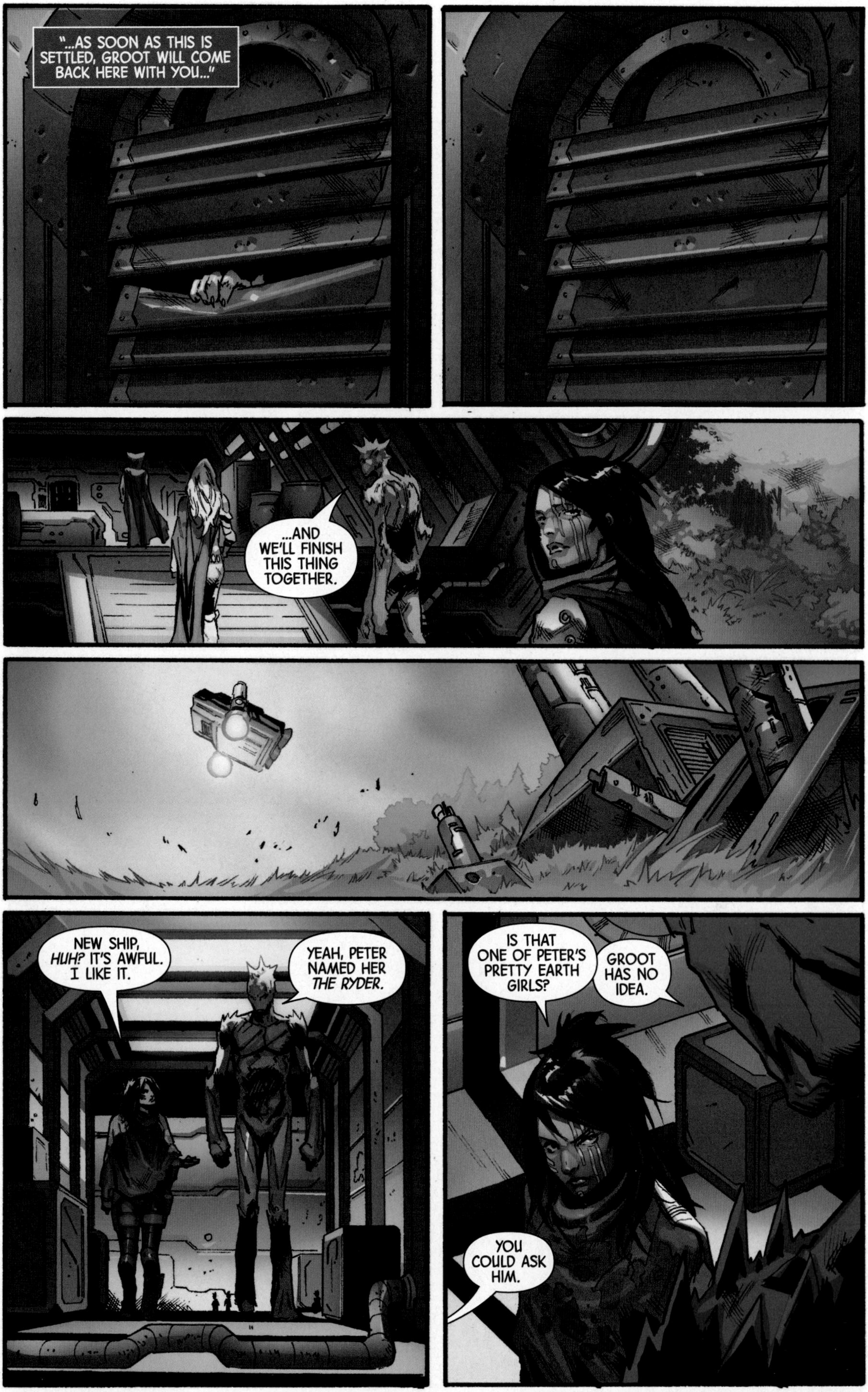
"...AS SOON AS THIS IS SETTLED, GROOT WILL COME BACK HERE WITH YOU..."
...AND WE'LL FINISH THIS THING TOGETHER.
NEW SHIP, *HUH?* IT'S AWFUL. I LIKE IT.
YEAH, PETER NAMED HER *THE RYDER*.
IS THAT ONE OF PETER'S PRETTY EARTH GIRLS?
GROOT HAS NO IDEA.
YOU COULD ASK HIM.

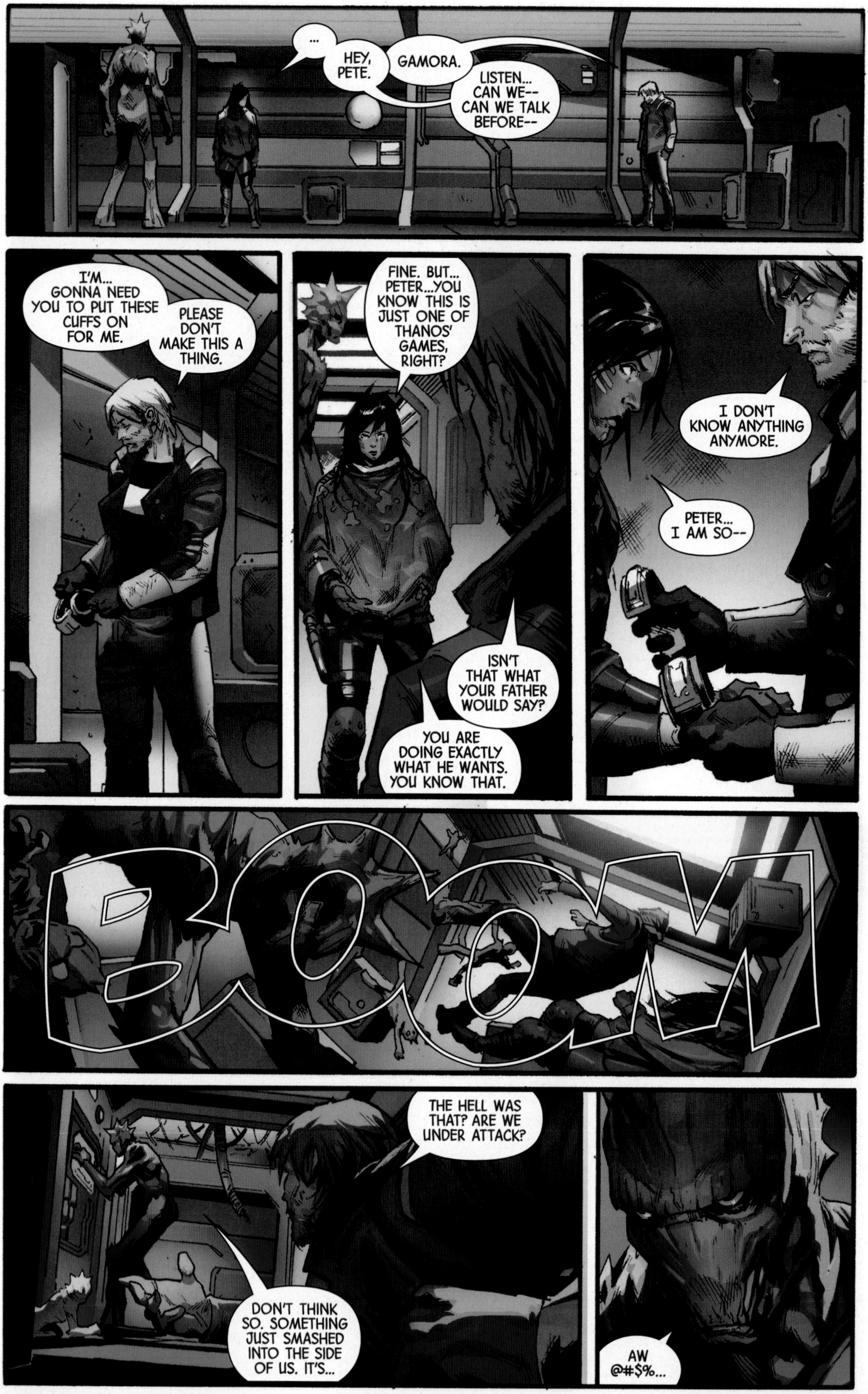
...
HEY, PETE.
GAMORA.
LISTEN... CAN WE-- CAN WE TALK BEFORE--
I'M... GONNA NEED YOU TO PUT THESE CUFFS ON FOR ME.
PLEASE DON'T MAKE THIS A THING.
FINE. BUT... PETER...YOU KNOW THIS IS JUST ONE OF THANOS' GAMES, RIGHT?
ISN'T THAT WHAT YOUR FATHER WOULD SAY?
YOU ARE DOING EXACTLY WHAT HE WANTS. YOU KNOW THAT.
I DON'T KNOW ANYTHING ANYMORE.
PETER... I AM SO--
BOOM
THE HELL WAS THAT? ARE WE UNDER ATTACK?
DON'T THINK SO. SOMETHING JUST SMASHED INTO THE SIDE OF US. IT'S...
AW @#$%...

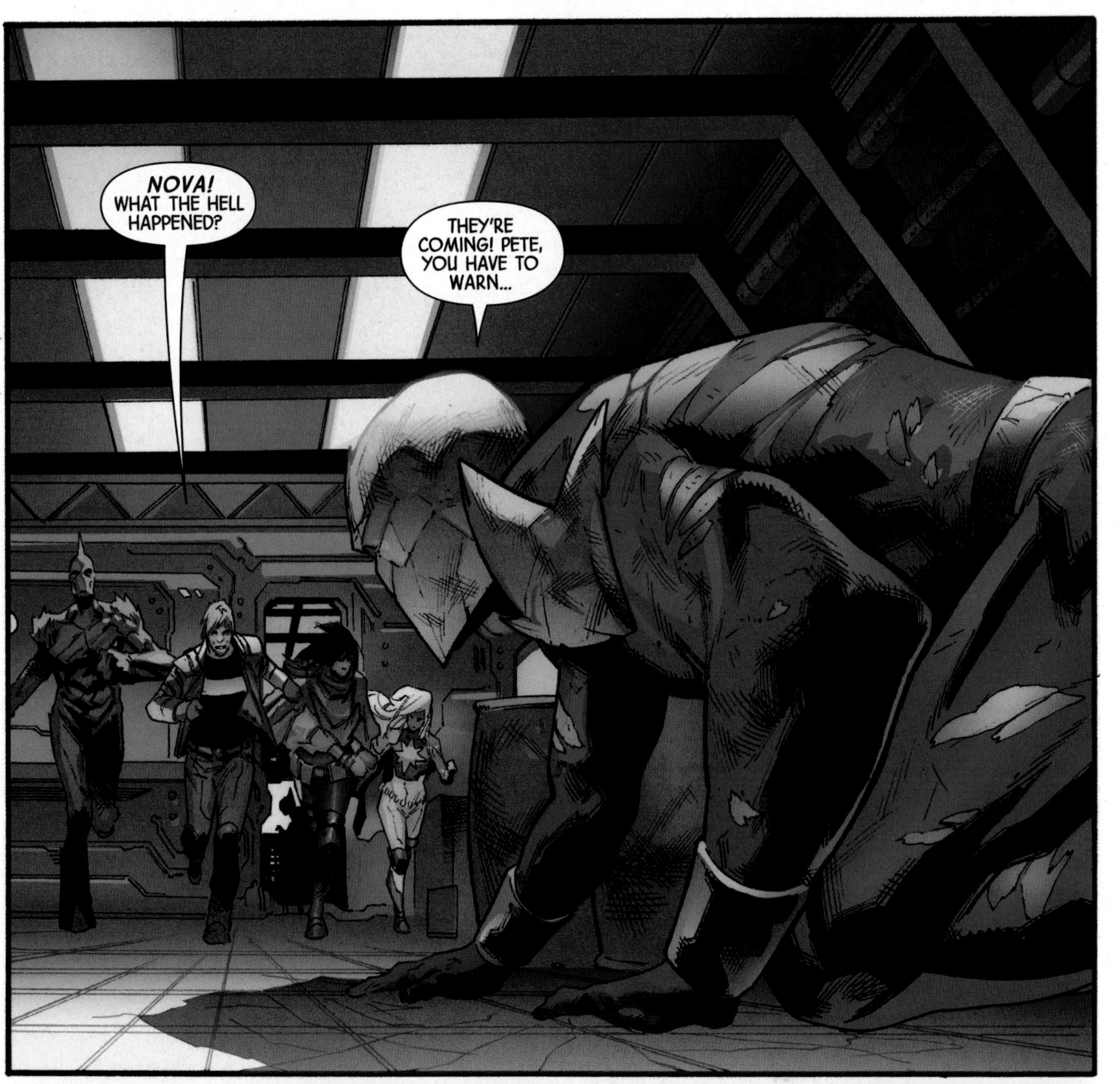
NOVA! WHAT THE HELL HAPPENED?
THEY'RE COMING! PETE, YOU HAVE TO WARN...

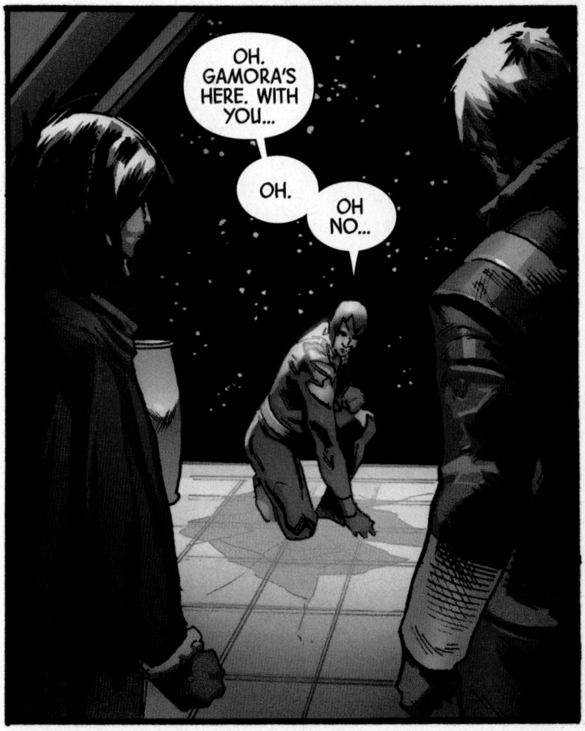
OH. GAMORA'S HERE. WITH YOU...
OH.
OH NO...

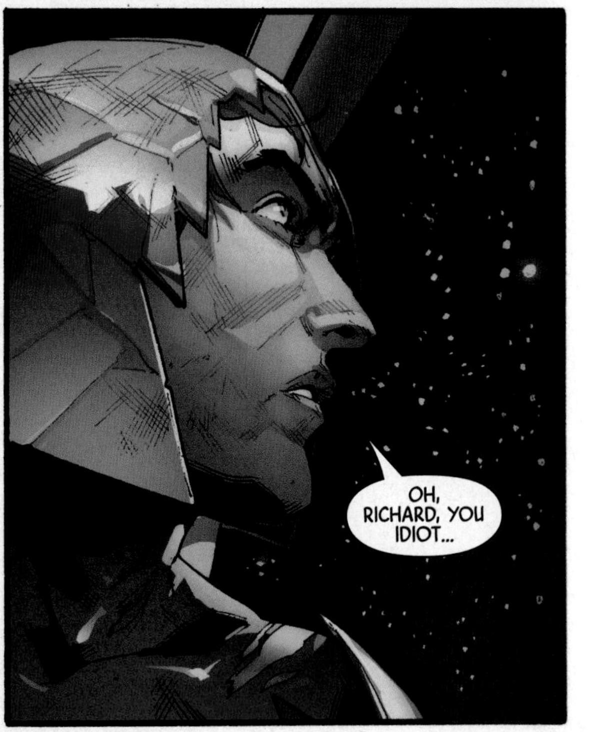
OH, RICHARD, YOU IDIOT...

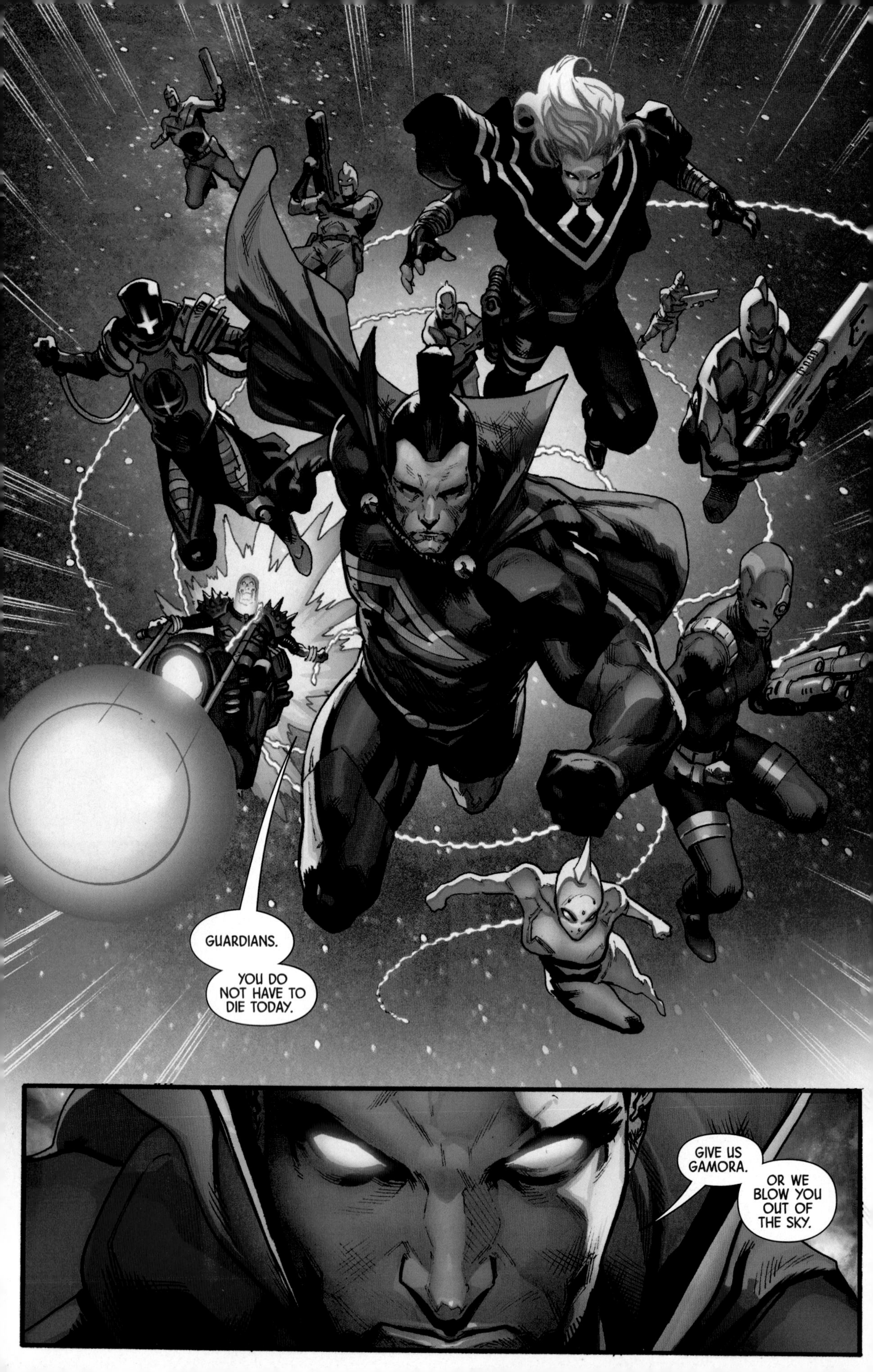
GUARDIANS.
YOU DO NOT HAVE TO DIE TODAY.
GIVE US GAMORA.
OR WE BLOW YOU OUT OF THE SKY.

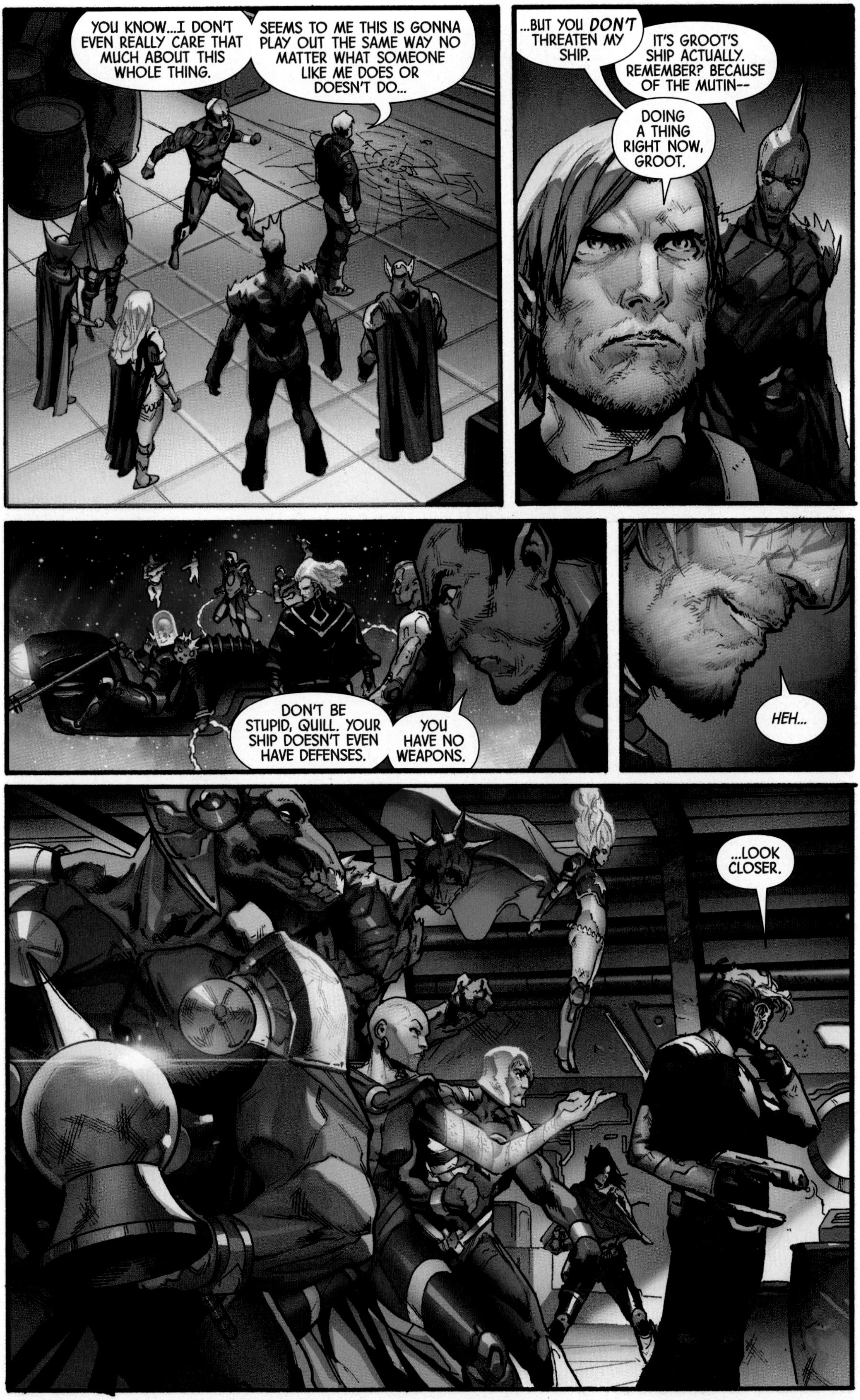
YOU KNOW...I DON'T EVEN REALLY CARE THAT MUCH ABOUT THIS WHOLE THING.
SEEMS TO ME THIS IS GONNA PLAY OUT THE SAME WAY NO MATTER WHAT SOMEONE LIKE ME DOES OR DOESN'T DO...
...BUT YOU DON'T THREATEN MY SHIP.
IT'S GROOT'S SHIP ACTUALLY. REMEMBER? BECAUSE OF THE MUTIN--
DOING A THING RIGHT NOW, GROOT.
DON'T BE STUPID, QUILL. YOUR SHIP DOESN'T EVEN HAVE DEFENSES.
YOU HAVE NO WEAPONS.
HEH...
...LOOK CLOSER.

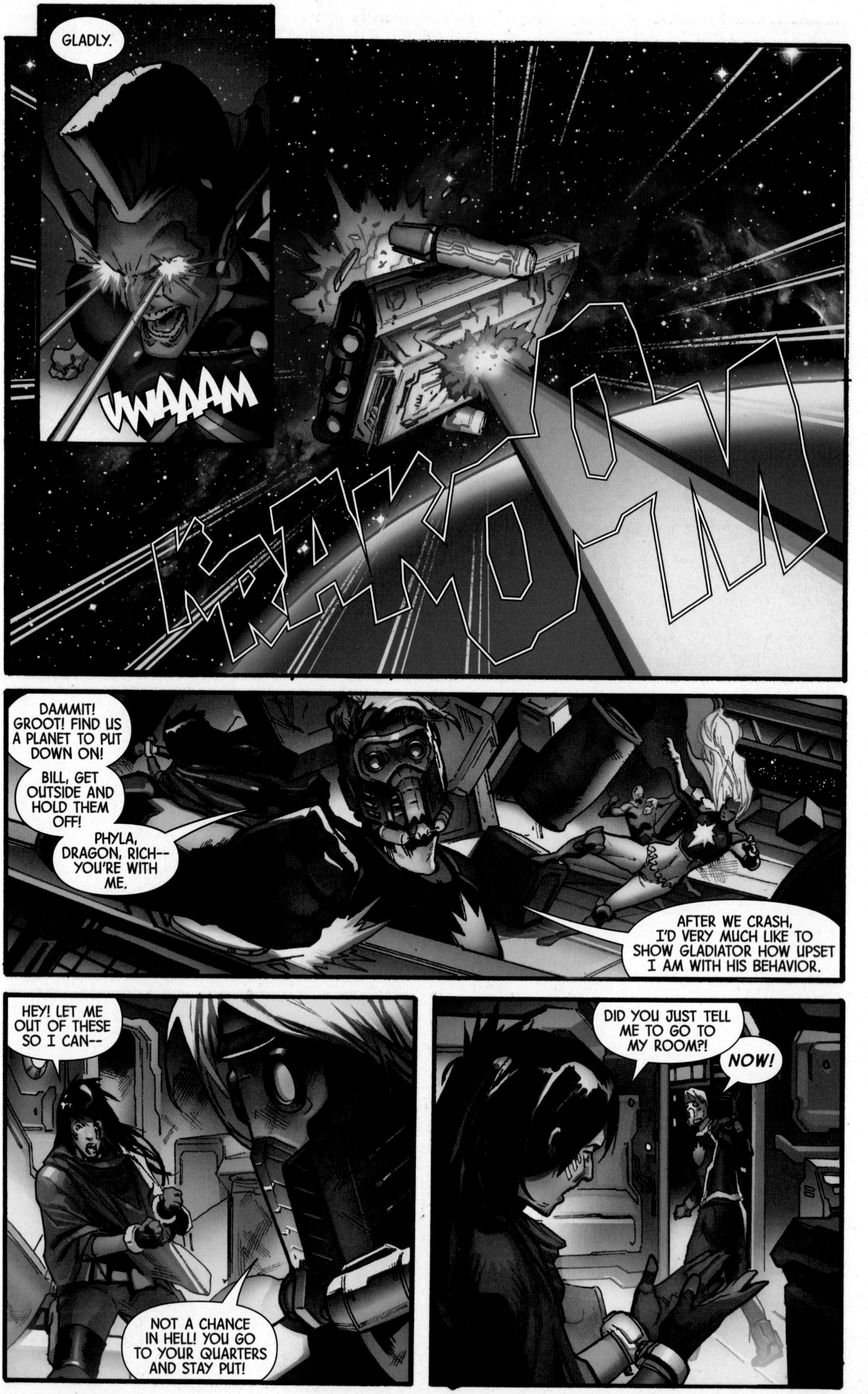
GLADLY.
VWAAAM
KRAKOOOM
DAMMIT! GROOT! FIND US A PLANET TO PUT DOWN ON!
BILL, GET OUTSIDE AND HOLD THEM OFF!
PHYLA, DRAGON, RICH-- YOU'RE WITH ME.
AFTER WE CRASH, I'D VERY MUCH LIKE TO SHOW GLADIATOR HOW UPSET I AM WITH HIS BEHAVIOR.
HEY! LET ME OUT OF THESE SO I CAN--
NOT A CHANCE IN HELL! YOU GO TO YOUR QUARTERS AND STAY PUT!
DID YOU JUST TELL ME TO GO TO MY ROOM?!
NOW!

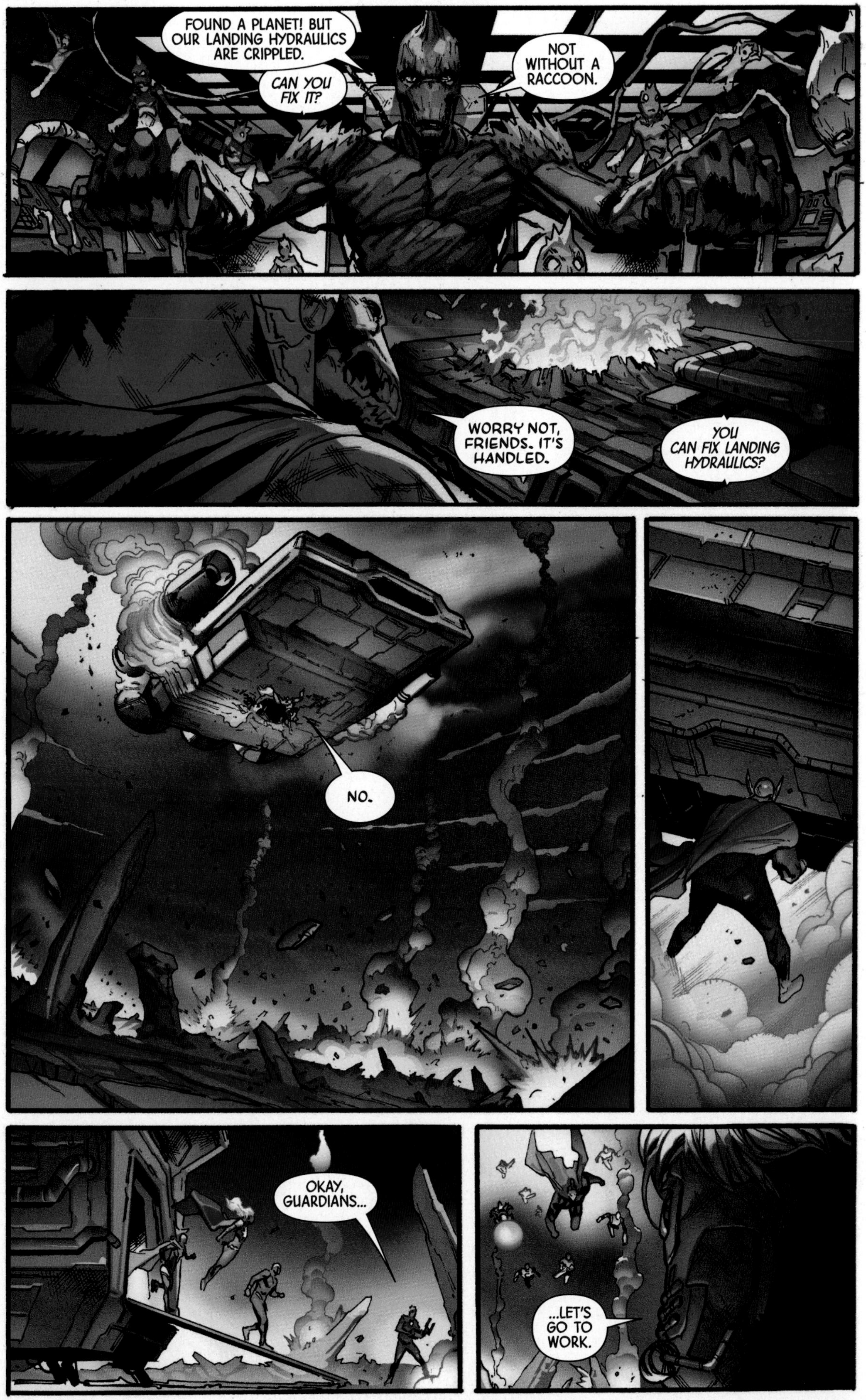
FOUND A PLANET! BUT OUR LANDING HYDRAULICS ARE CRIPPLED.
CAN YOU FIX IT?
NOT WITHOUT A RACCOON.
WORRY NOT, FRIENDS. IT'S HANDLED.
YOU CAN FIX LANDING HYDRAULICS?
NO.
OKAY, GUARDIANS...
...LET'S GO TO WORK.

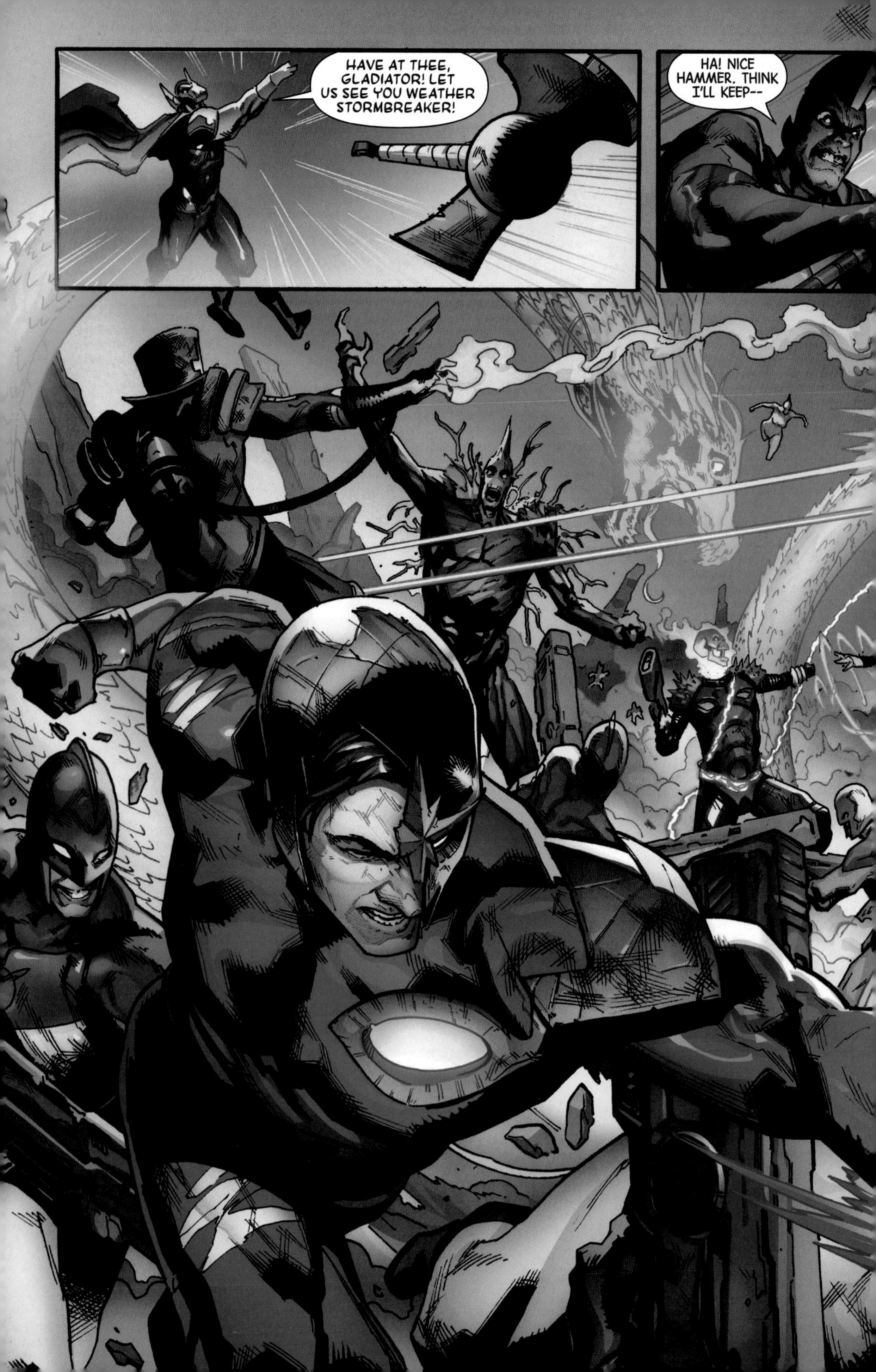
HAVE AT THEE, GLADIATOR! LET US SEE YOU WEATHER STORMBREAKER!
HA! NICE HAMMER. THINK I'LL KEEP--

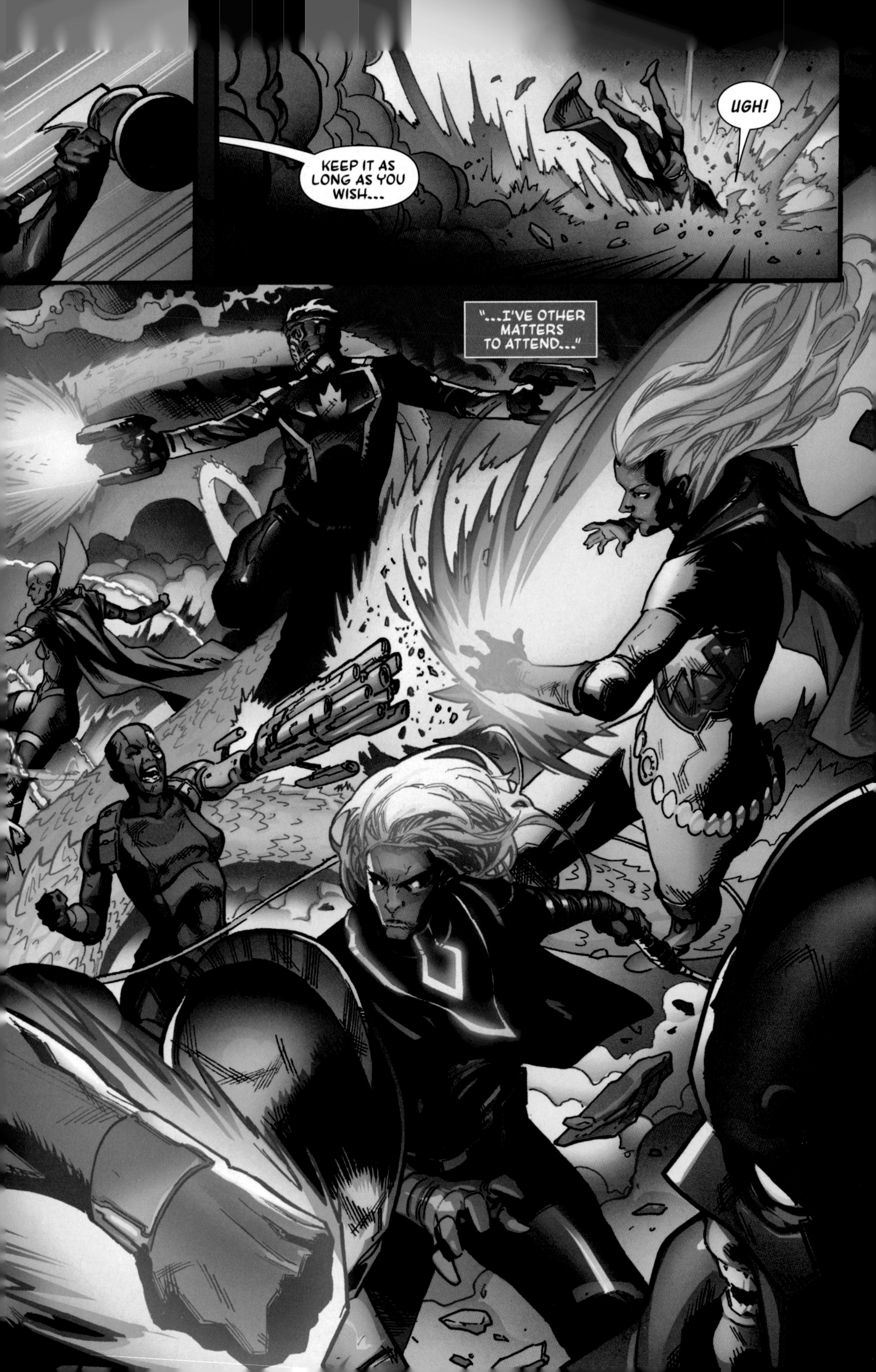
KEEP IT AS LONG AS YOU WISH...
UGH!
"...I'VE OTHER MATTERS TO ATTEND..."

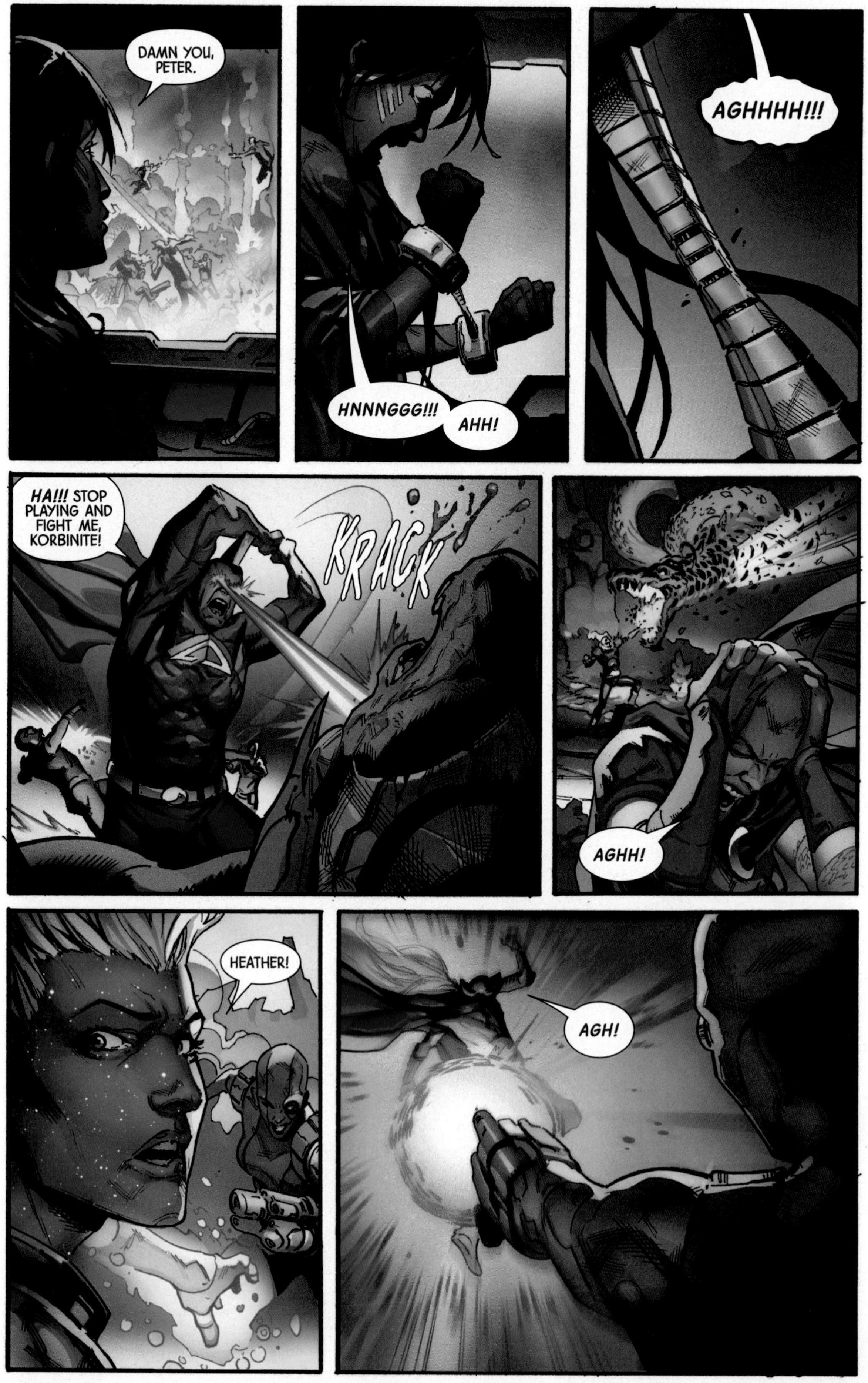
DAMN YOU, PETER.
HNNNGGG!!!
AHH!
AGHHHH!!!
HA!!! STOP PLAYING AND FIGHT ME, KORBINITE!
KRACK
AGHH!
HEATHER!
AGH!

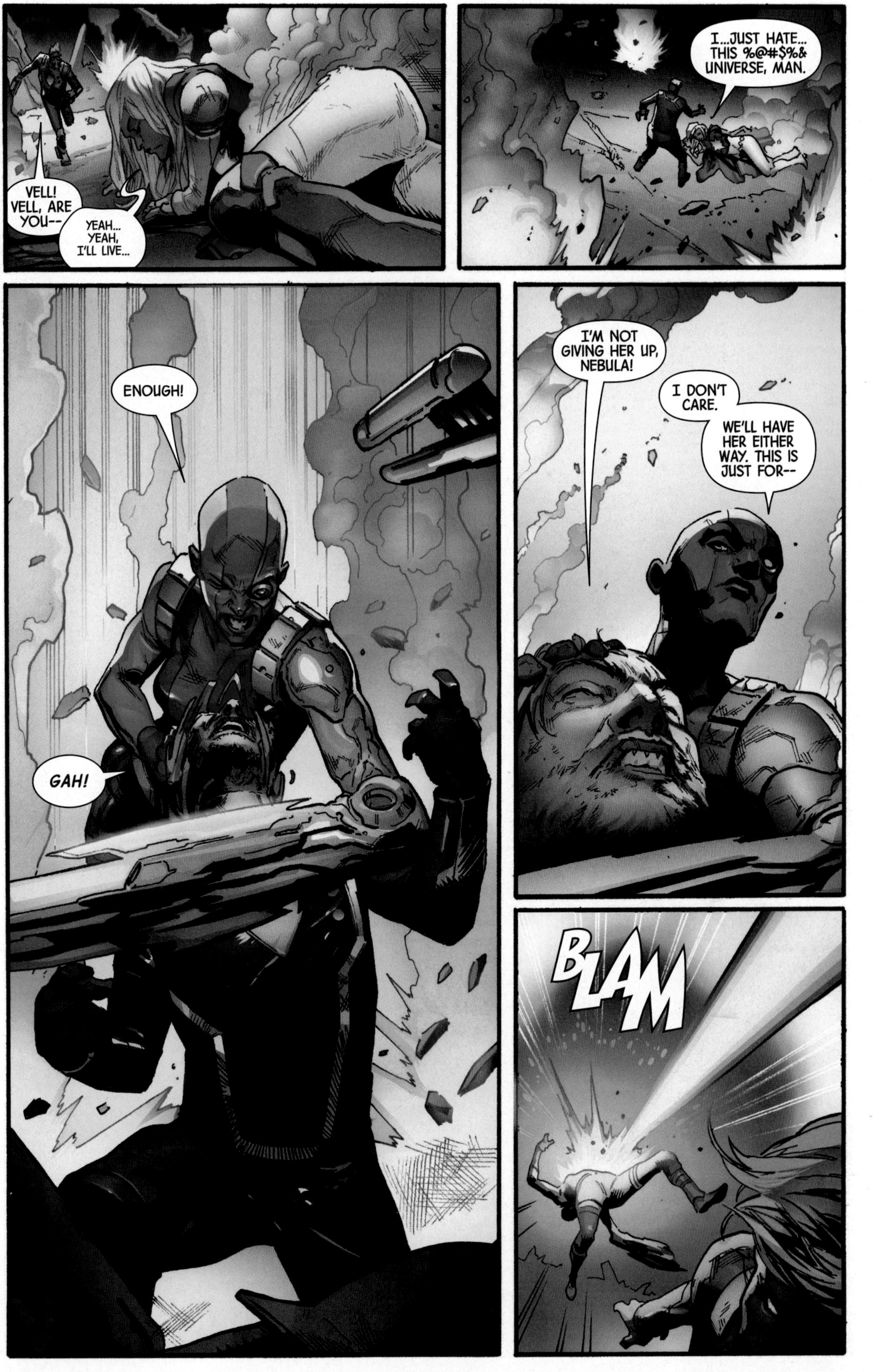
VELL! VELL, ARE YOU--
YEAH... YEAH, I'LL LIVE...
I...JUST HATE... THIS %@#$%& UNIVERSE, MAN.
ENOUGH!
GAH!
I'M NOT GIVING HER UP, NEBULA!
I DON'T CARE.
WE'LL HAVE HER EITHER WAY. THIS IS JUST FOR--
BLAM

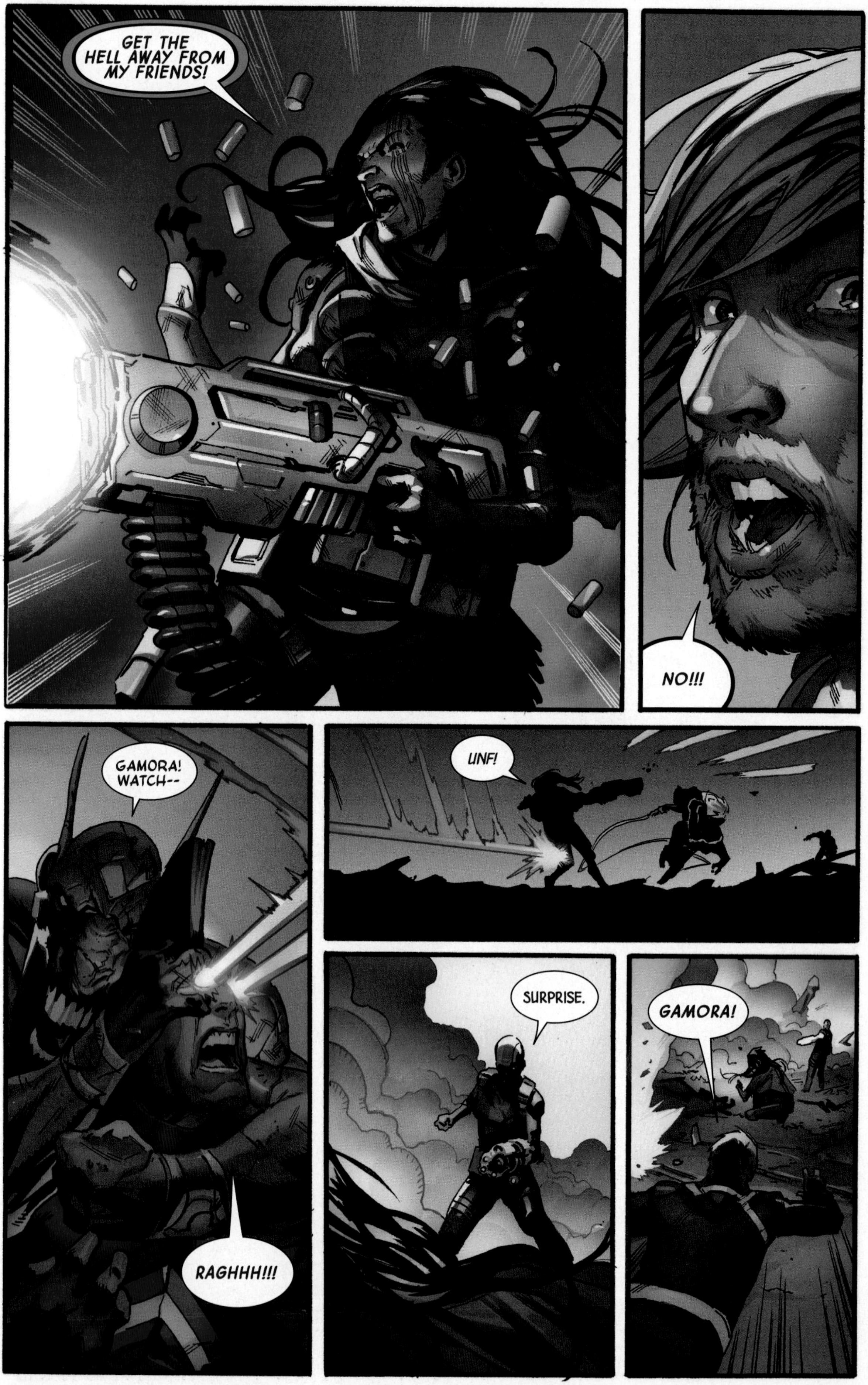
GET THE HELL AWAY FROM MY FRIENDS!
NO!!!
GAMORA! WATCH--
RAGHHH!!!
UNF!
SURPRISE.
GAMORA!

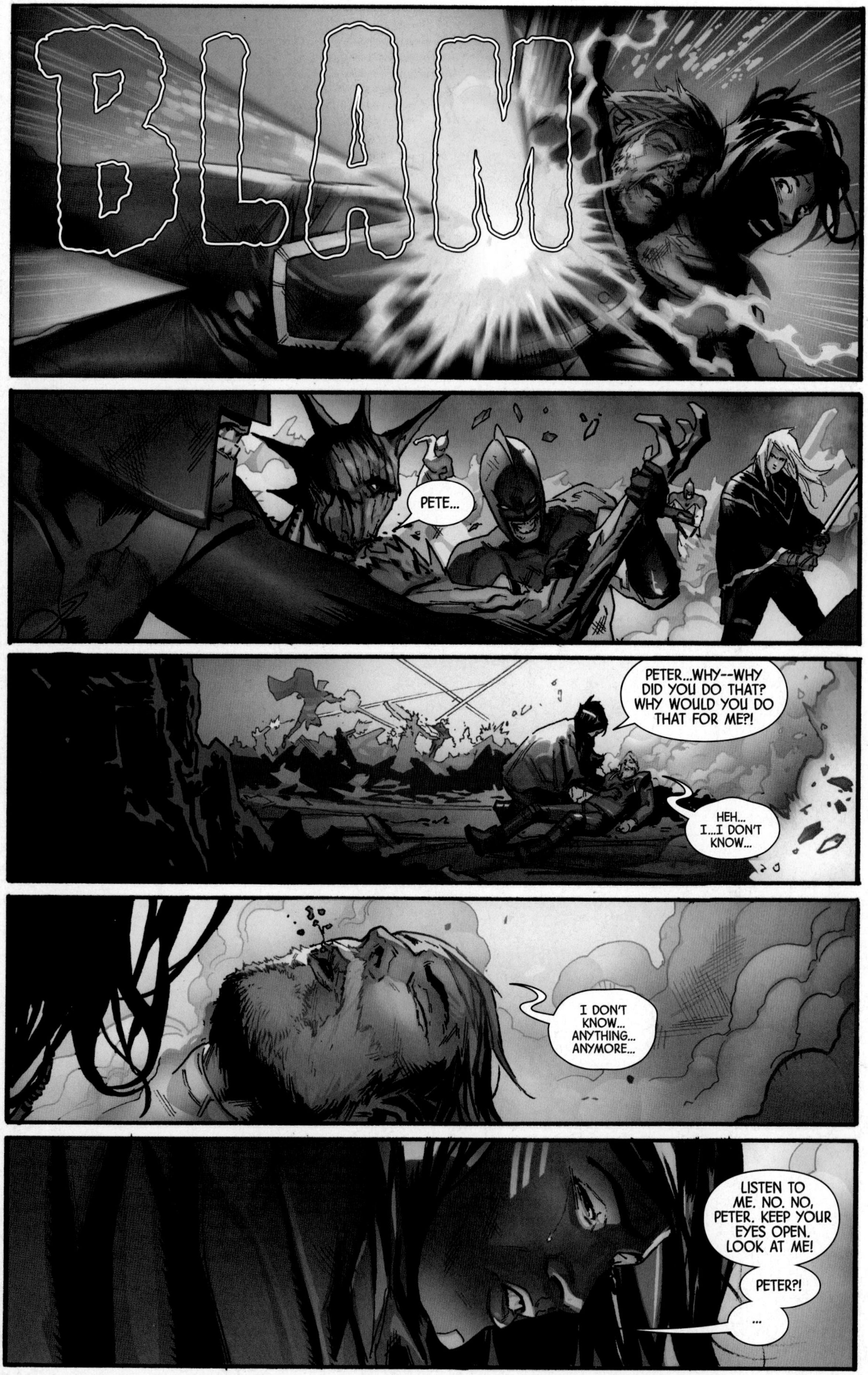
BLAM
PETE...
PETER...WHY--WHY DID YOU DO THAT? WHY WOULD YOU DO THAT FOR ME?!
HEH... I...I DON'T KNOW...
I DON'T KNOW... ANYTHING... ANYMORE...
LISTEN TO ME. NO. NO, PETER. KEEP YOUR EYES OPEN. LOOK AT ME!
PETER?!
...

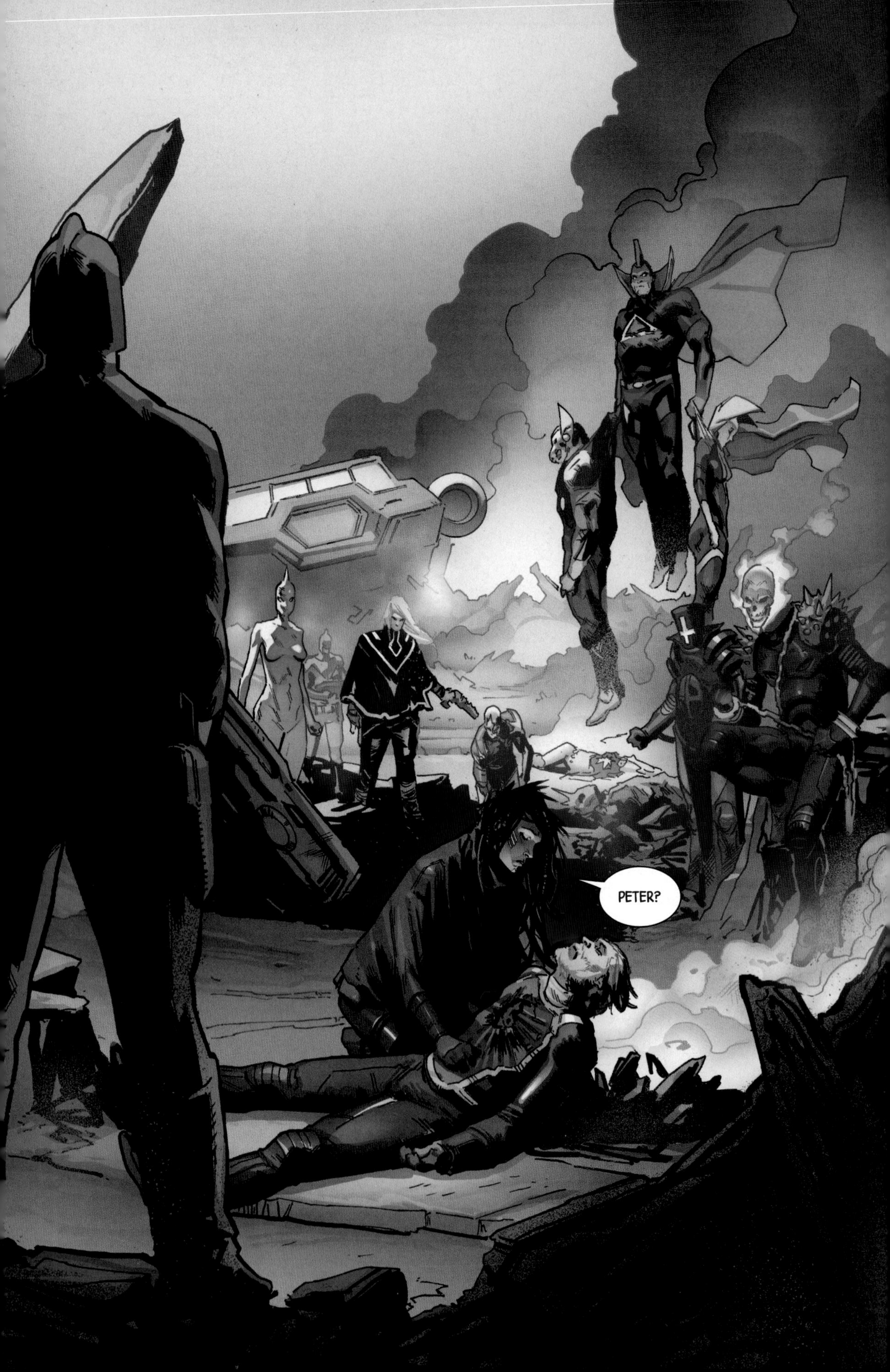
PETER?

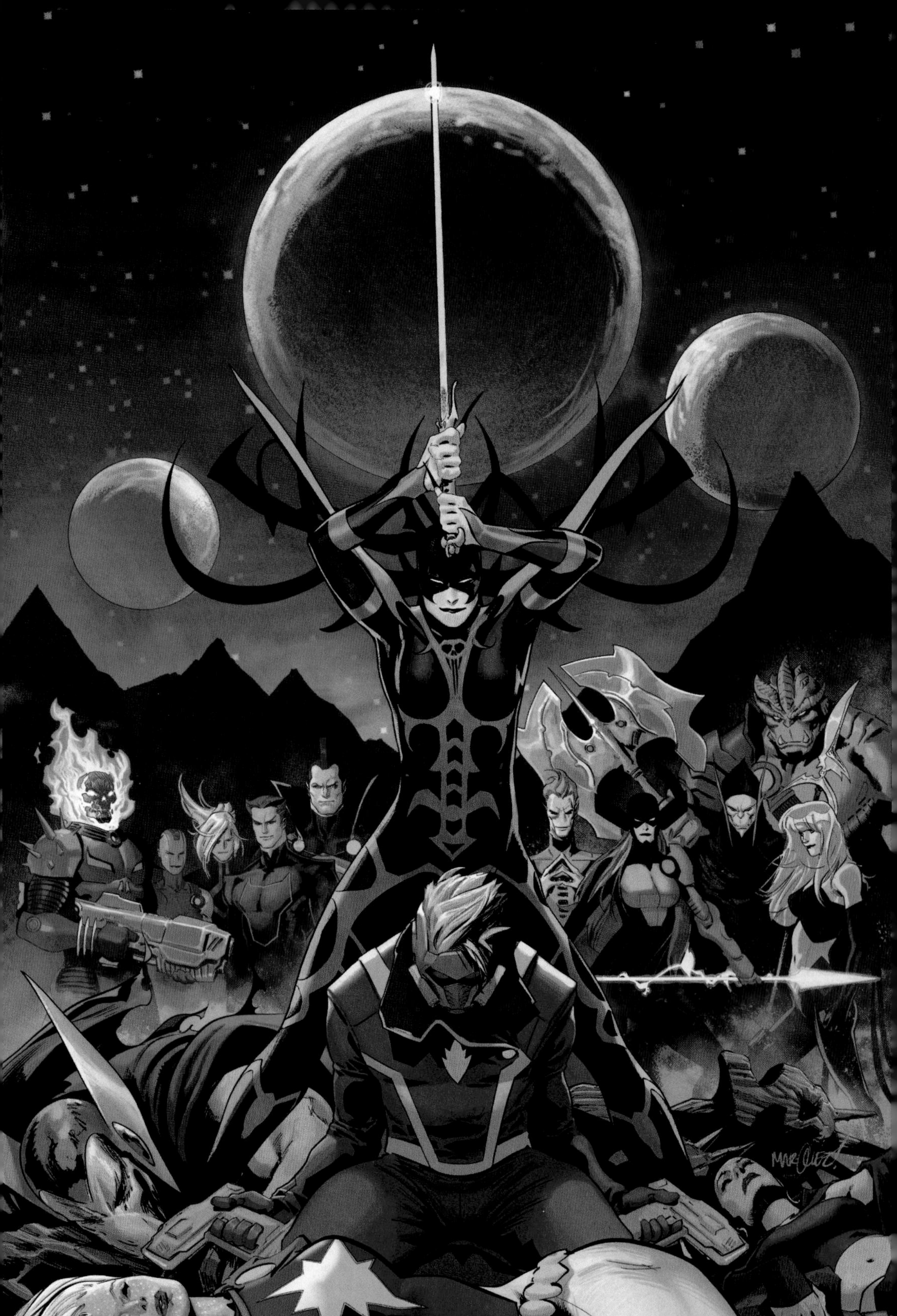

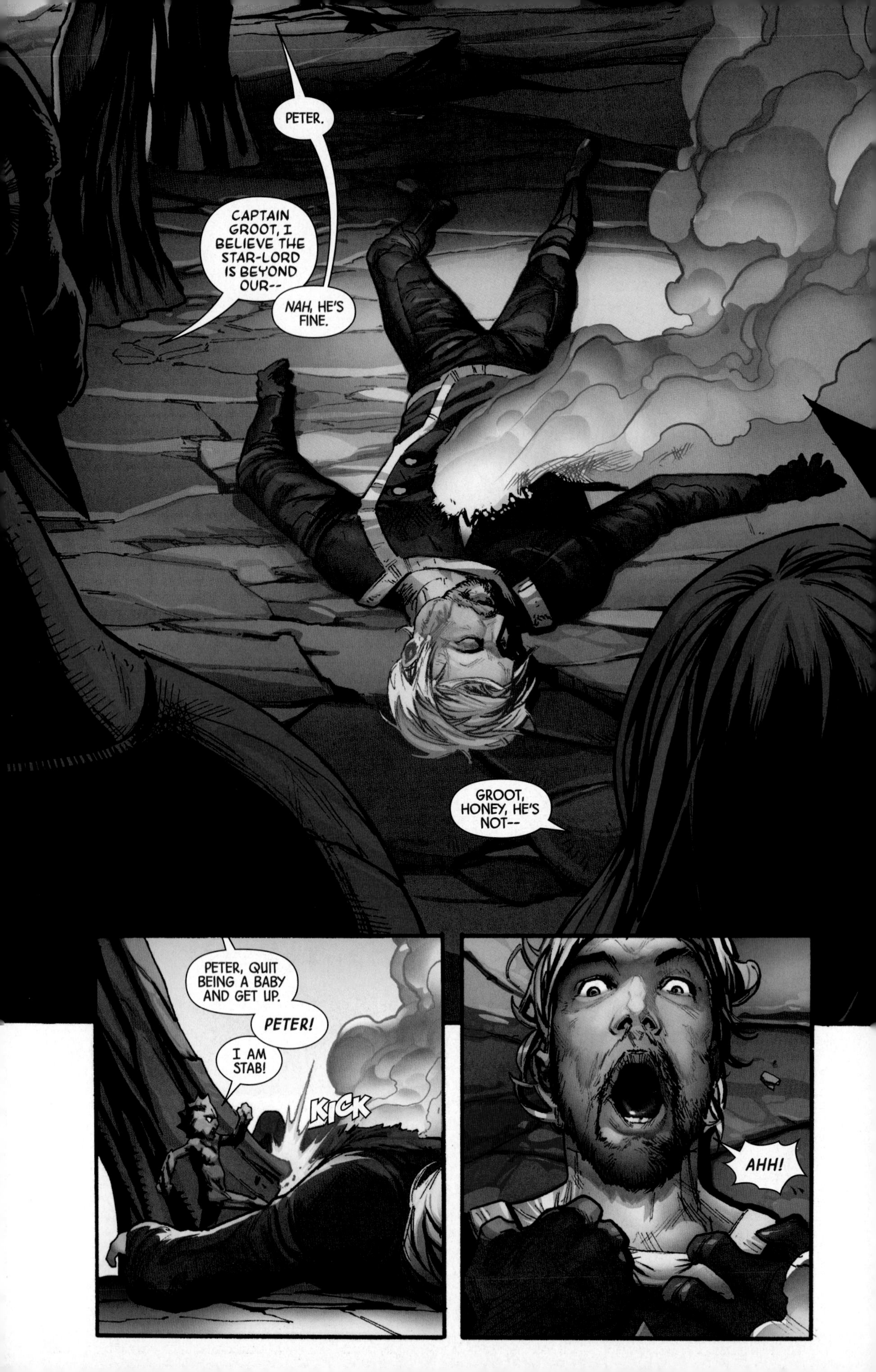
PETER.
CAPTAIN GROOT, I BELIEVE THE STAR-LORD IS BEYOND OUR--
NAH, HE'S FINE.
GROOT, HONEY, HE'S NOT--
PETER, QUIT BEING A BABY AND GET UP.
PETER!
I AM STAB!
KICK
AHH!

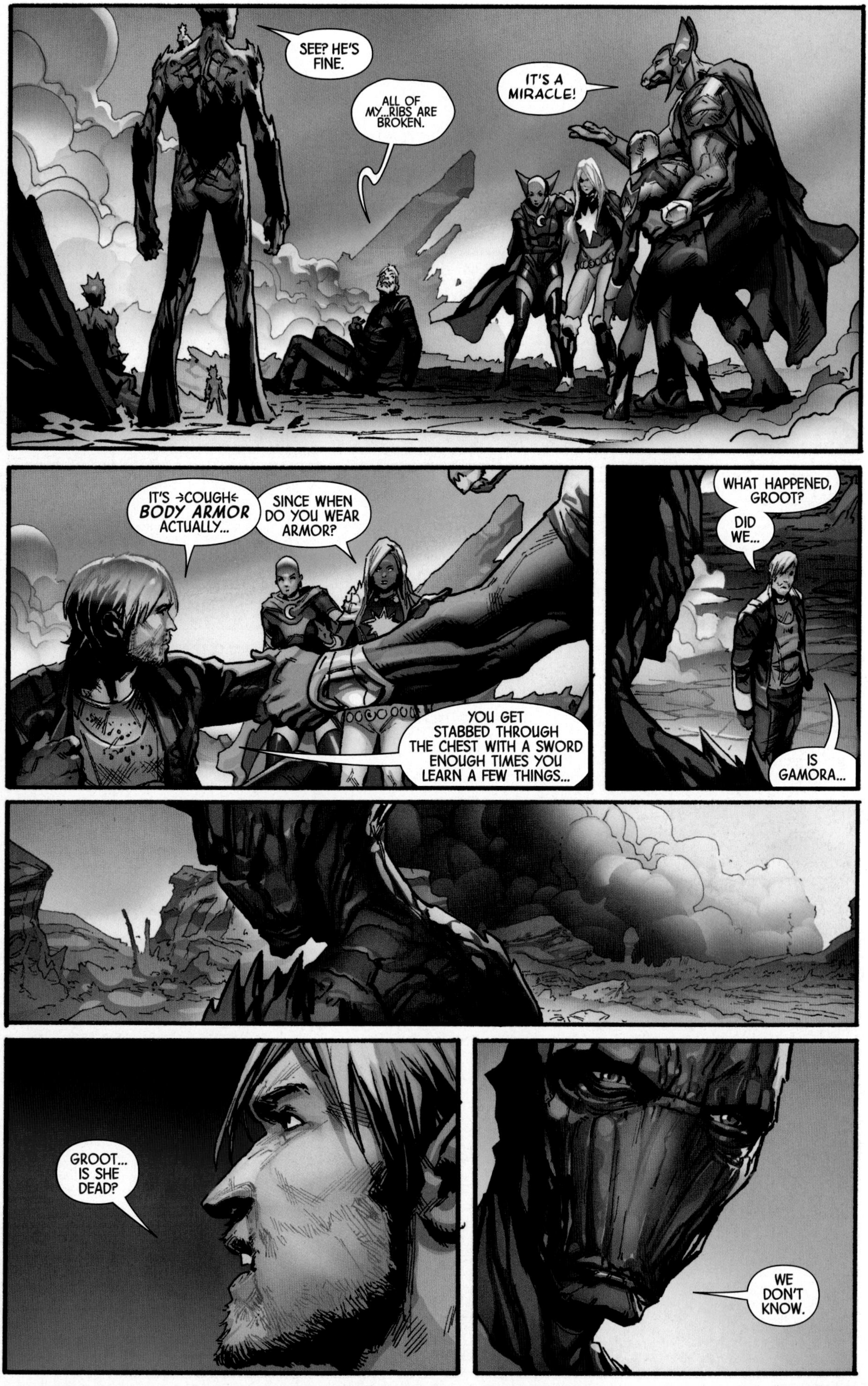
SEE? HE'S FINE.
ALL OF MY...RIBS ARE BROKEN.
IT'S A MIRACLE!
IT'S →COUGH← BODY ARMOR ACTUALLY...
SINCE WHEN DO YOU WEAR ARMOR?
YOU GET STABBED THROUGH THE CHEST WITH A SWORD ENOUGH TIMES YOU LEARN A FEW THINGS...
WHAT HAPPENED, GROOT?
DID WE...
IS GAMORA...
GROOT... IS SHE DEAD?
WE DON'T KNOW.

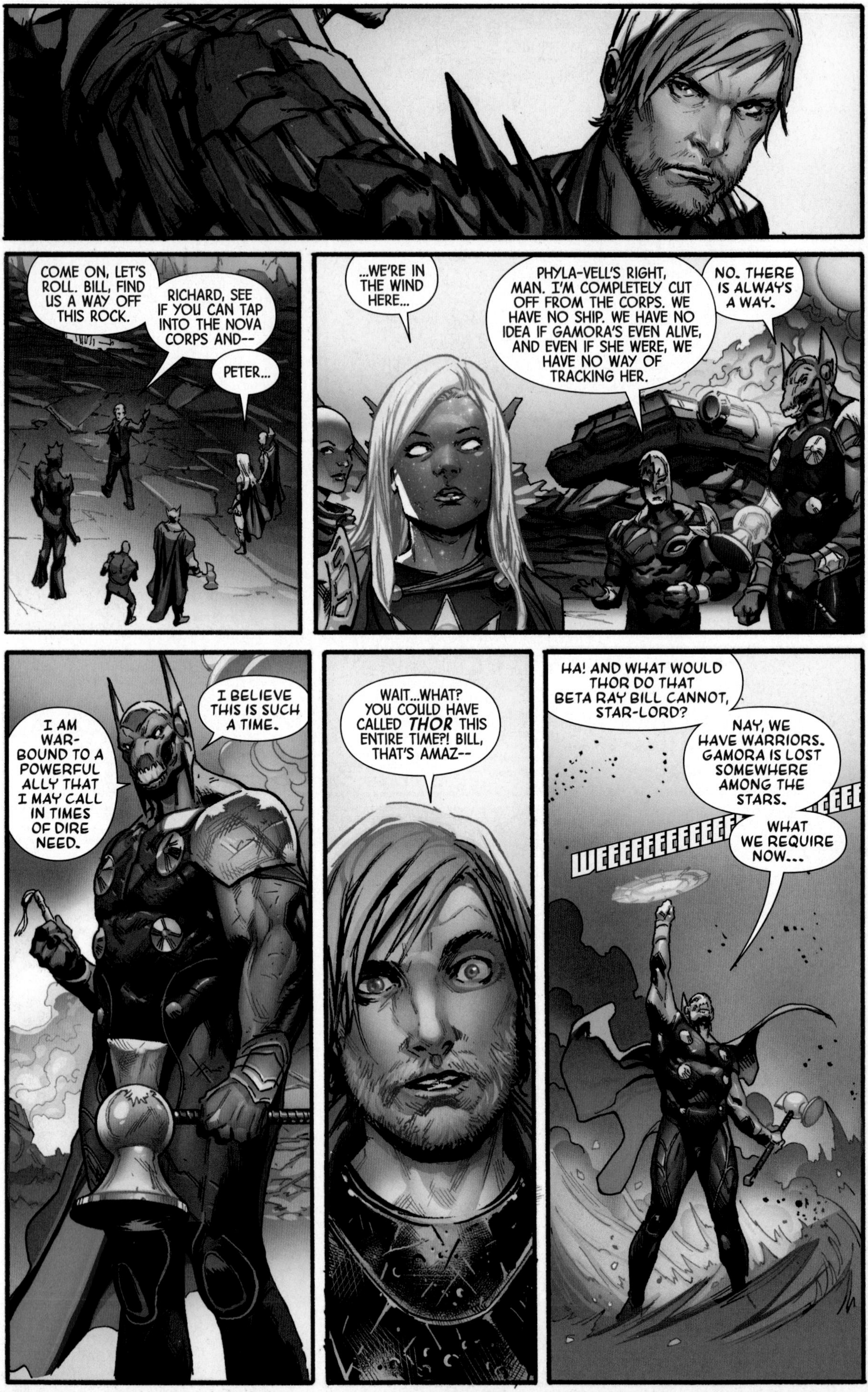
COME ON, LET'S ROLL. BILL, FIND US A WAY OFF THIS ROCK.
RICHARD, SEE IF YOU CAN TAP INTO THE NOVA CORPS AND--
PETER...
...WE'RE IN THE WIND HERE...
PHYLA-VELL'S RIGHT, MAN. I'M COMPLETELY CUT OFF FROM THE CORPS. WE HAVE NO SHIP. WE HAVE NO IDEA IF GAMORA'S EVEN ALIVE, AND EVEN IF SHE WERE, WE HAVE NO WAY OF TRACKING HER.
NO. THERE IS ALWAYS A WAY.
I AM WAR-BOUND TO A POWERFUL ALLY THAT I MAY CALL IN TIMES OF DIRE NEED.
I BELIEVE THIS IS SUCH A TIME.
WAIT...WHAT? YOU COULD HAVE CALLED THOR THIS ENTIRE TIME?! BILL, THAT'S AMAZ--
HA! AND WHAT WOULD THOR DO THAT BETA RAY BILL CANNOT, STAR-LORD?
NAY, WE HAVE WARRIORS. GAMORA IS LOST SOMEWHERE AMONG THE STARS.
WEEEEEEEEEEEEEEEEEE
WHAT WE REQUIRE NOW...

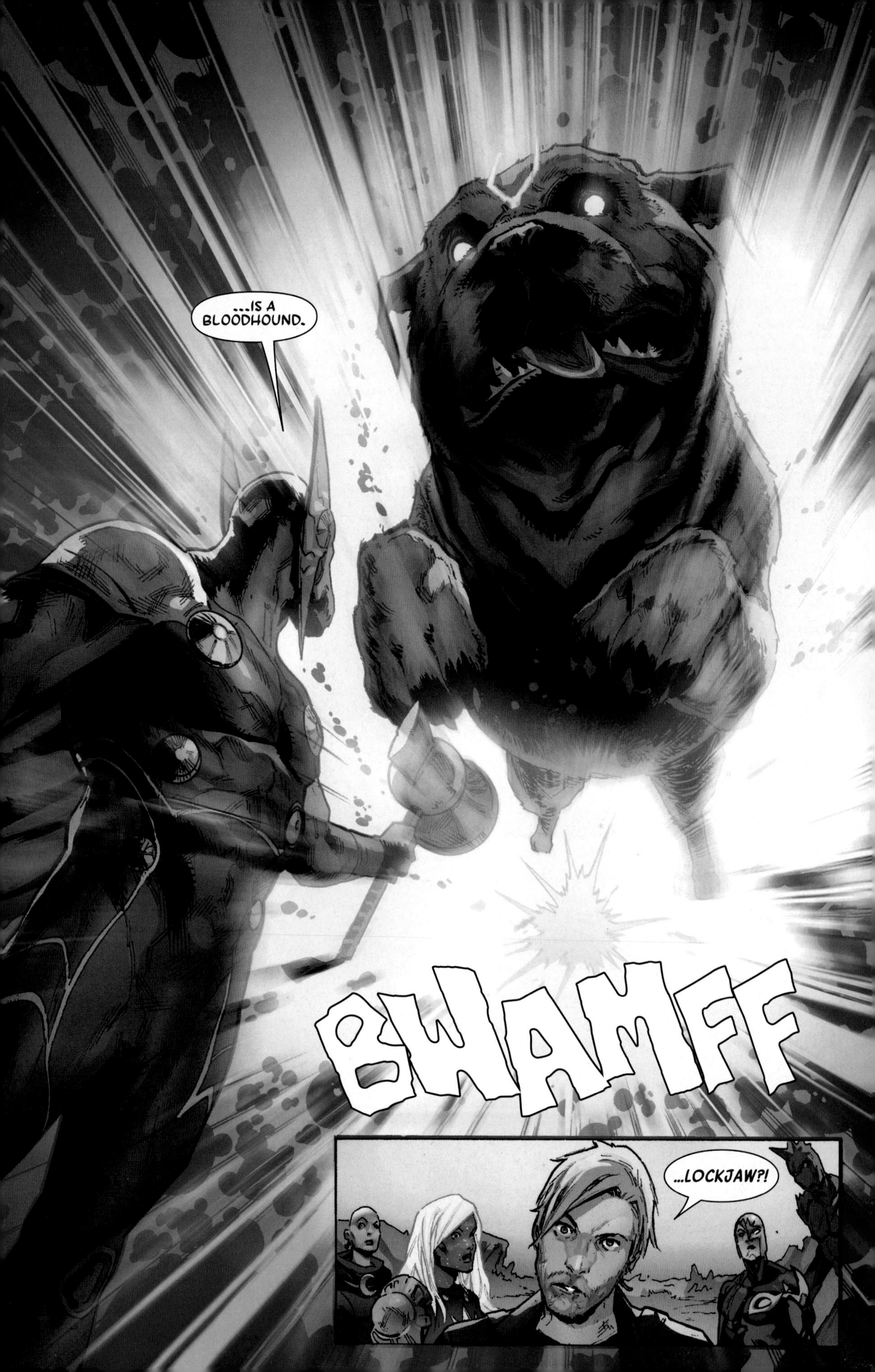
...IS A BLOODHOUND.
BWAMFF
...LOCKJAW?!

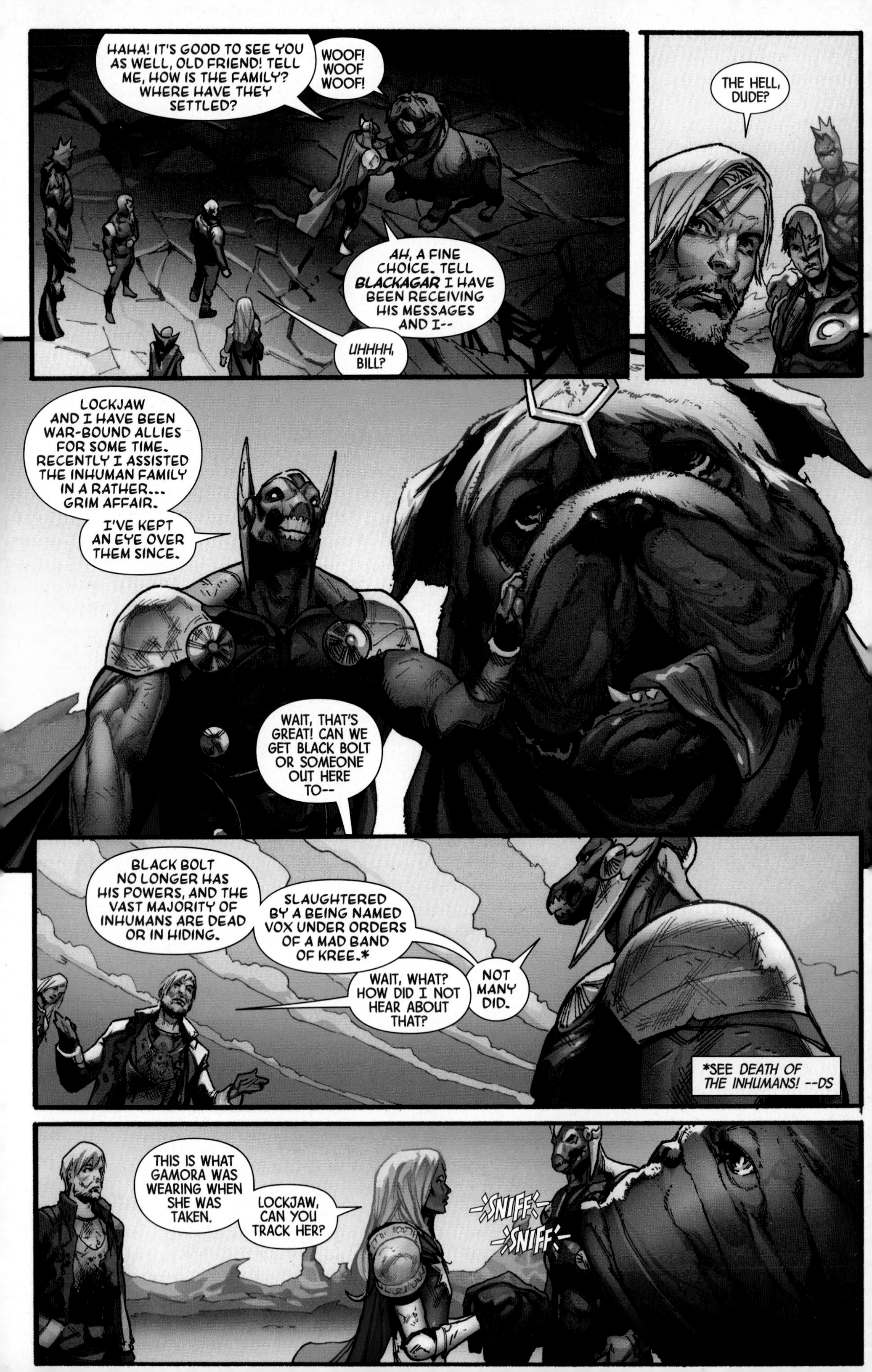
HAHA! IT'S GOOD TO SEE YOU AS WELL, OLD FRIEND! TELL ME, HOW IS THE FAMILY? WHERE HAVE THEY SETTLED?
WOOF! WOOF WOOF!
AH, A FINE CHOICE. TELL BLACKAGAR I HAVE BEEN RECEIVING HIS MESSAGES AND I--
UHHHH, BILL?
THE HELL, DUDE?
LOCKJAW AND I HAVE BEEN WAR-BOUND ALLIES FOR SOME TIME. RECENTLY I ASSISTED THE INHUMAN FAMILY IN A RATHER... GRIM AFFAIR.
I'VE KEPT AN EYE OVER THEM SINCE.
WAIT, THAT'S GREAT! CAN WE GET BLACK BOLT OR SOMEONE OUT HERE TO--
BLACK BOLT NO LONGER HAS HIS POWERS, AND THE VAST MAJORITY OF INHUMANS ARE DEAD OR IN HIDING.
SLAUGHTERED BY A BEING NAMED VOX UNDER ORDERS OF A MAD BAND OF KREE.*
WAIT, WHAT? HOW DID I NOT HEAR ABOUT THAT?
NOT MANY DID.
*SEE DEATH OF THE INHUMANS! --DS
THIS IS WHAT GAMORA WAS WEARING WHEN SHE WAS TAKEN.
LOCKJAW, CAN YOU TRACK HER?
SNIFF
SNIFF

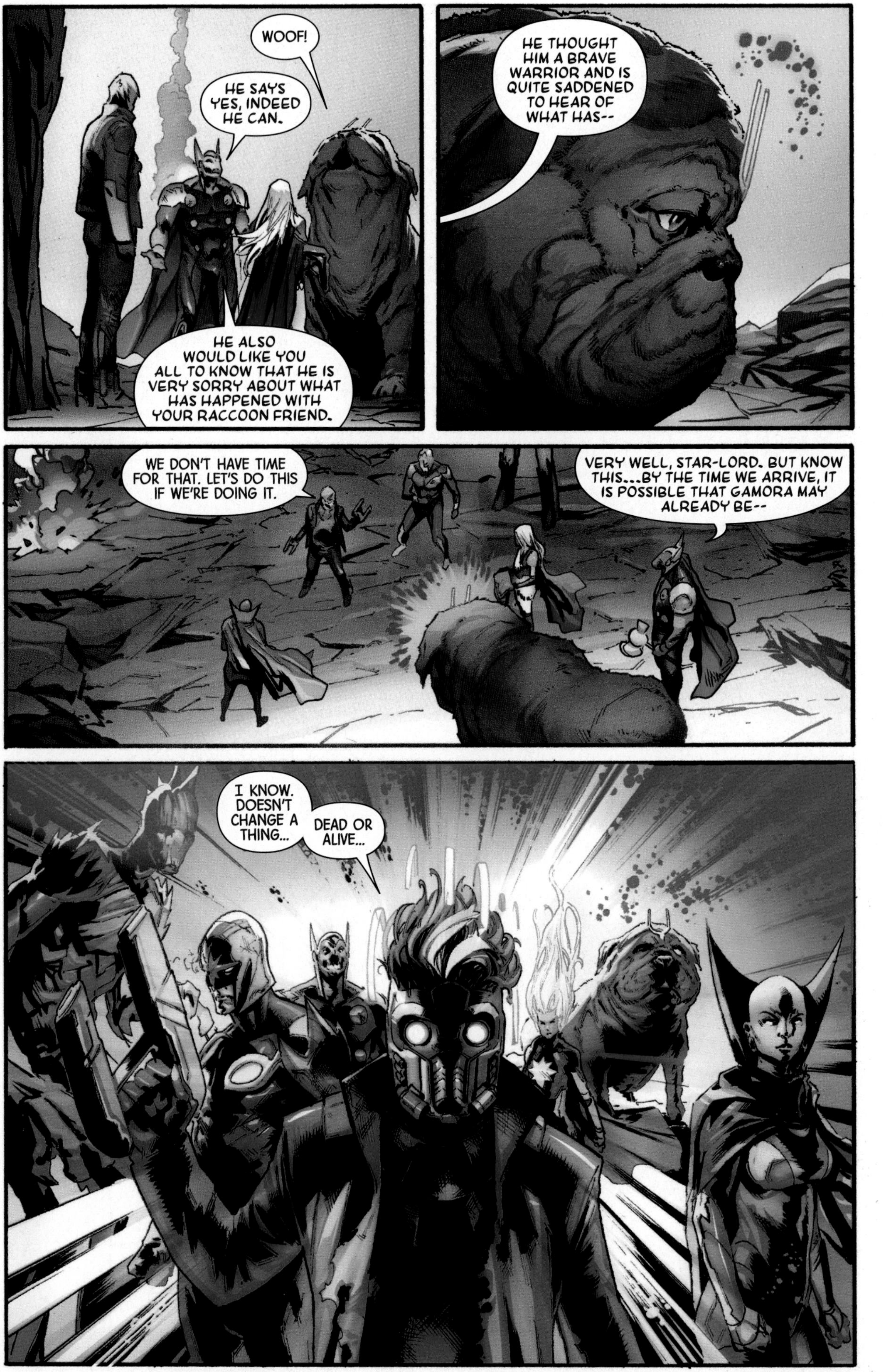
WOOF!
HE SAYS YES, INDEED HE CAN.
HE ALSO WOULD LIKE YOU ALL TO KNOW THAT HE IS VERY SORRY ABOUT WHAT HAS HAPPENED WITH YOUR RACCOON FRIEND.
HE THOUGHT HIM A BRAVE WARRIOR AND IS QUITE SADDENED TO HEAR OF WHAT HAS--
WE DON'T HAVE TIME FOR THAT. LET'S DO THIS IF WE'RE DOING IT.
VERY WELL, STAR-LORD. BUT KNOW THIS...BY THE TIME WE ARRIVE, IT IS POSSIBLE THAT GAMORA MAY ALREADY BE--
I KNOW. DOESN'T CHANGE A THING...
DEAD OR ALIVE...

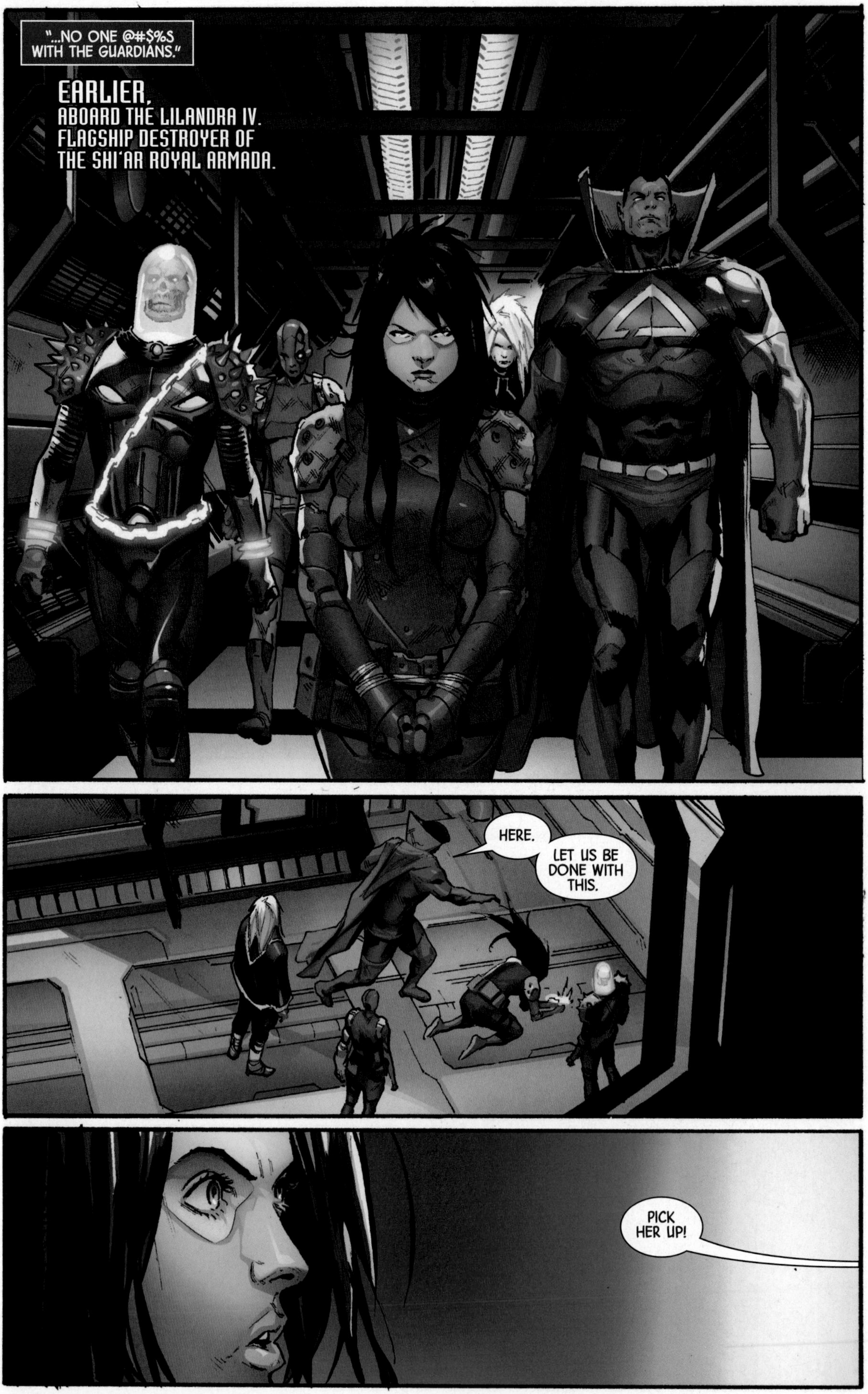
"...NO ONE @#$%S WITH THE GUARDIANS."
EARLIER,
ABOARD THE LILANDRA IV. FLAGSHIP DESTROYER OF THE SHI'AR ROYAL ARMADA.
HERE.
LET US BE DONE WITH THIS.
PICK HER UP!

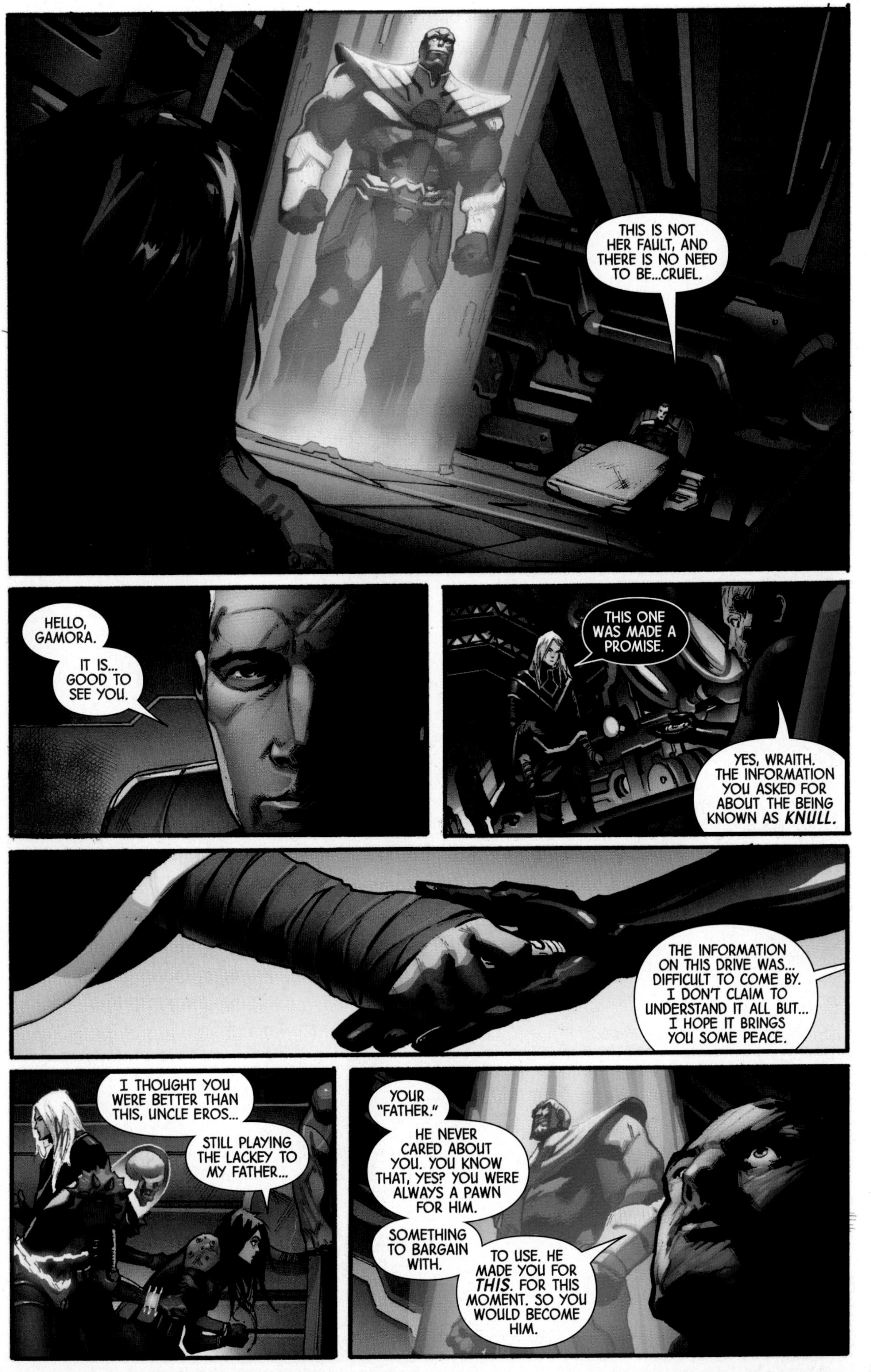

THIS IS NOT HER FAULT, AND THERE IS NO NEED TO BE...CRUEL.
HELLO, GAMORA.
IT IS... GOOD TO SEE YOU.
THIS ONE WAS MADE A PROMISE.
YES, WRAITH. THE INFORMATION YOU ASKED FOR ABOUT THE BEING KNOWN AS KNULL.
THE INFORMATION ON THIS DRIVE WAS... DIFFICULT TO COME BY. I DON'T CLAIM TO UNDERSTAND IT ALL BUT... I HOPE IT BRINGS YOU SOME PEACE.
I THOUGHT YOU WERE BETTER THAN THIS, UNCLE EROS...
STILL PLAYING THE LACKEY TO MY FATHER...
YOUR "FATHER."
HE NEVER CARED ABOUT YOU. YOU KNOW THAT, YES? YOU WERE ALWAYS A PAWN FOR HIM.
SOMETHING TO BARGAIN WITH.
TO USE. HE MADE YOU FOR THIS, FOR THIS MOMENT. SO YOU WOULD BECOME HIM.

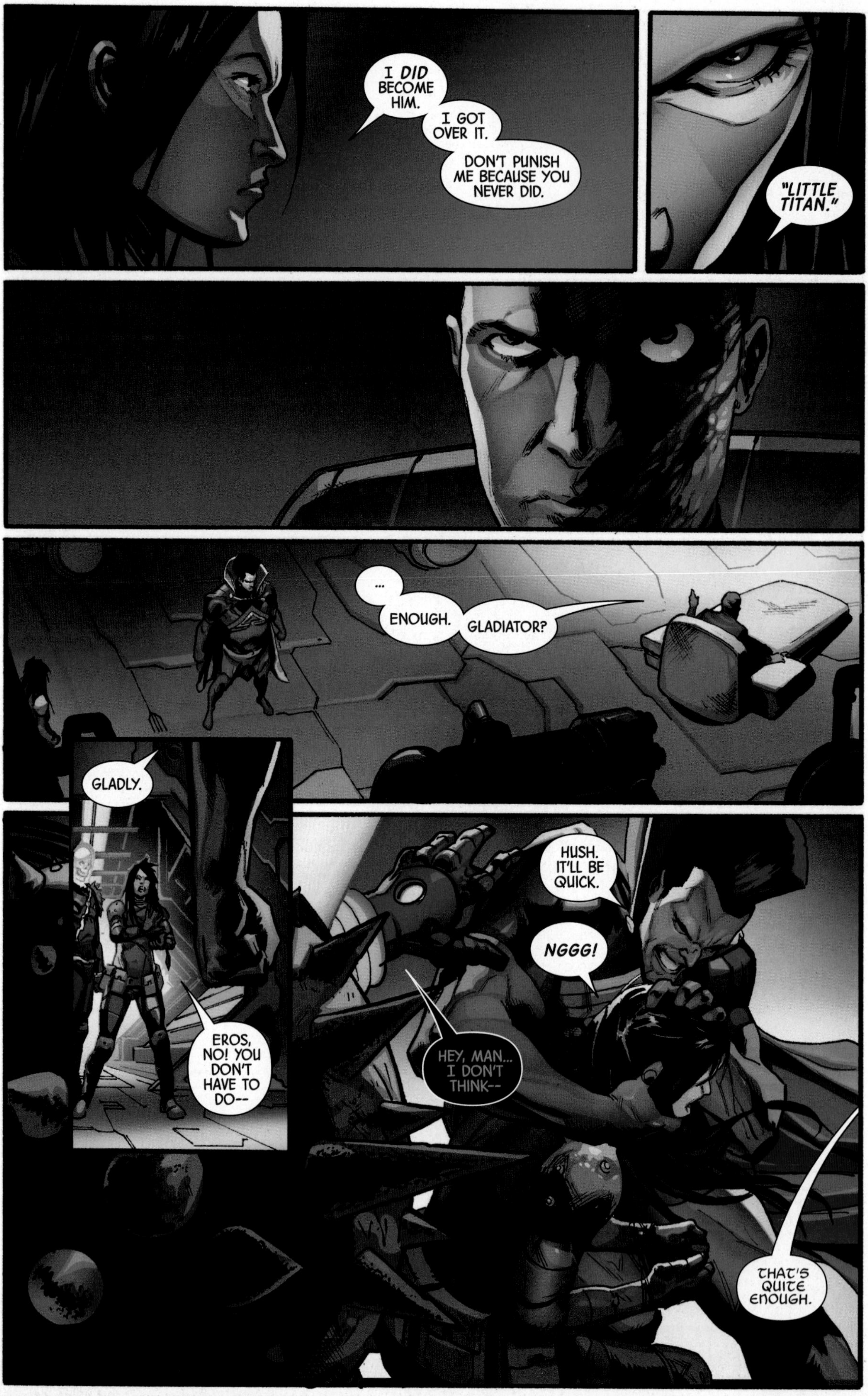
I *DID* BECOME HIM.
I GOT OVER IT.
DON'T PUNISH ME BECAUSE YOU NEVER DID.
"LITTLE TITAN."
...
ENOUGH.
GLADIATOR?
GLADLY.
HUSH. IT'LL BE QUICK.
NGGG!
EROS, NO! YOU DON'T HAVE TO DO--
HEY, MAN... I DON'T THINK--
THAT'S QUITE ENOUGH.

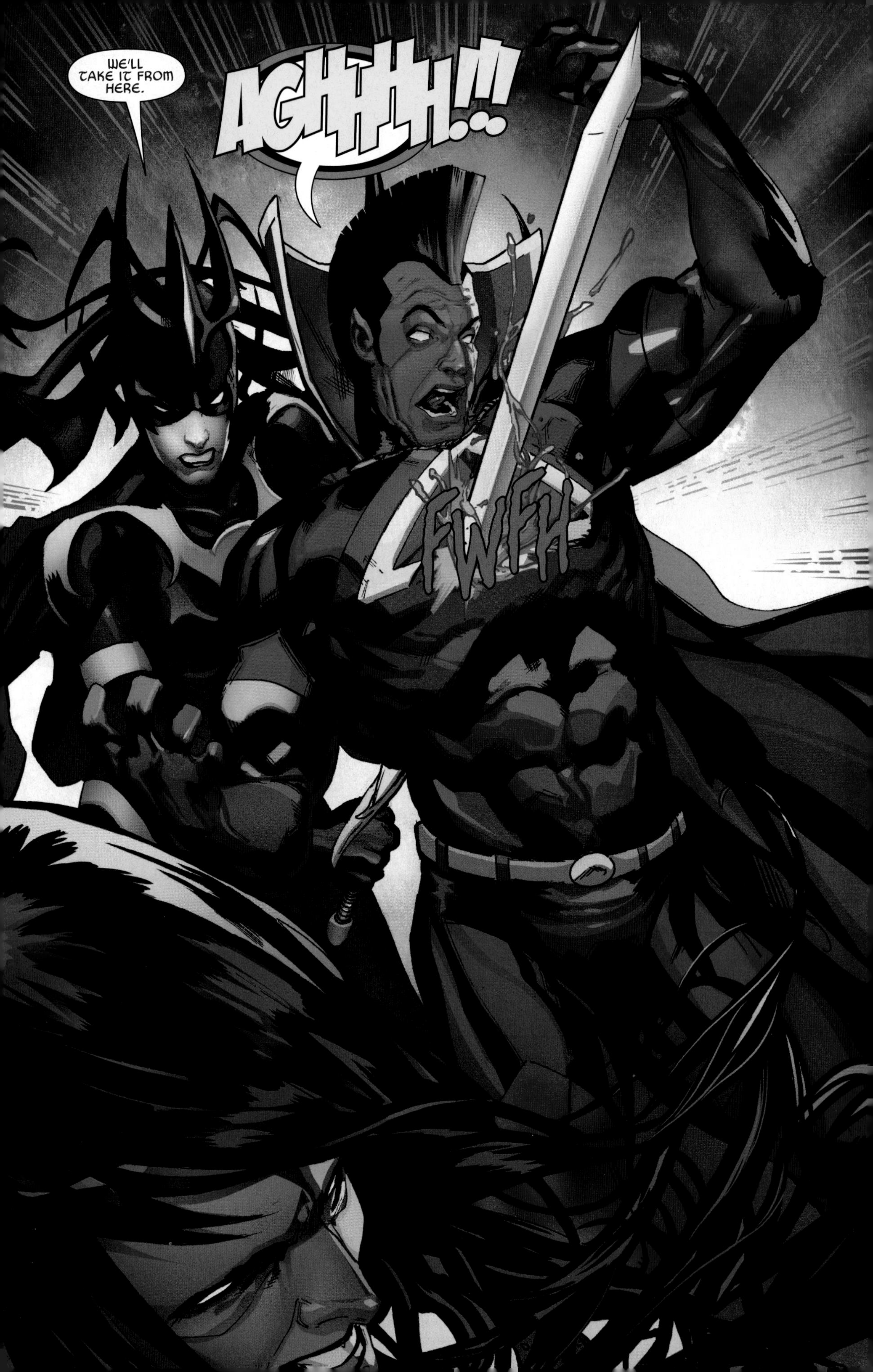
WE'LL TAKE IT FROM HERE.
AGHHHH!!!
FWFH

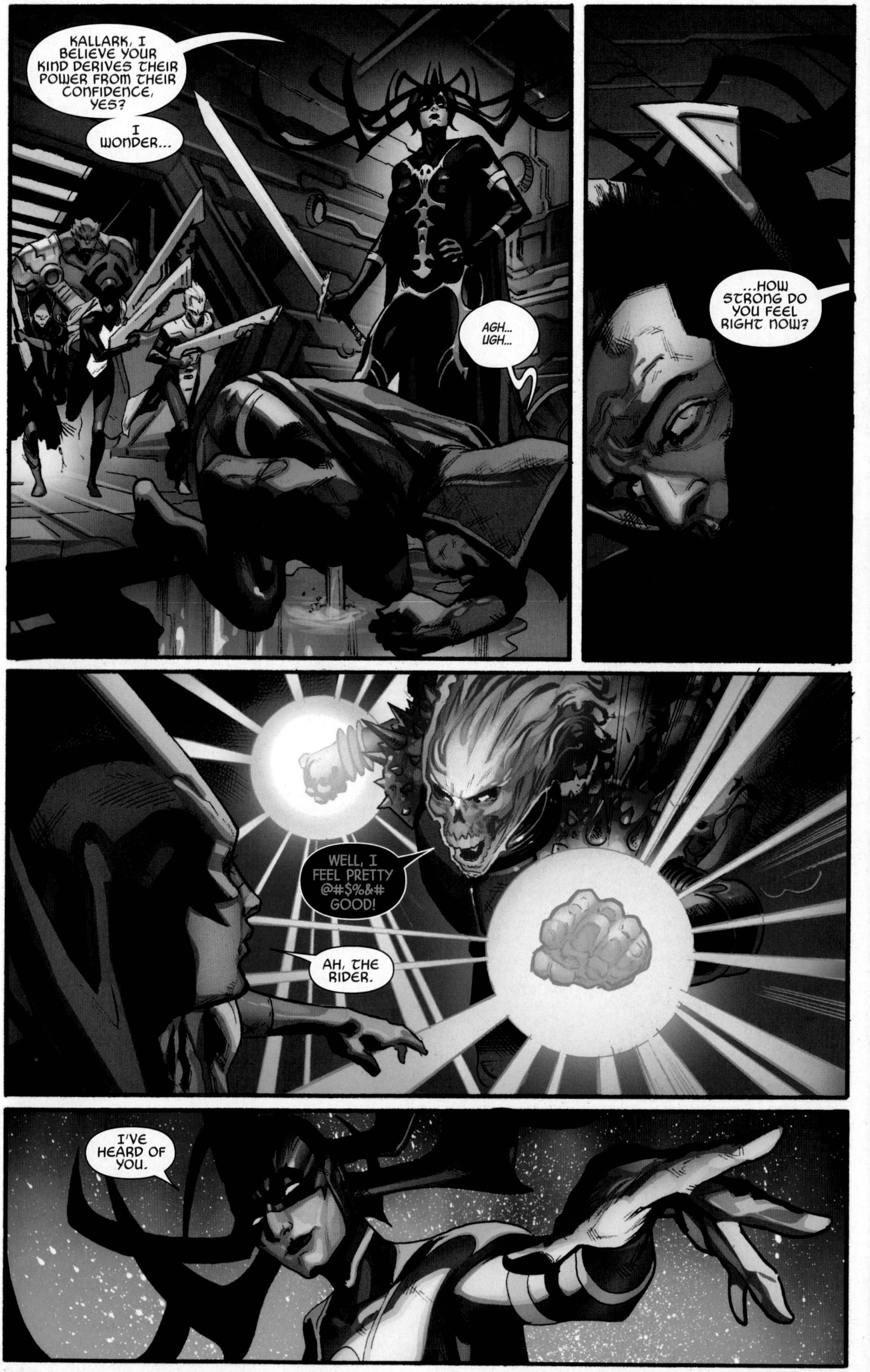
KALLARK, I BELIEVE YOUR KIND DERIVES THEIR POWER FROM THEIR CONFIDENCE, YES?
I WONDER...
AGH... UGH...
...HOW STRONG DO YOU FEEL RIGHT NOW?
WELL, I FEEL PRETTY @#$%&# GOOD!
AH, THE RIDER.
I'VE HEARD OF YOU.

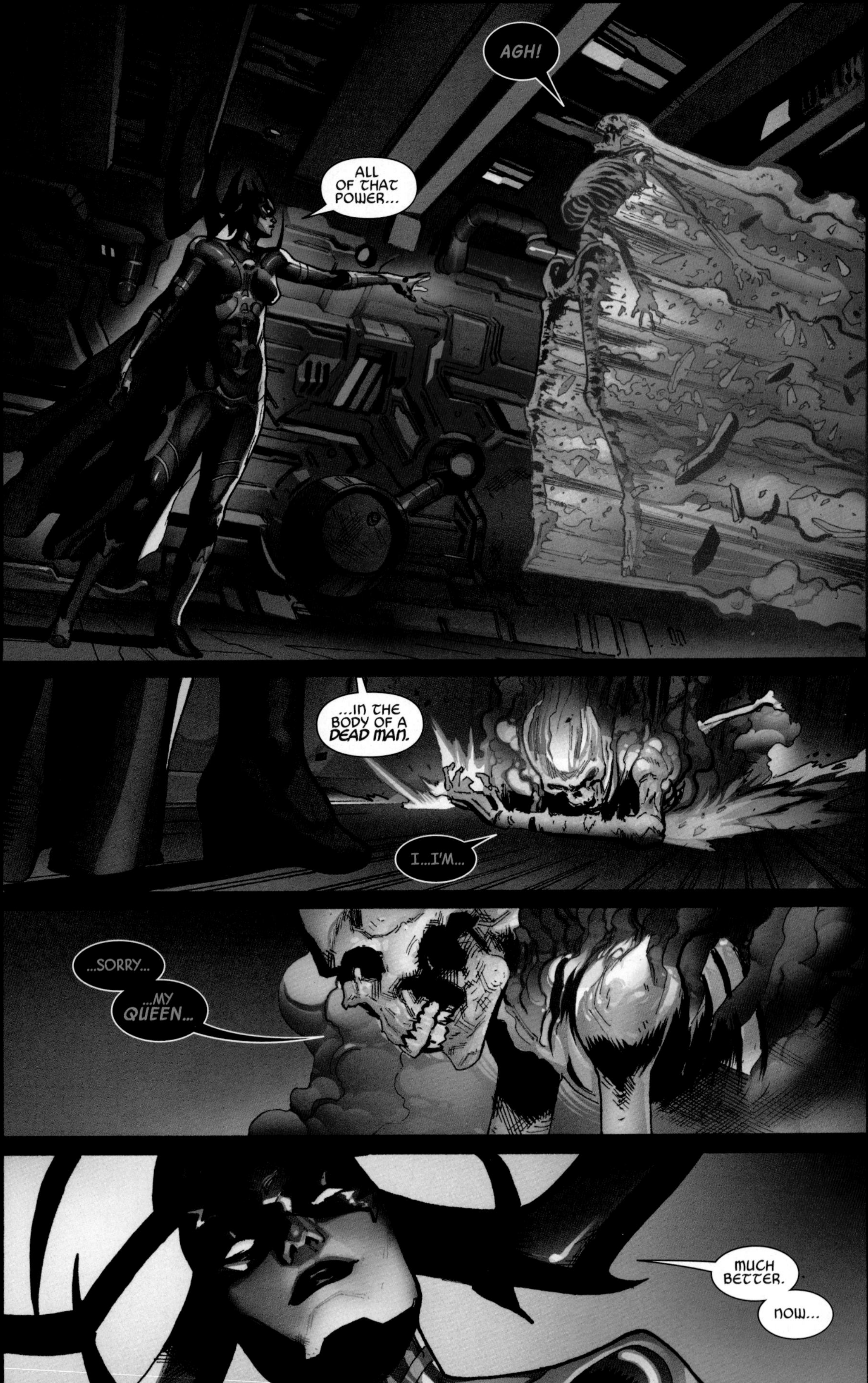
AGH!
ALL OF THAT POWER...
...IN THE BODY OF A DEAD MAN.
I...I'M...
...SORRY...
...MY QUEEN...
MUCH BETTER.
NOW...

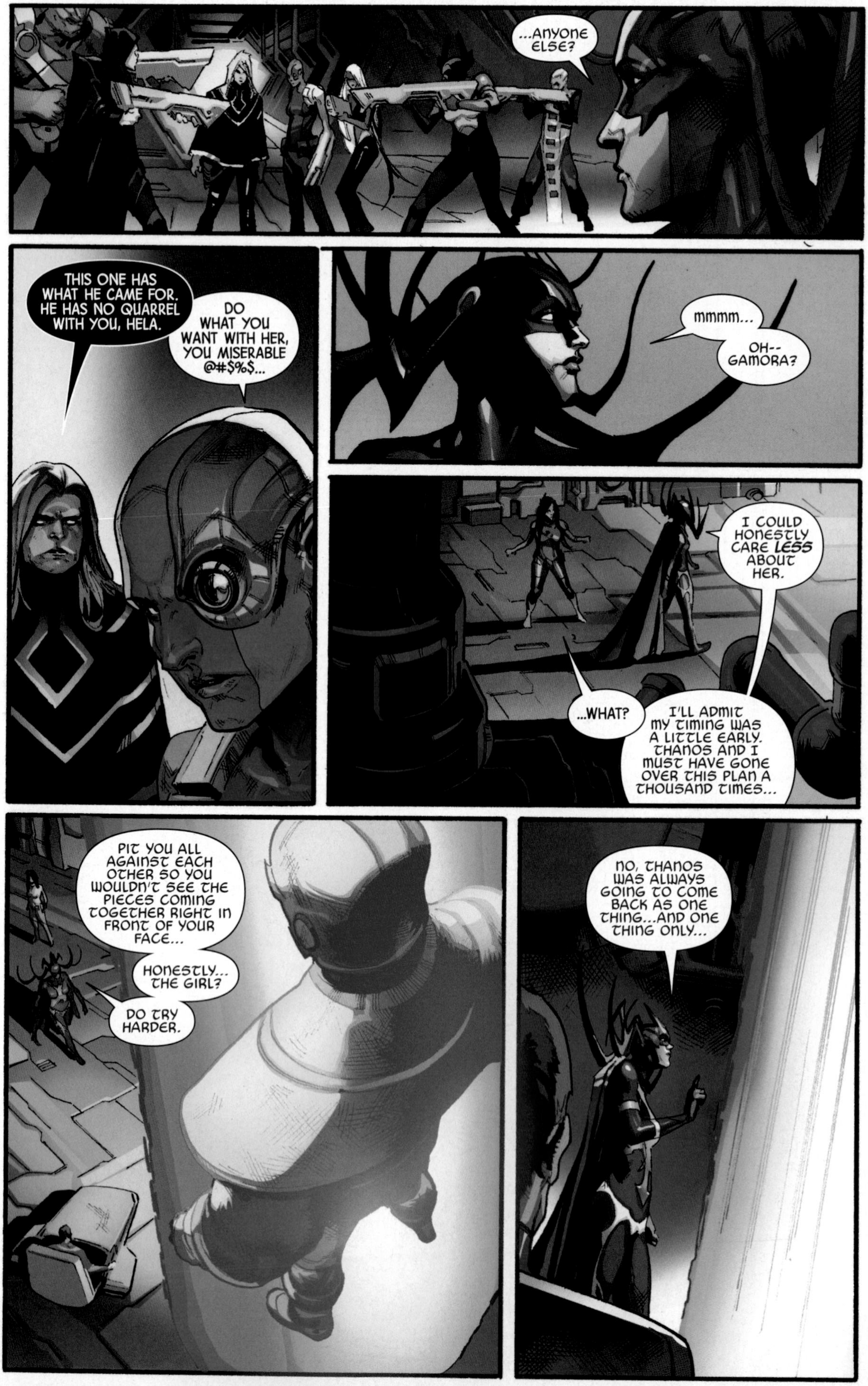
...ANYONE ELSE?
THIS ONE HAS WHAT HE CAME FOR. HE HAS NO QUARREL WITH YOU, HELA.
DO WHAT YOU WANT WITH HER, YOU MISERABLE @#$%$...
mmmm...
OH-- GAMORA?
I COULD HONESTLY CARE LESS ABOUT HER.
...WHAT?
I'LL ADMIT MY TIMING WAS A LITTLE EARLY. THANOS AND I MUST HAVE GONE OVER THIS PLAN A THOUSAND TIMES...
PIT YOU ALL AGAINST EACH OTHER SO YOU WOULDN'T SEE THE PIECES COMING TOGETHER RIGHT IN FRONT OF YOUR FACE...
HONESTLY... THE GIRL?
DO TRY HARDER.
NO, THANOS WAS ALWAYS GOING TO COME BACK AS ONE THING...AND ONE THING ONLY...

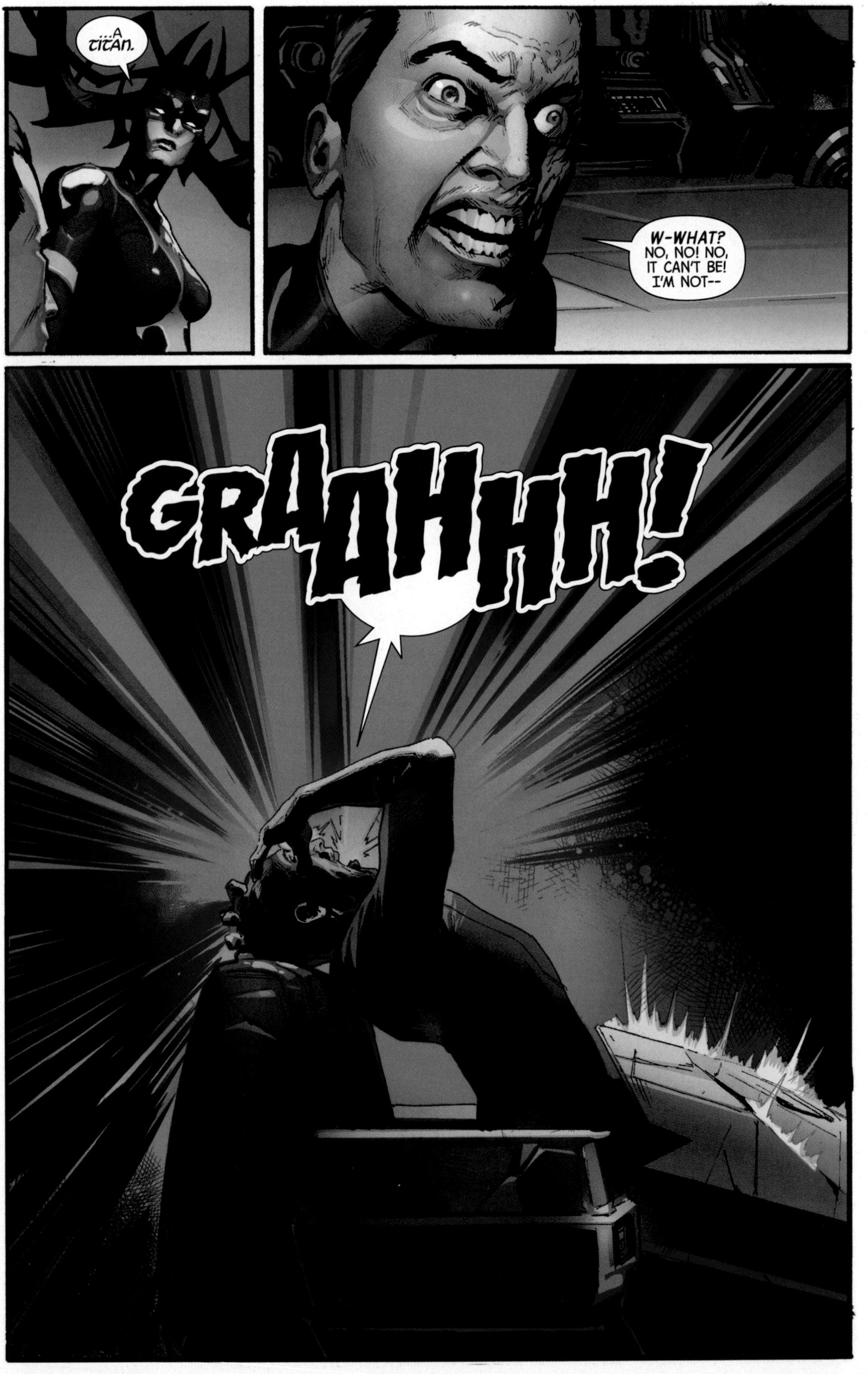
...A TITAN.
W-WHAT? NO, NO! NO, IT CAN'T BE! I'M NOT--
GRAAHHHH!

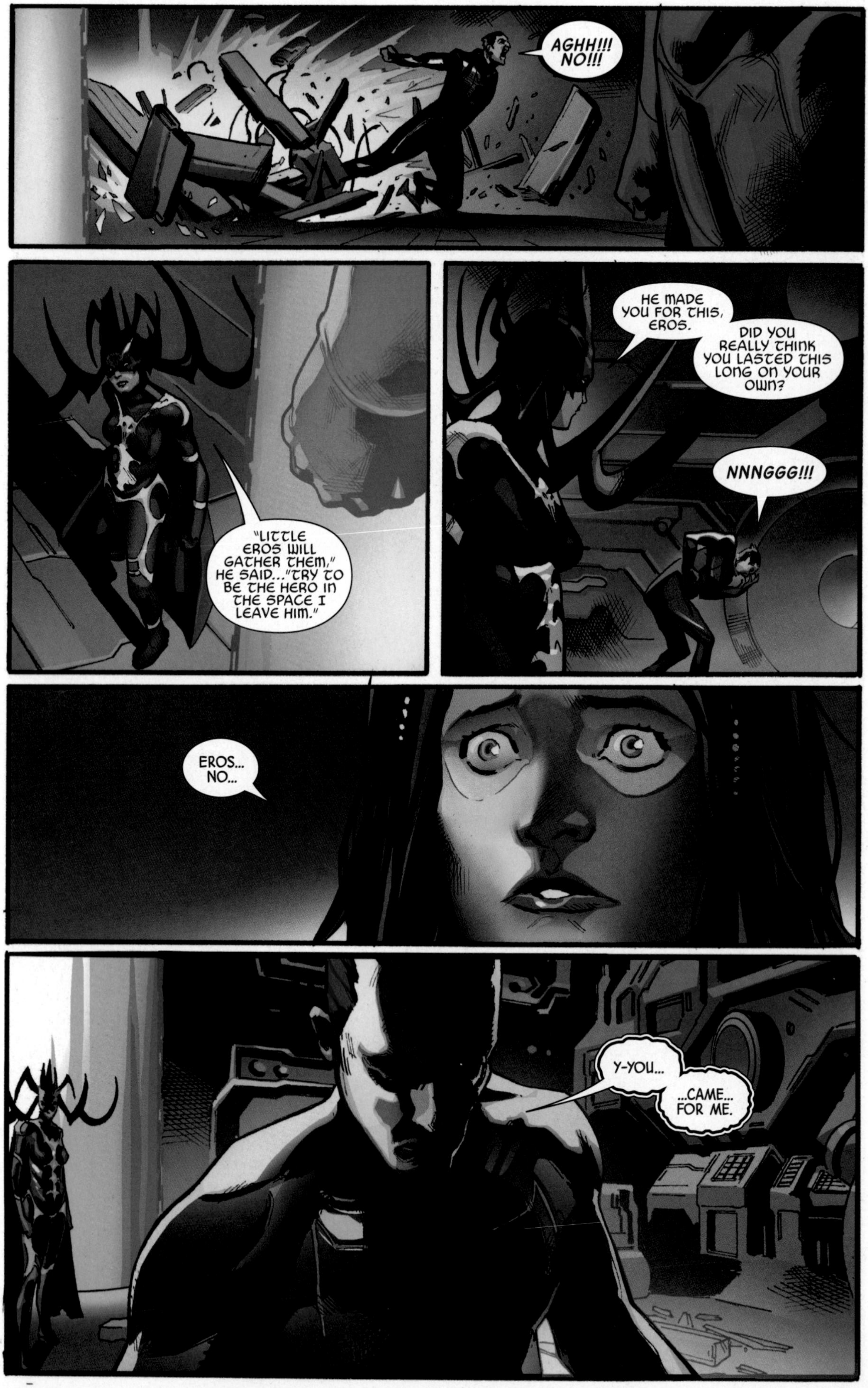
AGHH!!! NO!!!
"LITTLE EROS WILL GATHER THEM," HE SAID..."TRY TO BE THE HERO IN THE SPACE I LEAVE HIM."
HE MADE YOU FOR THIS, EROS.
DID YOU REALLY THINK YOU LASTED THIS LONG ON YOUR OWN?
NNNGGG!!!
EROS... NO...
Y-YOU...
...CAME... FOR ME.

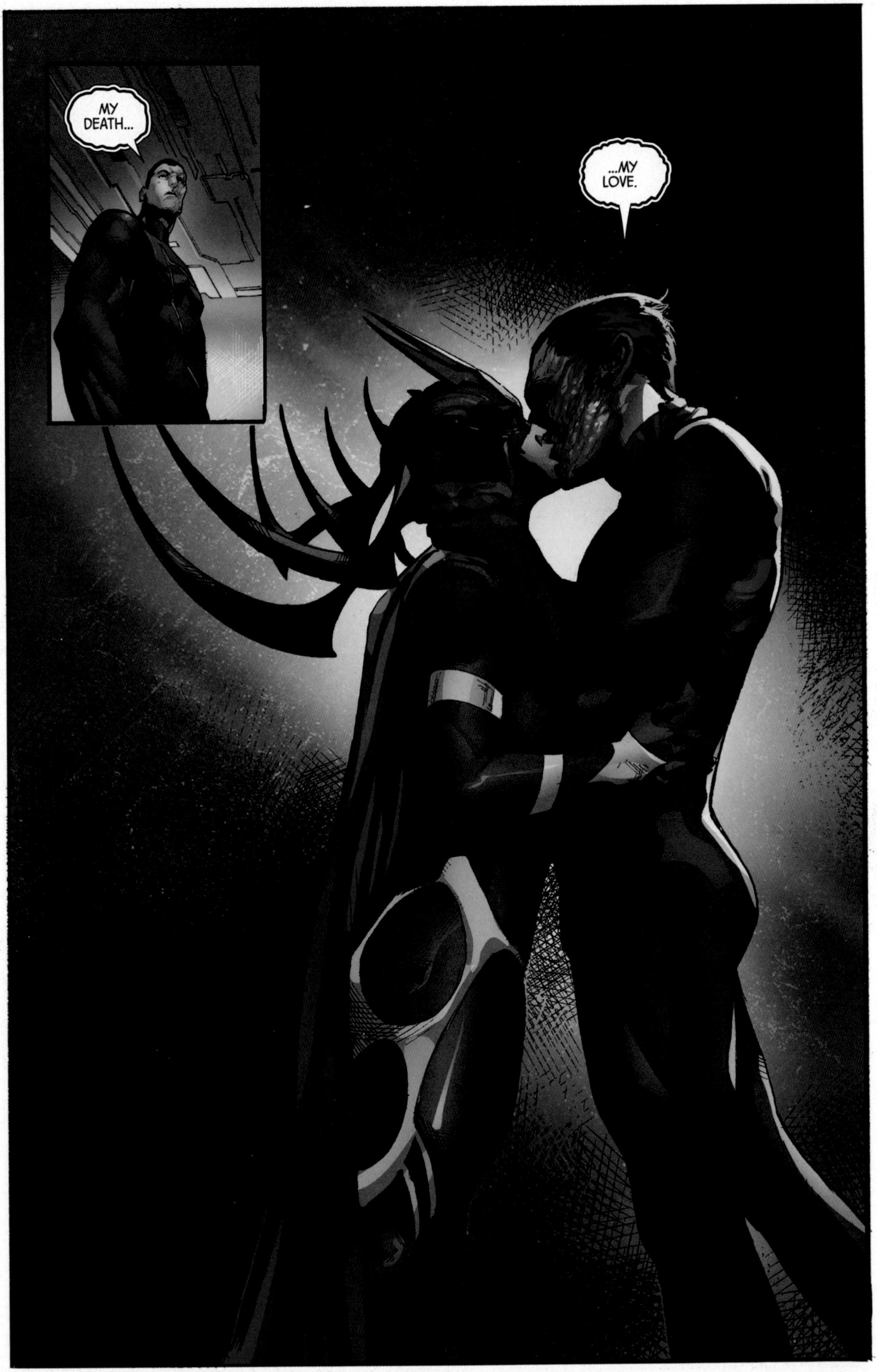
MY DEATH...
...MY LOVE.

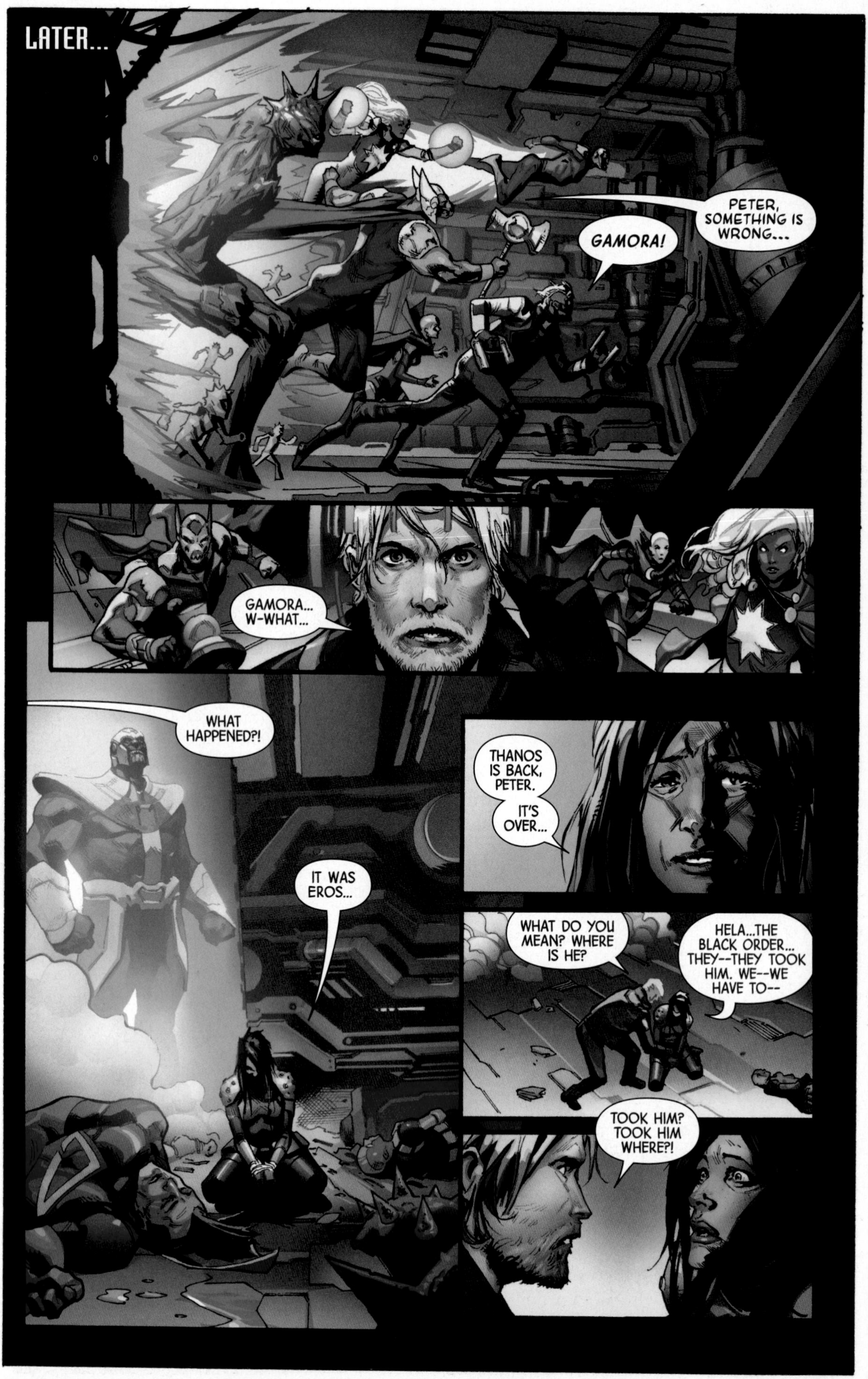
LATER...
PETER, SOMETHING IS WRONG...
GAMORA!
GAMORA... W-WHAT...
WHAT HAPPENED?!
THANOS IS BACK, PETER.
IT'S OVER...
IT WAS EROS...
WHAT DO YOU MEAN? WHERE IS HE?
HELA...THE BLACK ORDER... THEY--THEY TOOK HIM. WE--WE HAVE TO--
TOOK HIM? TOOK HIM WHERE?!

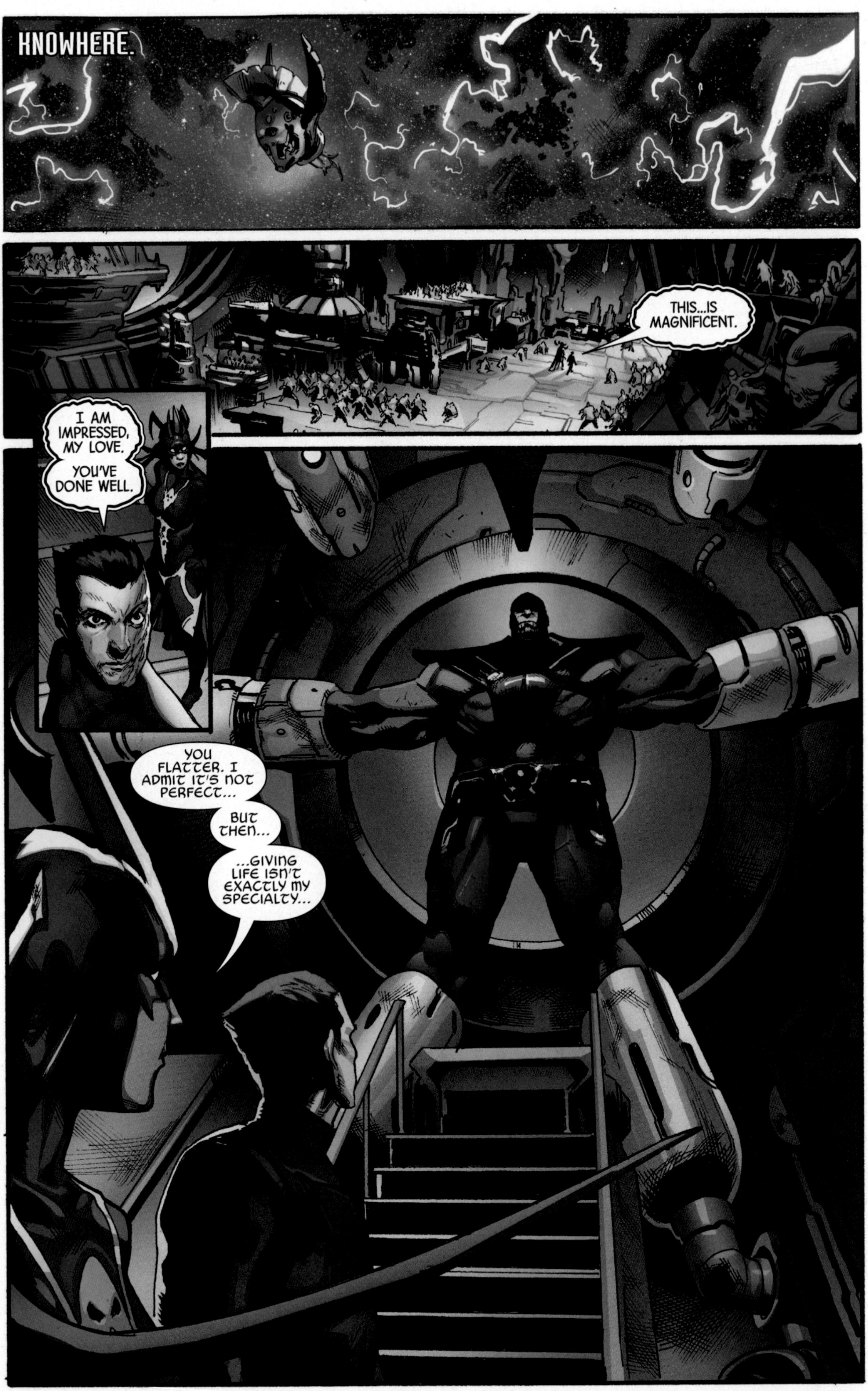
KNOWHERE.
THIS...IS MAGNIFICENT.
I AM IMPRESSED, MY LOVE.
YOU'VE DONE WELL.
YOU FLATTER. I ADMIT IT'S NOT PERFECT...
BUT THEN...
...GIVING LIFE ISN'T EXACTLY MY SPECIALTY...

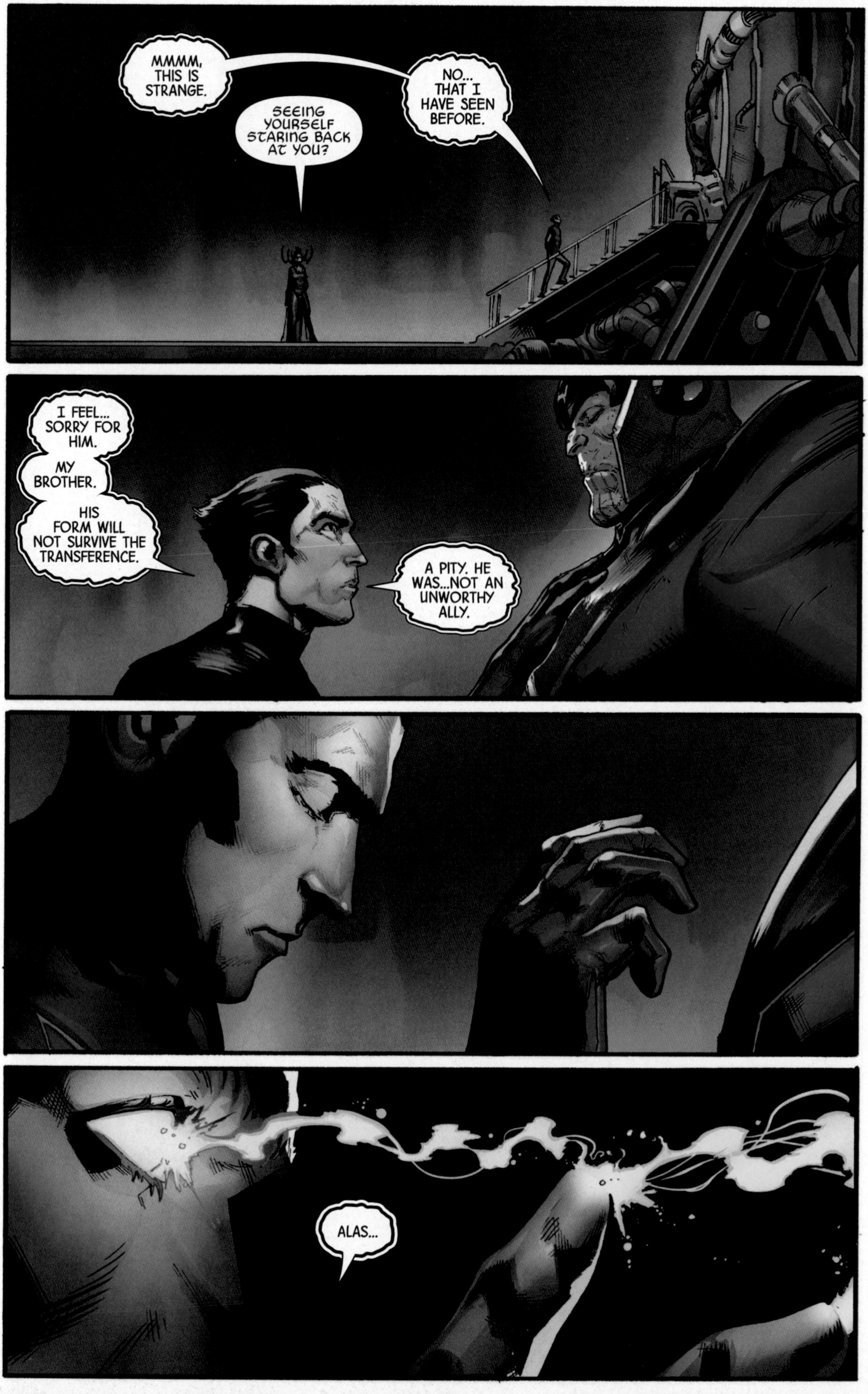
MMMM, THIS IS STRANGE.
SEEING YOURSELF STARING BACK AT YOU?
NO... THAT I HAVE SEEN BEFORE.
I FEEL... SORRY FOR HIM.
MY BROTHER.
HIS FORM WILL NOT SURVIVE THE TRANSFERENCE.
A PITY. HE WAS...NOT AN UNWORTHY ALLY.
ALAS...

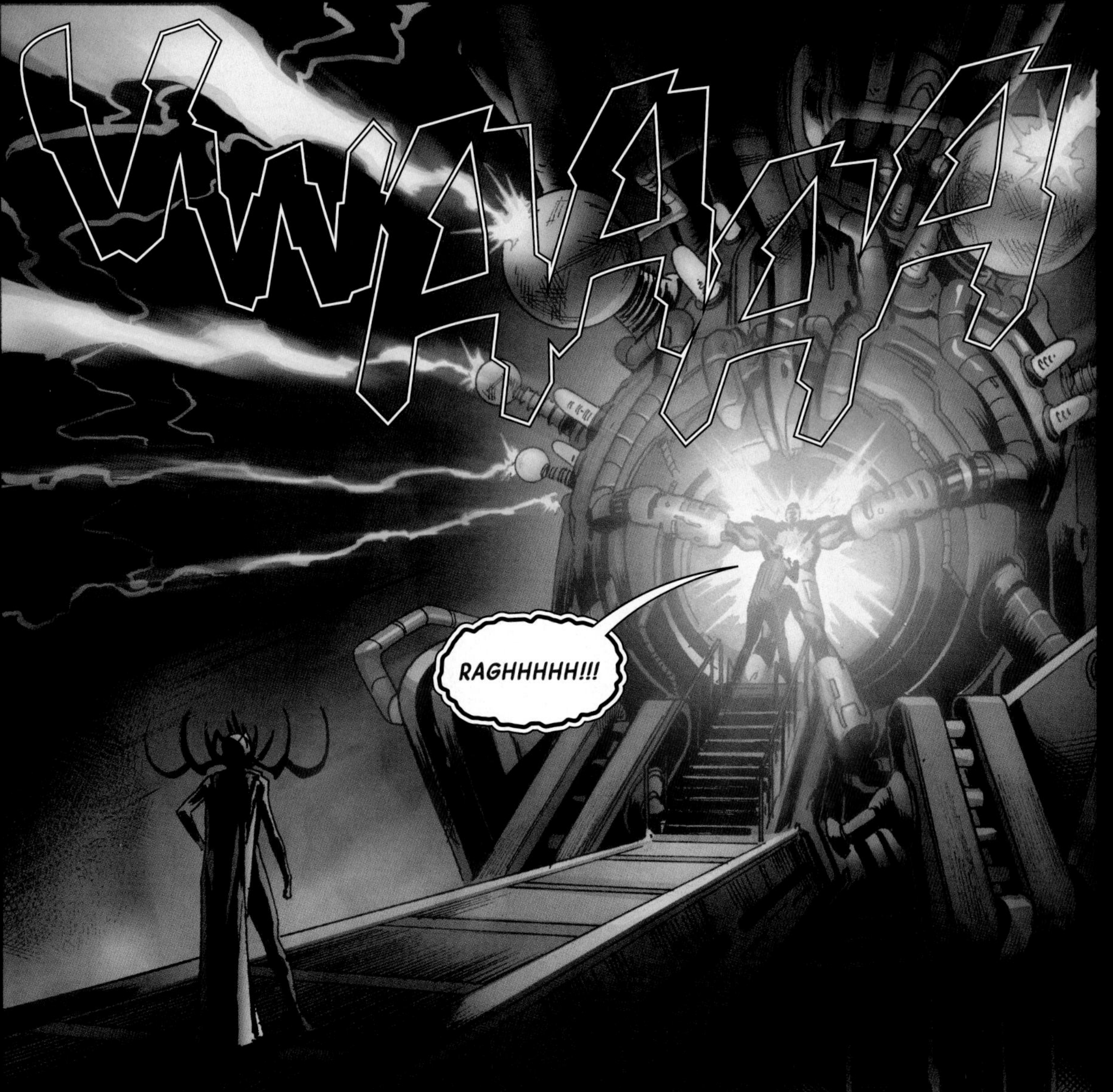
VWAAAA
RAGHHHHH!!!

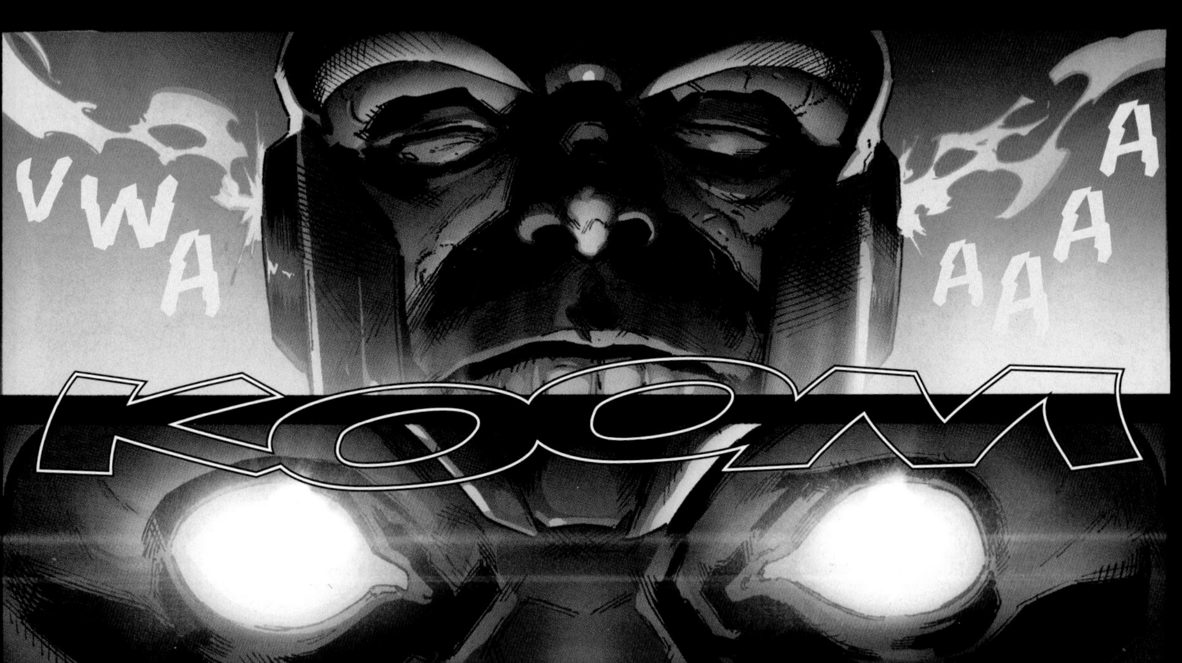
VWAAAAA
KOOM

SIX

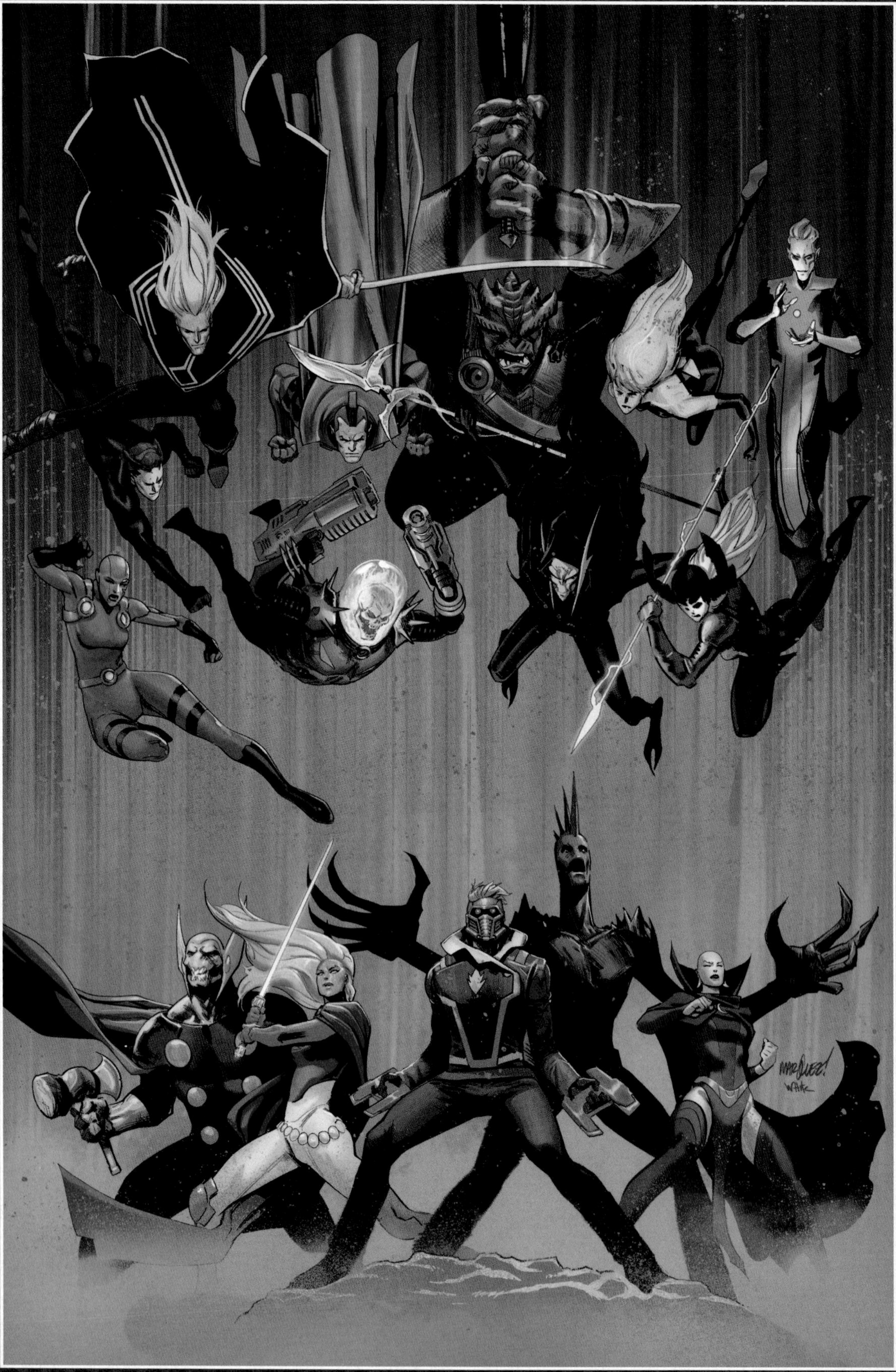

OKAY, LISTEN UP.

WE GOT PLAYED.

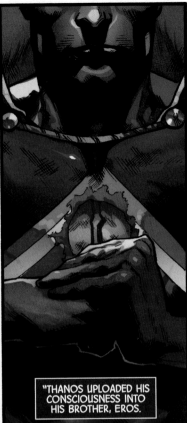

"THANOS UPLOADED HIS CONSCIOUSNESS INTO HIS BROTHER, EROS.

"AND WHILE WE WERE ALL CHASING OUR TAILS, HELA REASSEMBLED THANOS' BODY.

"NOW SHE'S TAKEN EROS TO KNOWHERE. TO DO WHAT? I DON'T KNOW. BUT IT ALL ADDS UP TO A NEW THANOS.

"SO HERE'S THE @#$%&@# DEAL.

"I KNOW WE ALL HATE EACH OTHER AND WE ALL TRIED TO KILL ONE ANOTHER.

"BUT FROM NOW ON, AND UNTIL THE JOB IS DONE..."

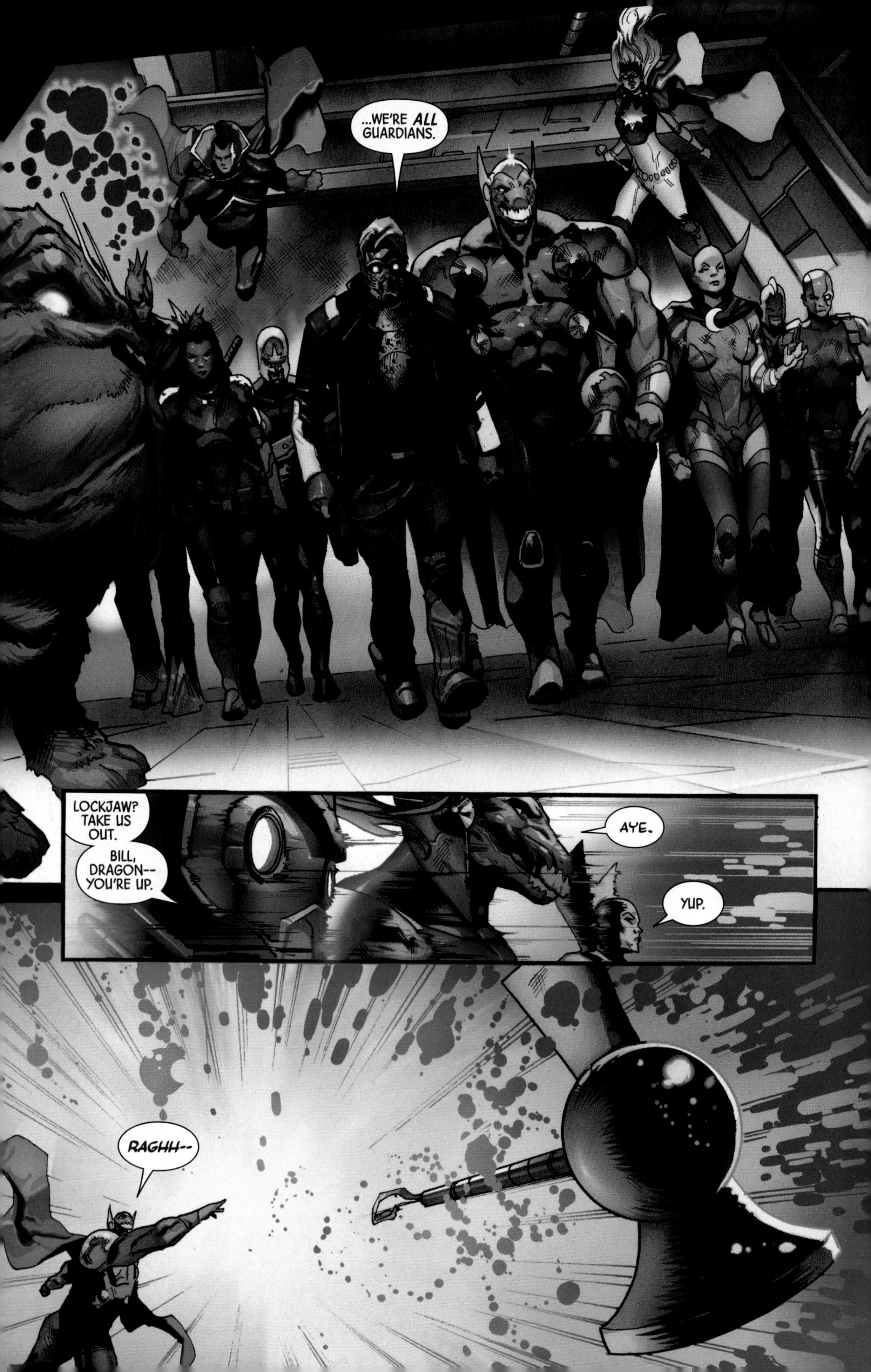
...WE'RE ALL GUARDIANS.
LOCKJAW? TAKE US OUT.
BILL, DRAGON-- YOU'RE UP.
AYE.
YUP.
RAGHH--

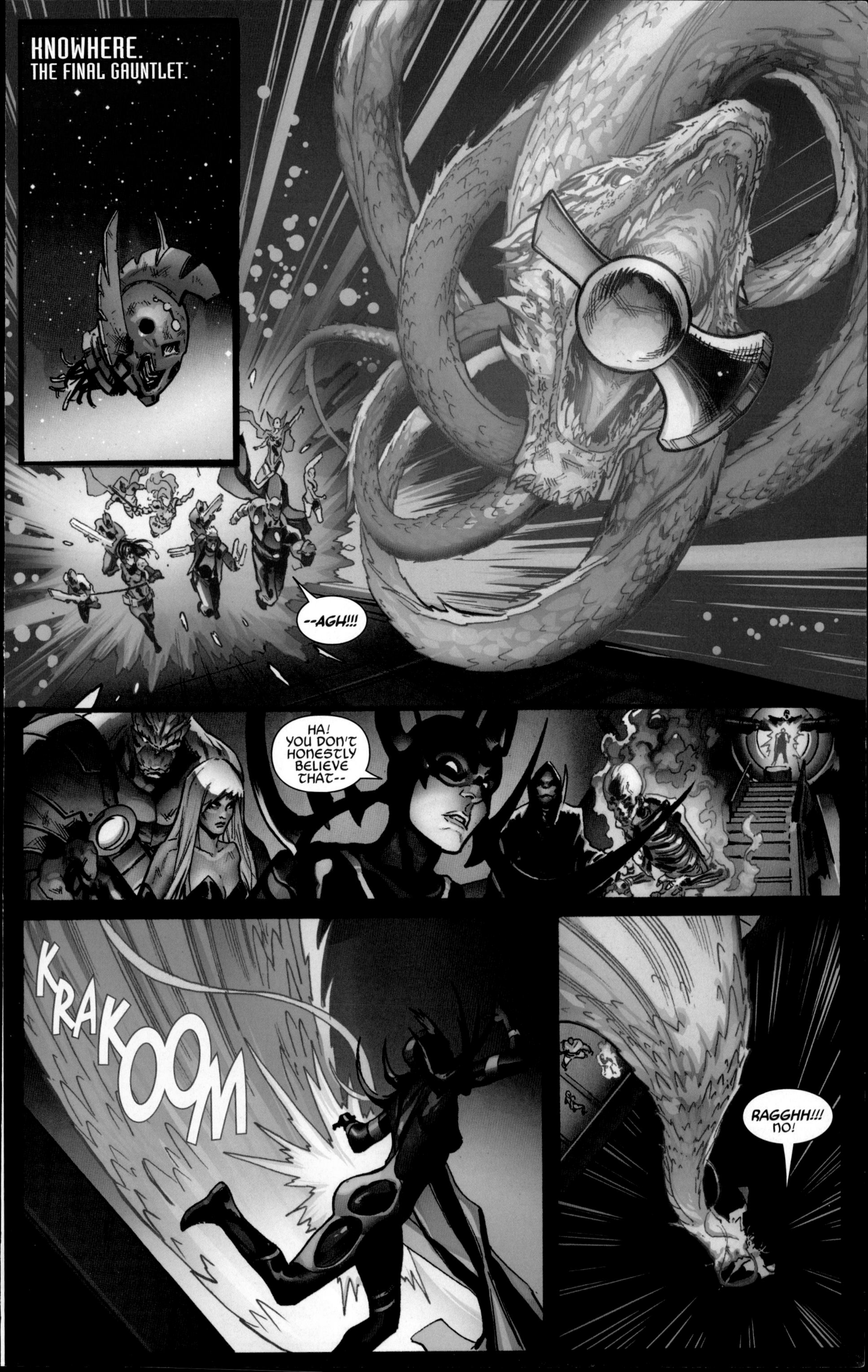
KNOWHERE.
THE FINAL GAUNTLET.
--AGH!!!
HA! YOU DON'T HONESTLY BELIEVE THAT--
KRAKOOM
RAGGHH!!! NO!

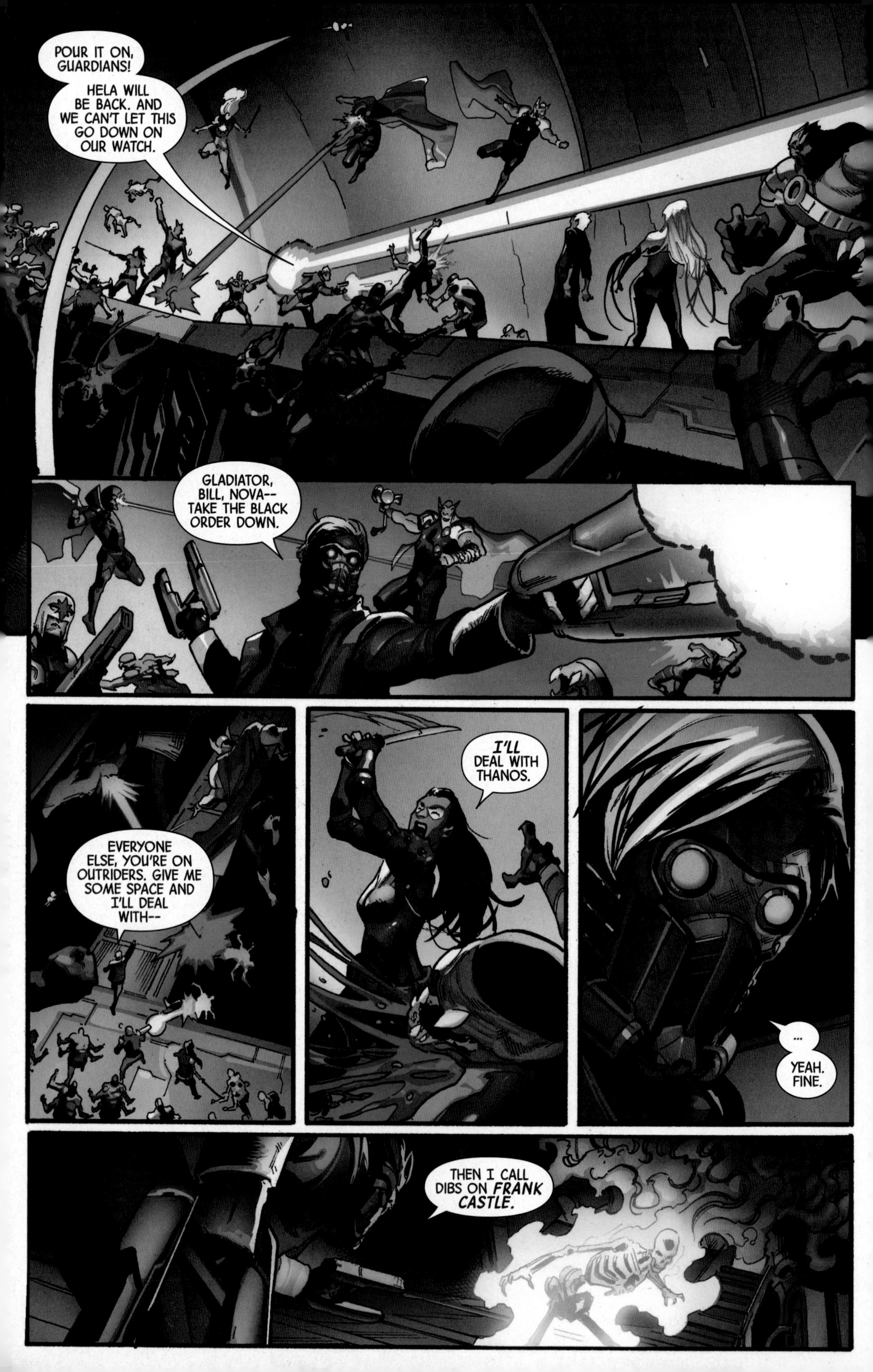
POUR IT ON, GUARDIANS!
HELA WILL BE BACK. AND WE CAN'T LET THIS GO DOWN ON OUR WATCH.
GLADIATOR, BILL, NOVA-- TAKE THE BLACK ORDER DOWN.
EVERYONE ELSE, YOU'RE ON OUTRIDERS. GIVE ME SOME SPACE AND I'LL DEAL WITH--
I'LL DEAL WITH THANOS.
...
YEAH. FINE.
THEN I CALL DIBS ON *FRANK CASTLE*.

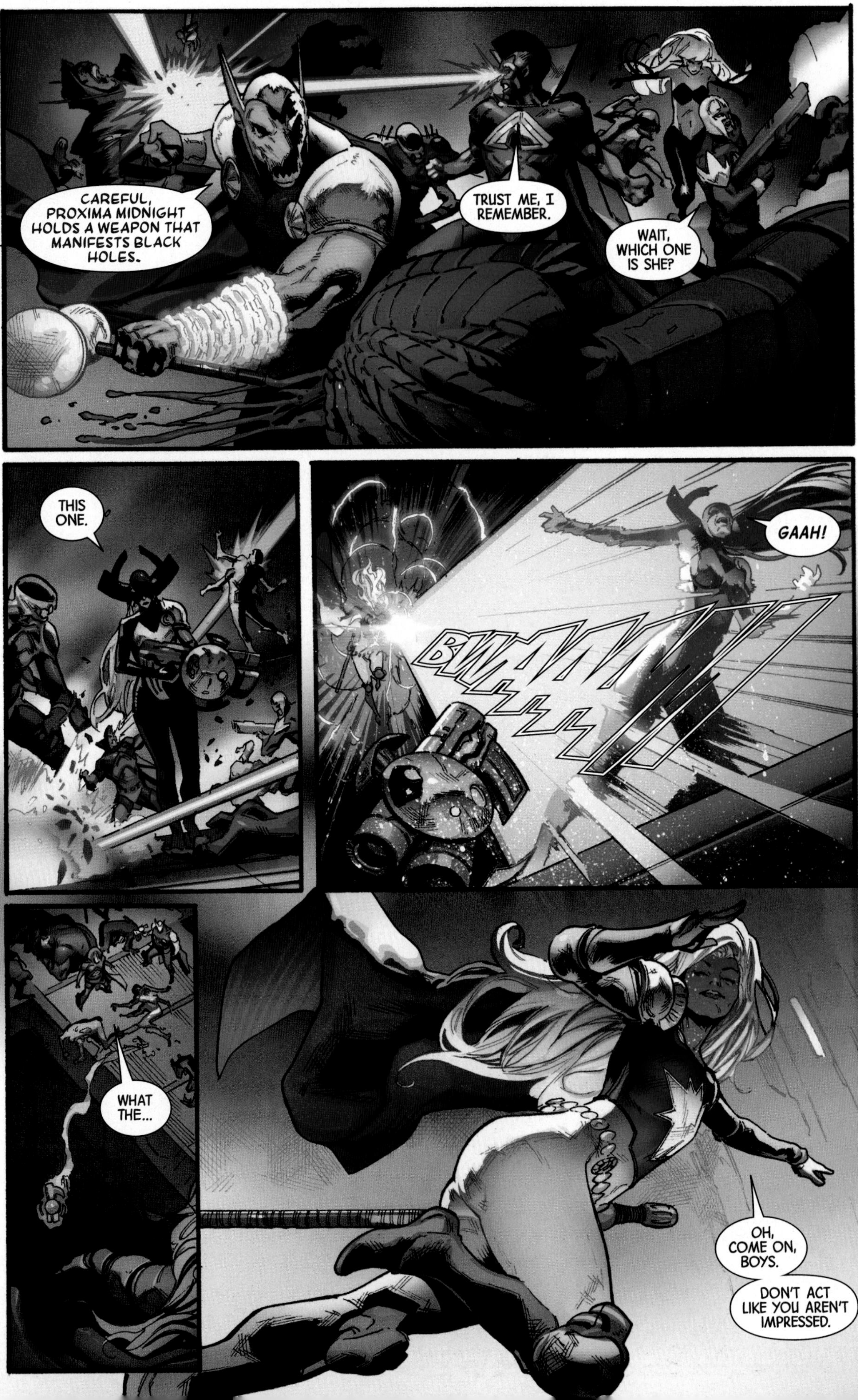
CAREFUL, PROXIMA MIDNIGHT HOLDS A WEAPON THAT MANIFESTS BLACK HOLES.
TRUST ME, I REMEMBER.
WAIT, WHICH ONE IS SHE?
THIS ONE.
GAAH!
BUHMM
WHAT THE...
OH, COME ON, BOYS.
DON'T ACT LIKE YOU AREN'T IMPRESSED.

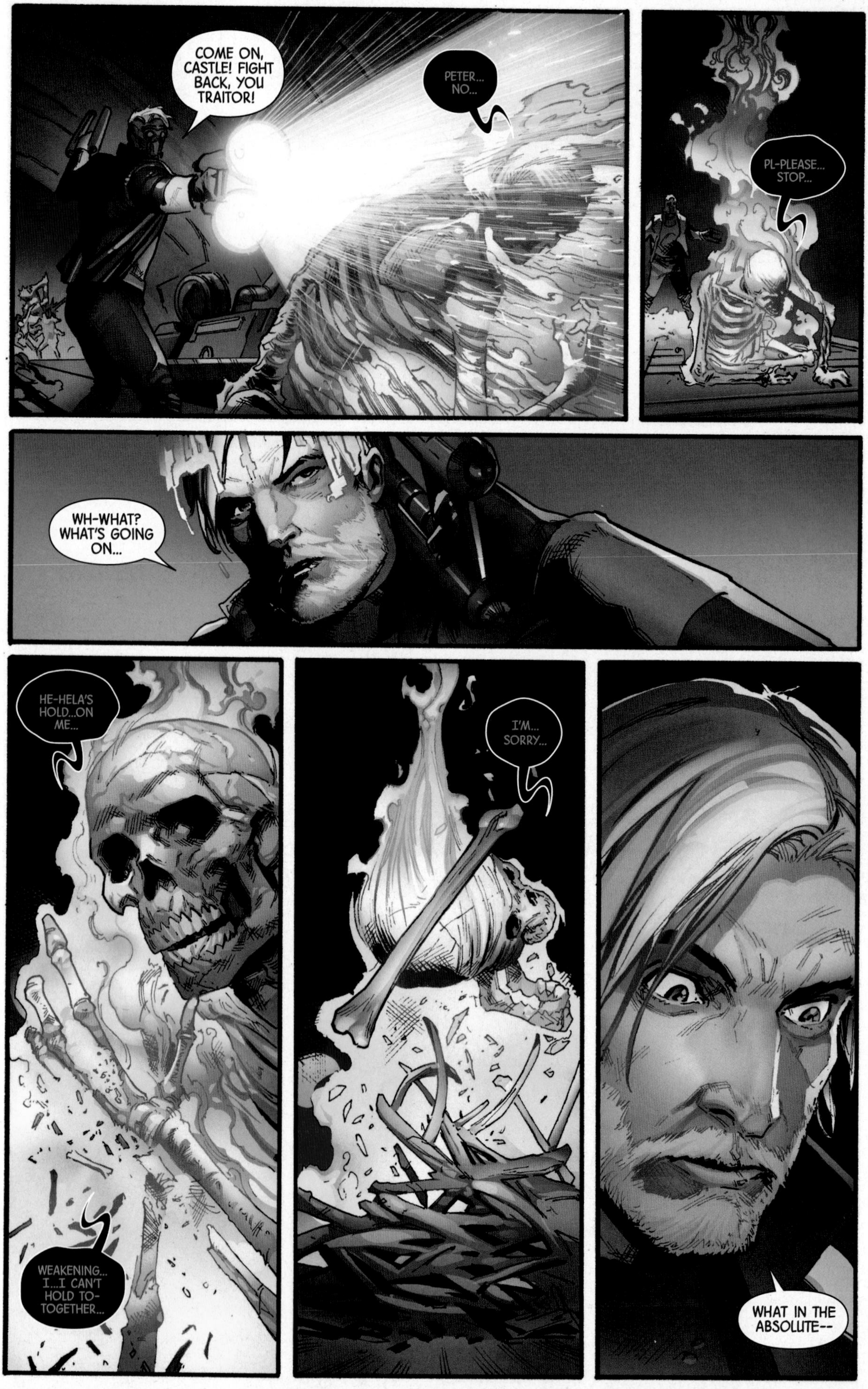
COME ON, CASTLE! FIGHT BACK, YOU TRAITOR!
PETER... NO...
PL-PLEASE... STOP...
WH-WHAT? WHAT'S GOING ON...
HE-HELA'S HOLD...ON ME...
WEAKENING... I...I CAN'T HOLD TO-TOGETHER...
I'M... SORRY...
WHAT IN THE ABSOLUTE--

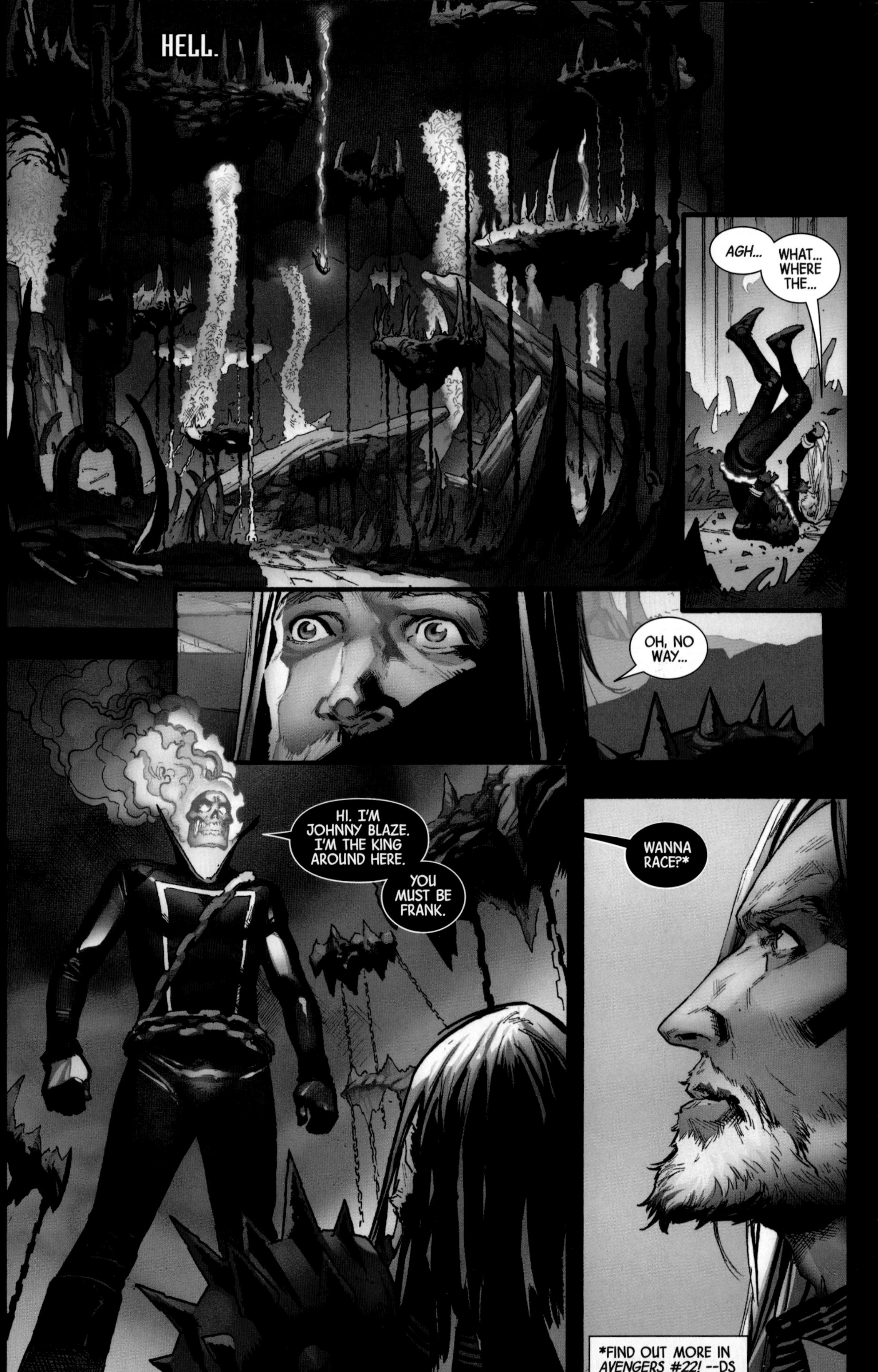
HELL.
AGH...
WHAT... WHERE THE...
OH, NO WAY...
HI. I'M JOHNNY BLAZE. I'M THE KING AROUND HERE.
YOU MUST BE FRANK.
WANNA RACE?*
*FIND OUT MORE IN AVENGERS #22! --DS

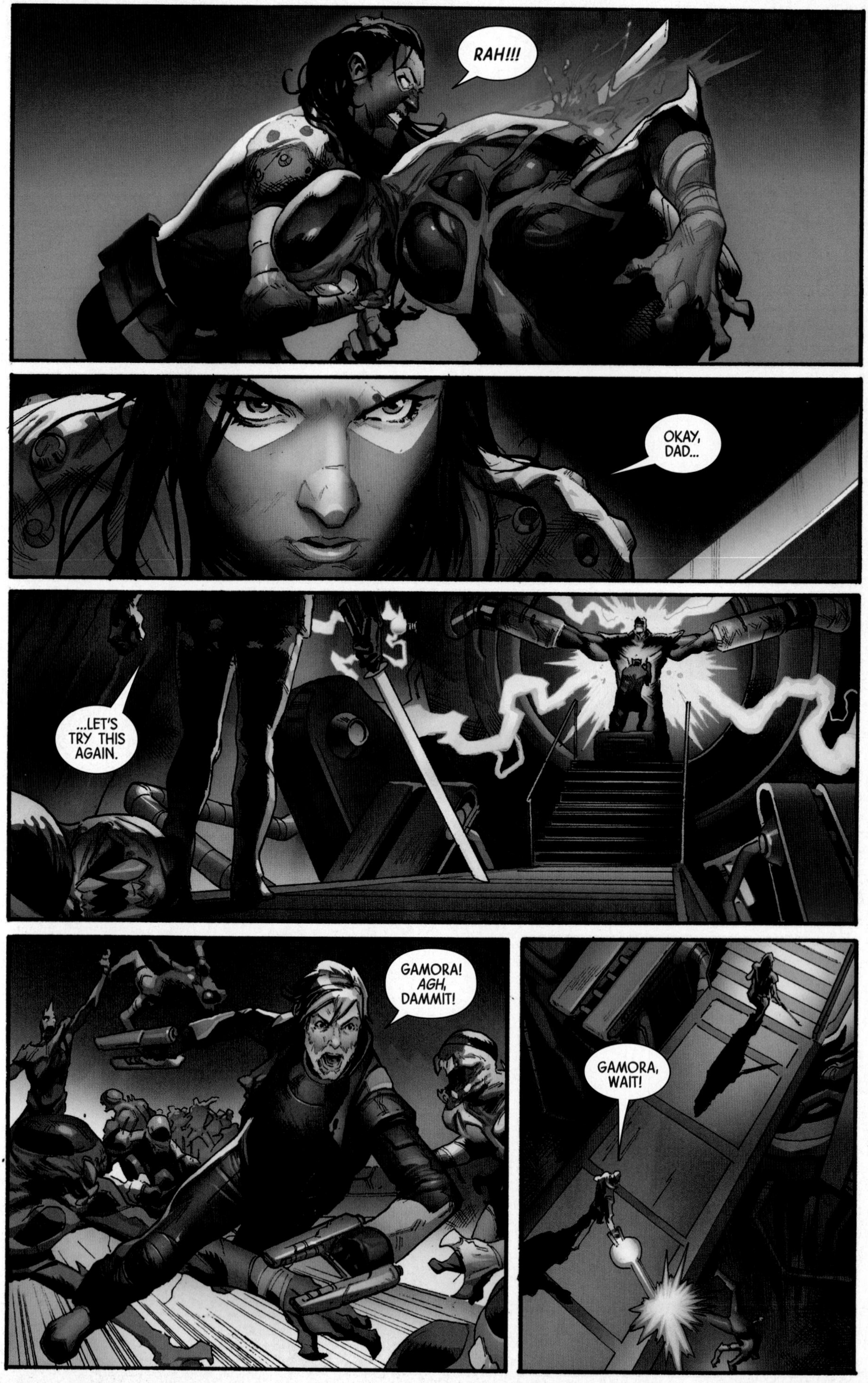
RAH!!!
OKAY, DAD...
...LET'S TRY THIS AGAIN.
GAMORA! AGH, DAMMIT!
GAMORA, WAIT!

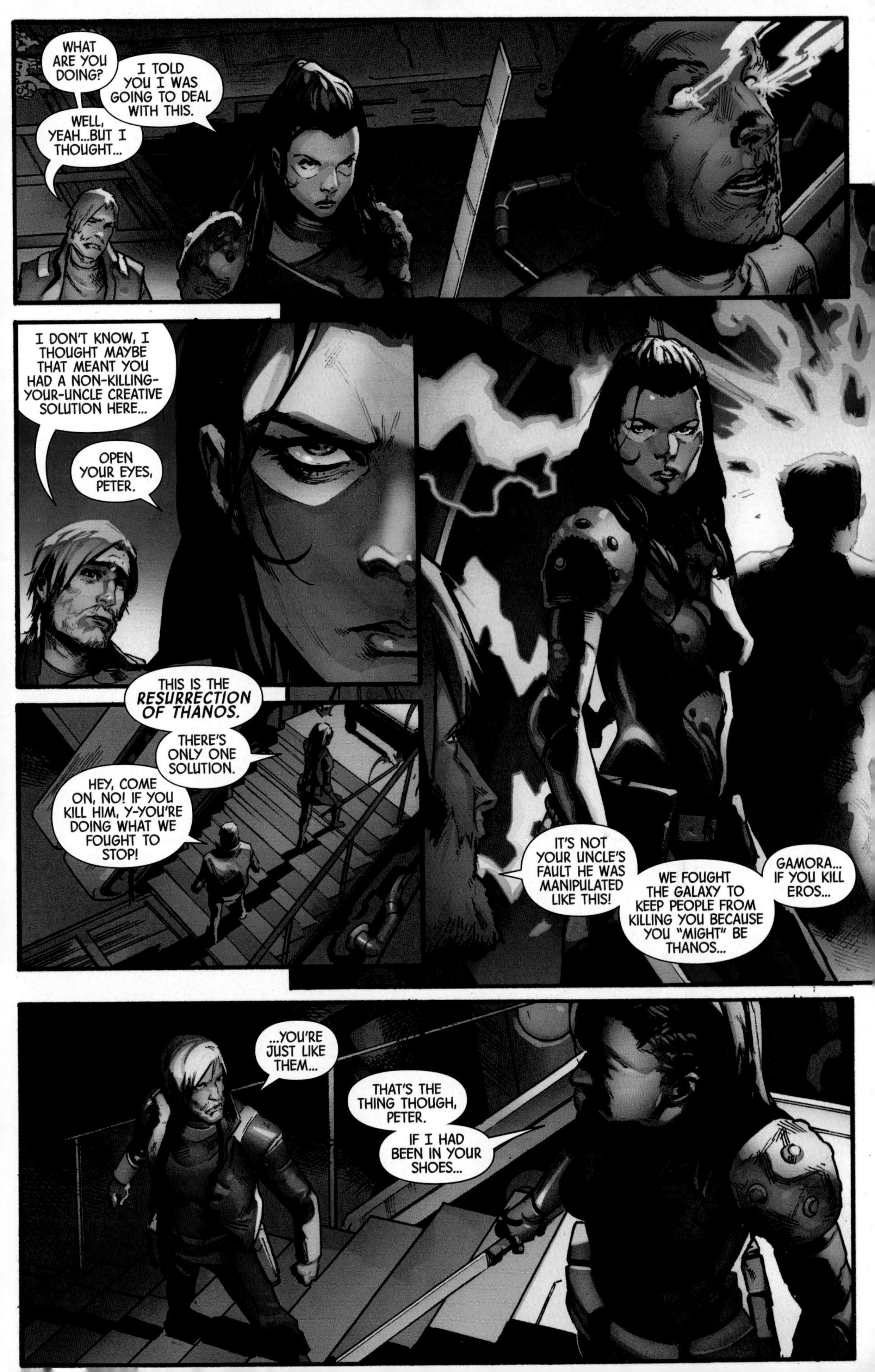
WHAT ARE YOU DOING?
I TOLD YOU I WAS GOING TO DEAL WITH THIS.
WELL, YEAH...BUT I THOUGHT...
I DON'T KNOW, I THOUGHT MAYBE THAT MEANT YOU HAD A NON-KILLING-YOUR-UNCLE CREATIVE SOLUTION HERE...
OPEN YOUR EYES, PETER.
THIS IS THE RESURRECTION OF THANOS.
THERE'S ONLY ONE SOLUTION.
HEY, COME ON, NO! IF YOU KILL HIM, Y-YOU'RE DOING WHAT WE FOUGHT TO STOP!
GAMORA... IF YOU KILL EROS...
WE FOUGHT THE GALAXY TO KEEP PEOPLE FROM KILLING YOU BECAUSE YOU "MIGHT" BE THANOS...
IT'S NOT YOUR UNCLE'S FAULT HE WAS MANIPULATED LIKE THIS!
...YOU'RE JUST LIKE THEM...
THAT'S THE THING THOUGH, PETER.
IF I HAD BEEN IN YOUR SHOES...

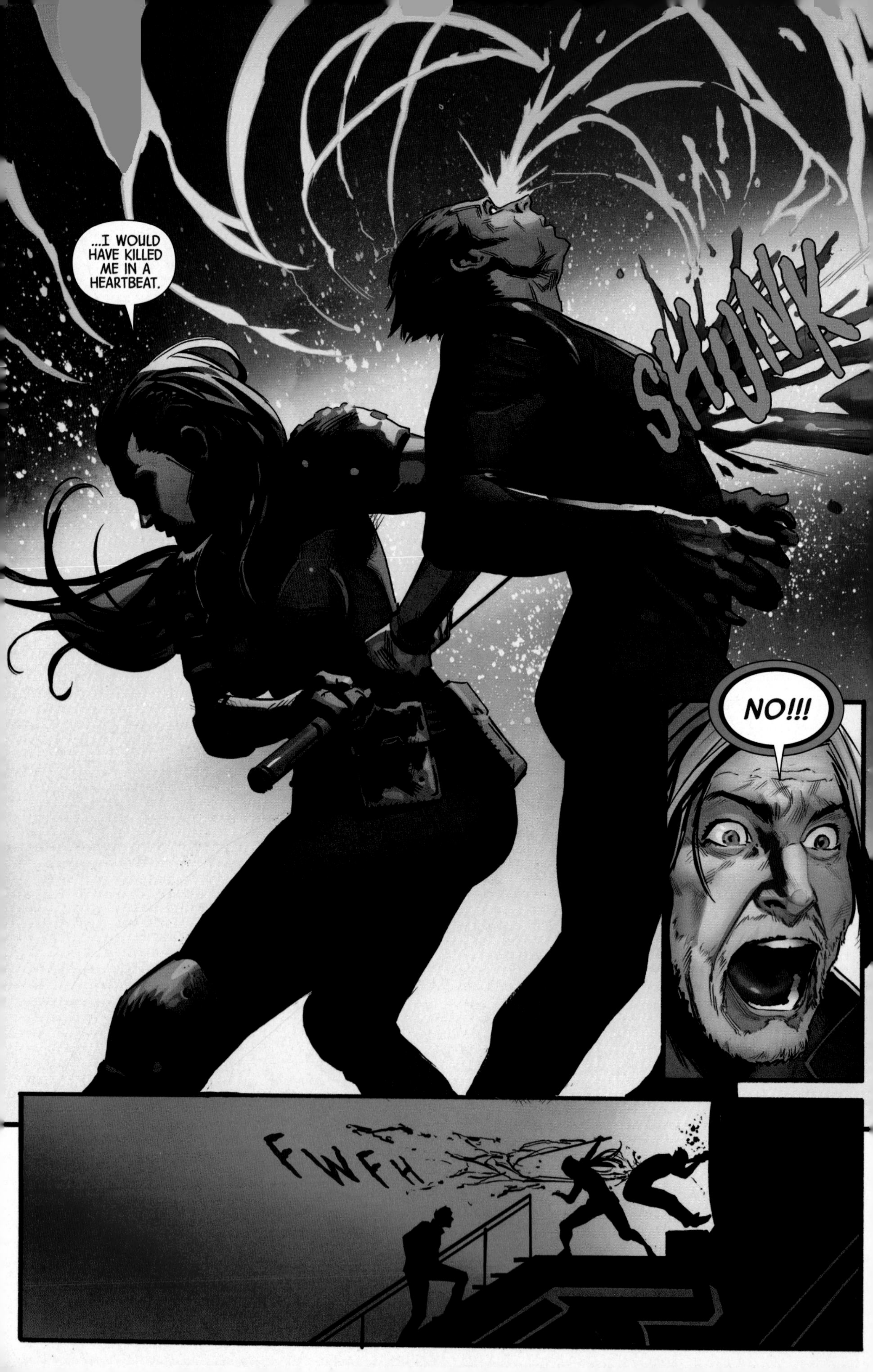
...I WOULD HAVE KILLED ME IN A HEARTBEAT.
SHUNK
NO!!!
FWFH

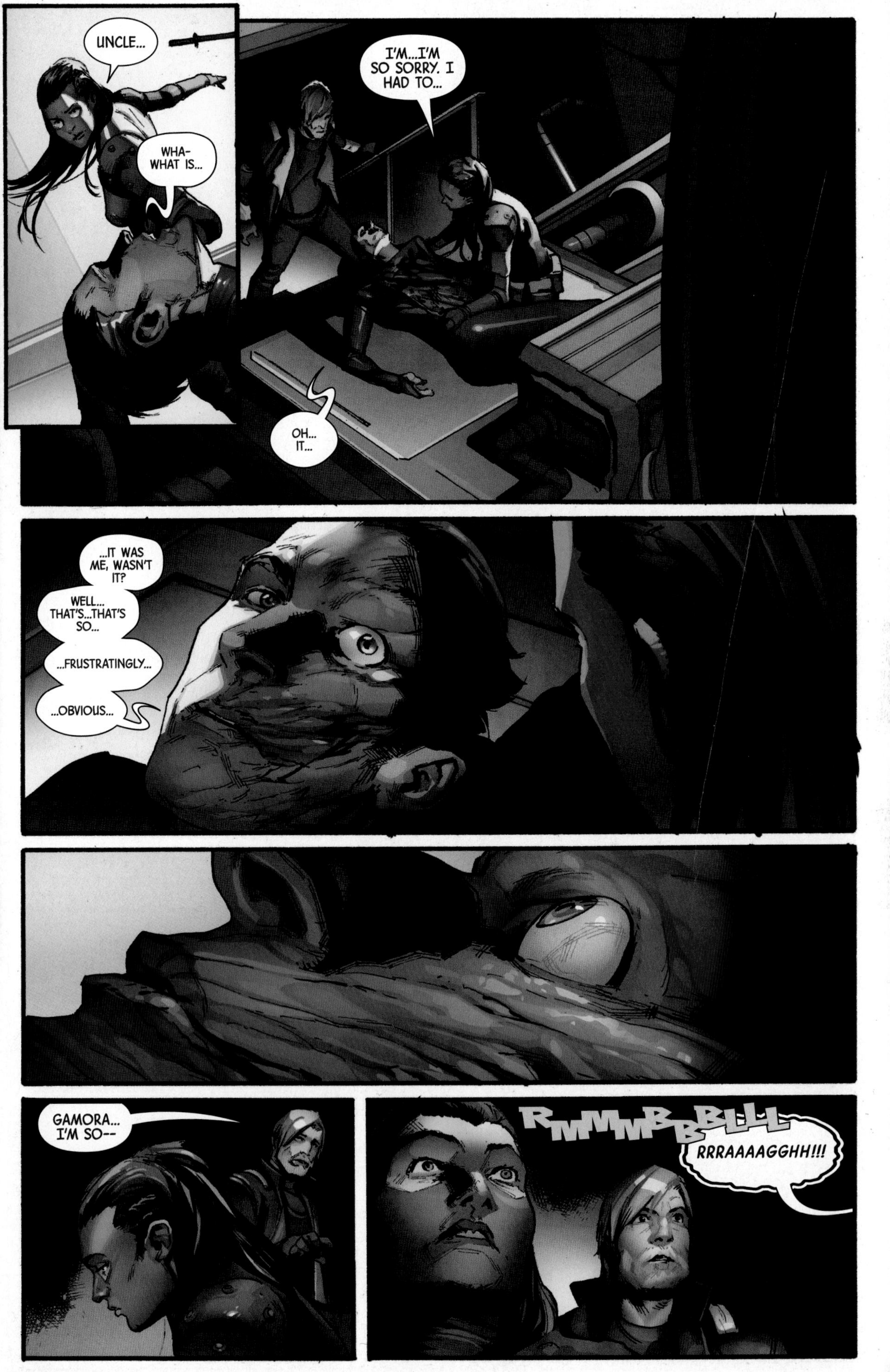
UNCLE...
WHA-WHAT IS...
I'M...I'M SO SORRY. I HAD TO...
OH... IT...
...IT WAS ME, WASN'T IT?
WELL... THAT'S...THAT'S SO...
...FRUSTRATINGLY...
...OBVIOUS...
GAMORA... I'M SO--
RMMMBBBLLL
RRRAAAAGGHH!!!

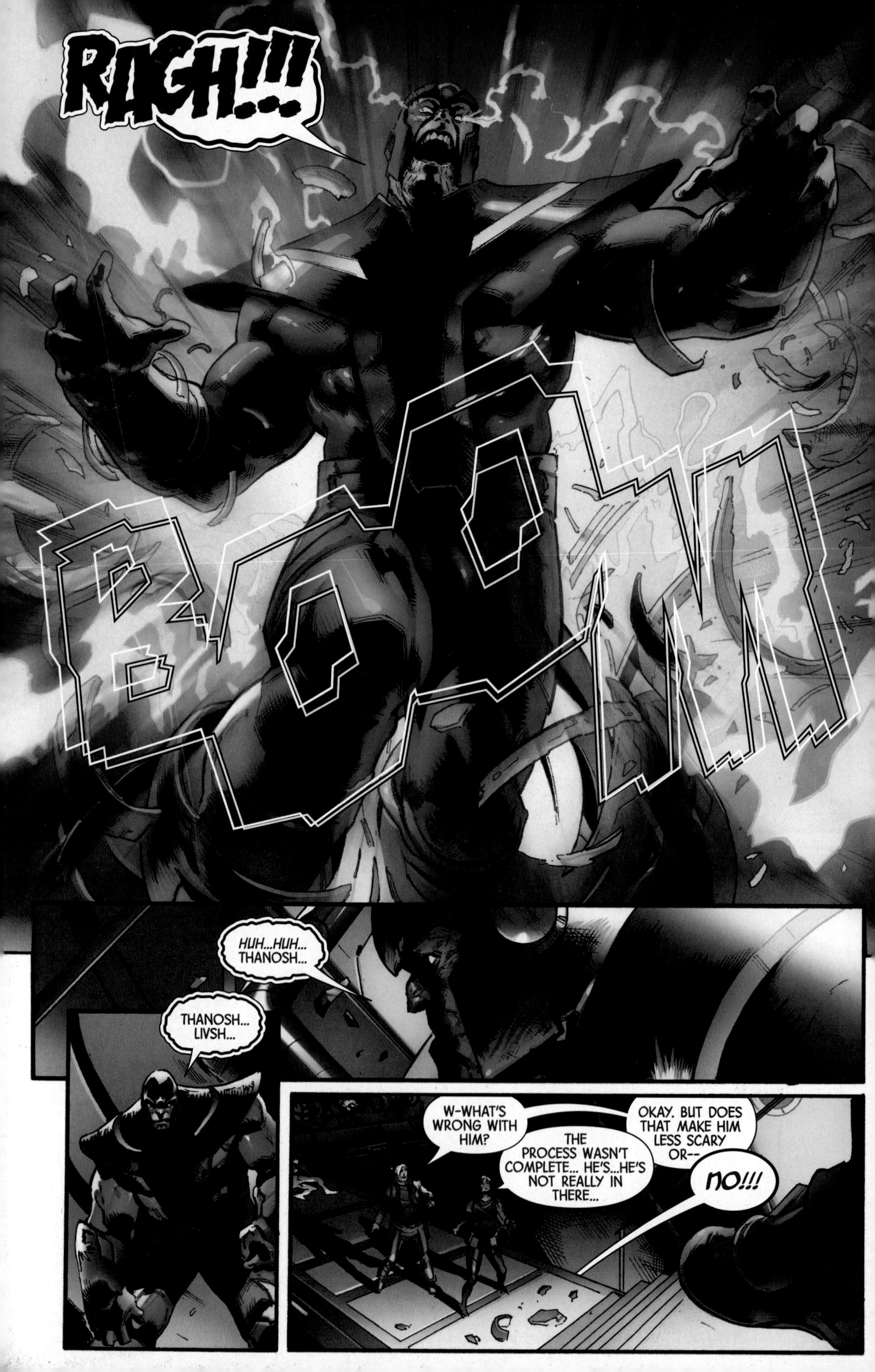
RAGH!!!...
BOOM
HUH...HUH... THANOSH...
THANOSH... LIVSH...
W-WHAT'S WRONG WITH HIM?
THE PROCESS WASN'T COMPLETE... HE'S...HE'S NOT REALLY IN THERE...
OKAY. BUT DOES THAT MAKE HIM LESS SCARY OR--
NO!!!

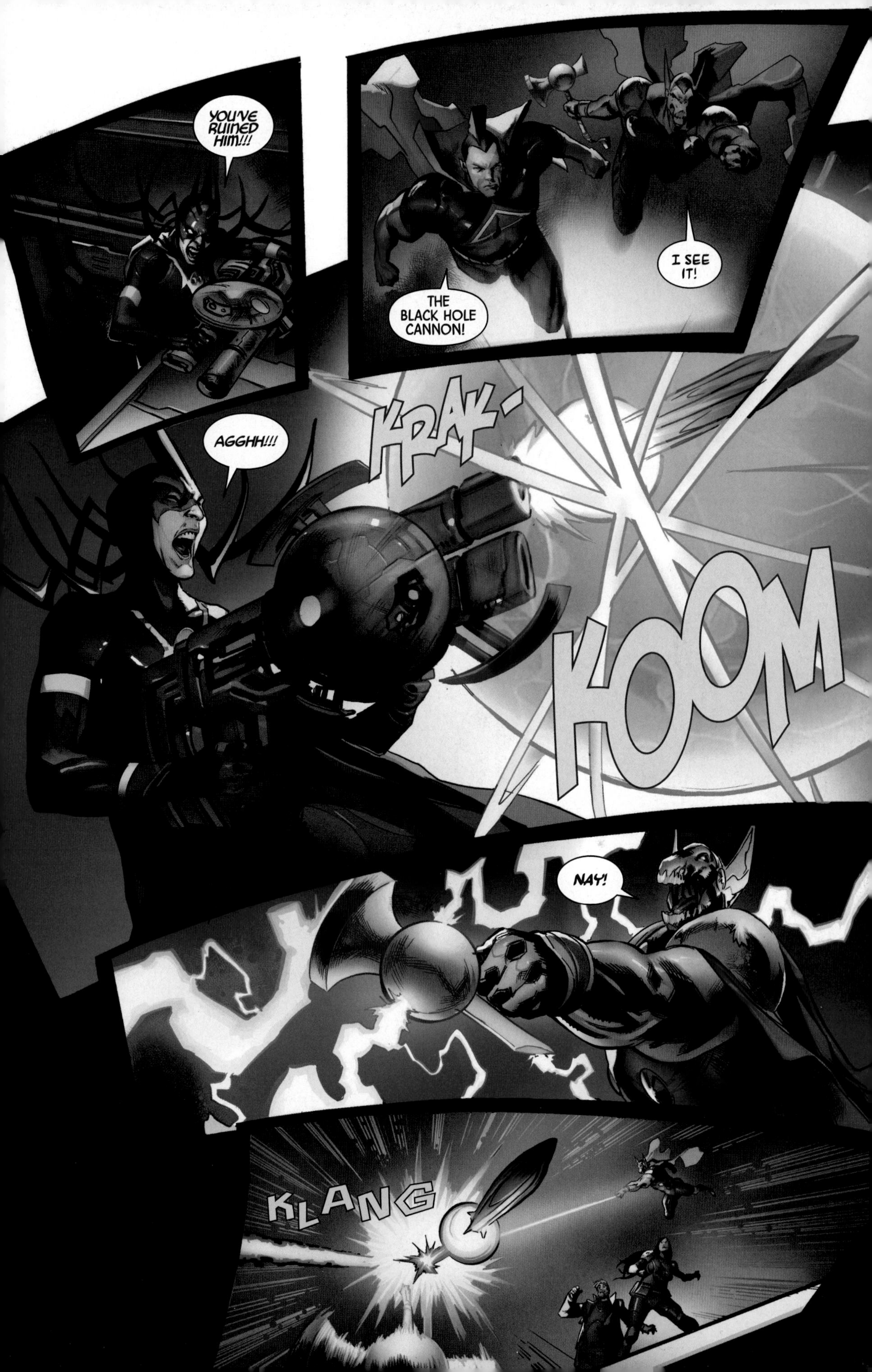
YOU'VE RUINED HIM!!!
THE BLACK HOLE CANNON!
I SEE IT!
AGGHH!!!
KRAK-
KOOM
NAY!
KLANG

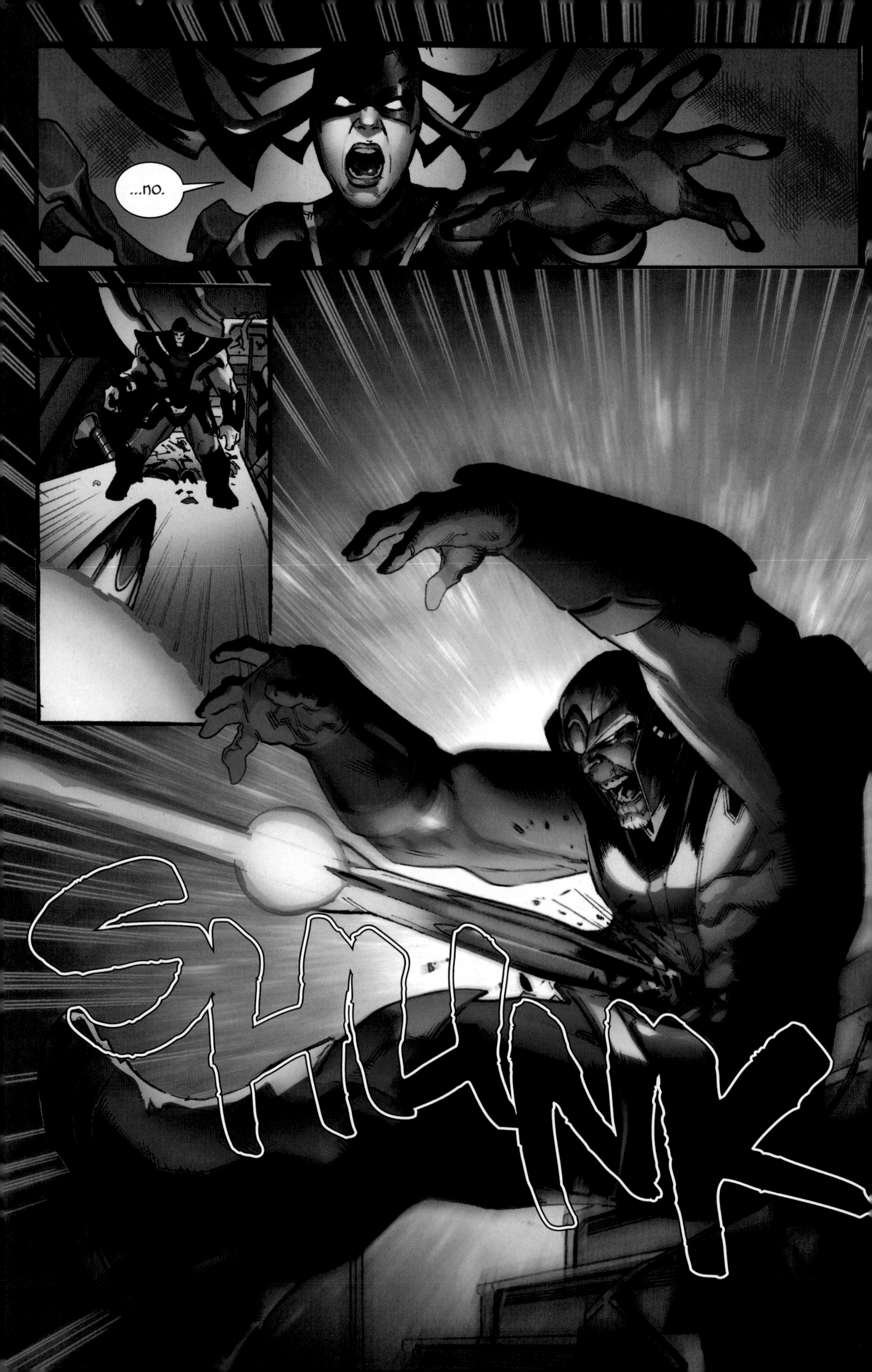
...no.
SHLUNK

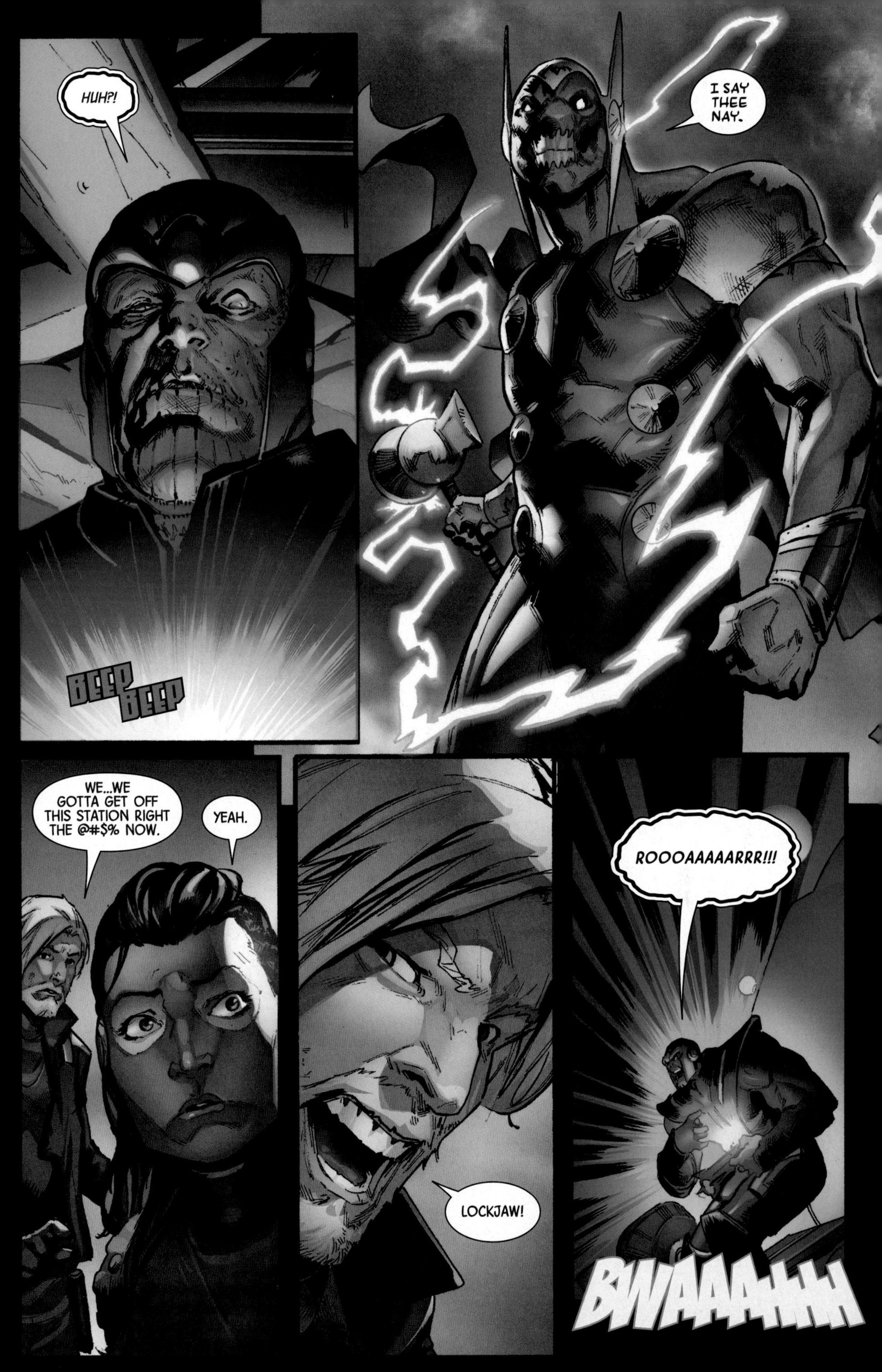
HUH?!
BEEP BEEP
I SAY THEE NAY.
WE...WE GOTTA GET OFF THIS STATION RIGHT THE @#$% NOW.
YEAH.
LOCKJAW!
ROOOAAAAARRR!!!
BWAAAhhhh

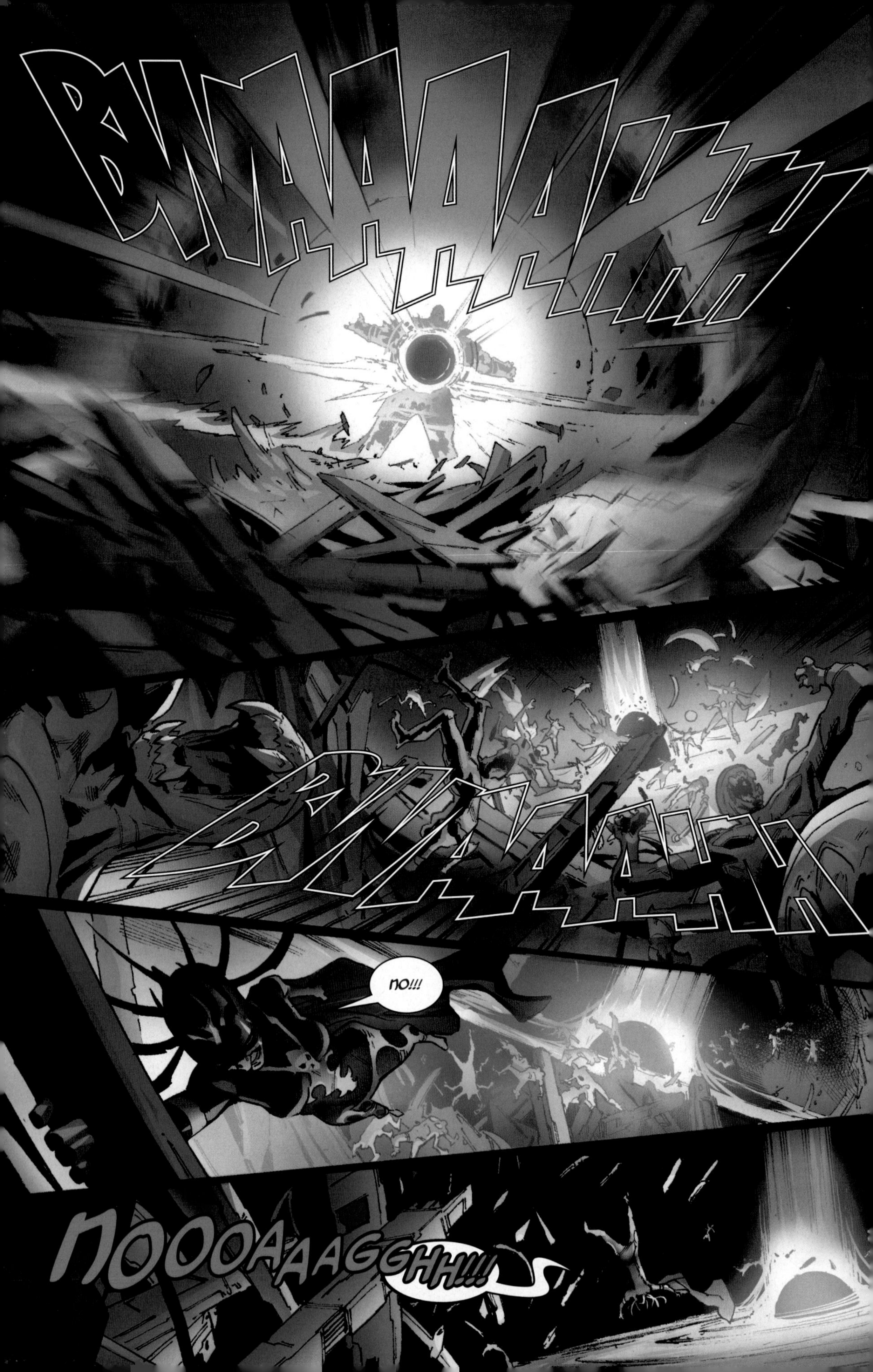
NO!!!
NOOOAAAAGGHH!!!

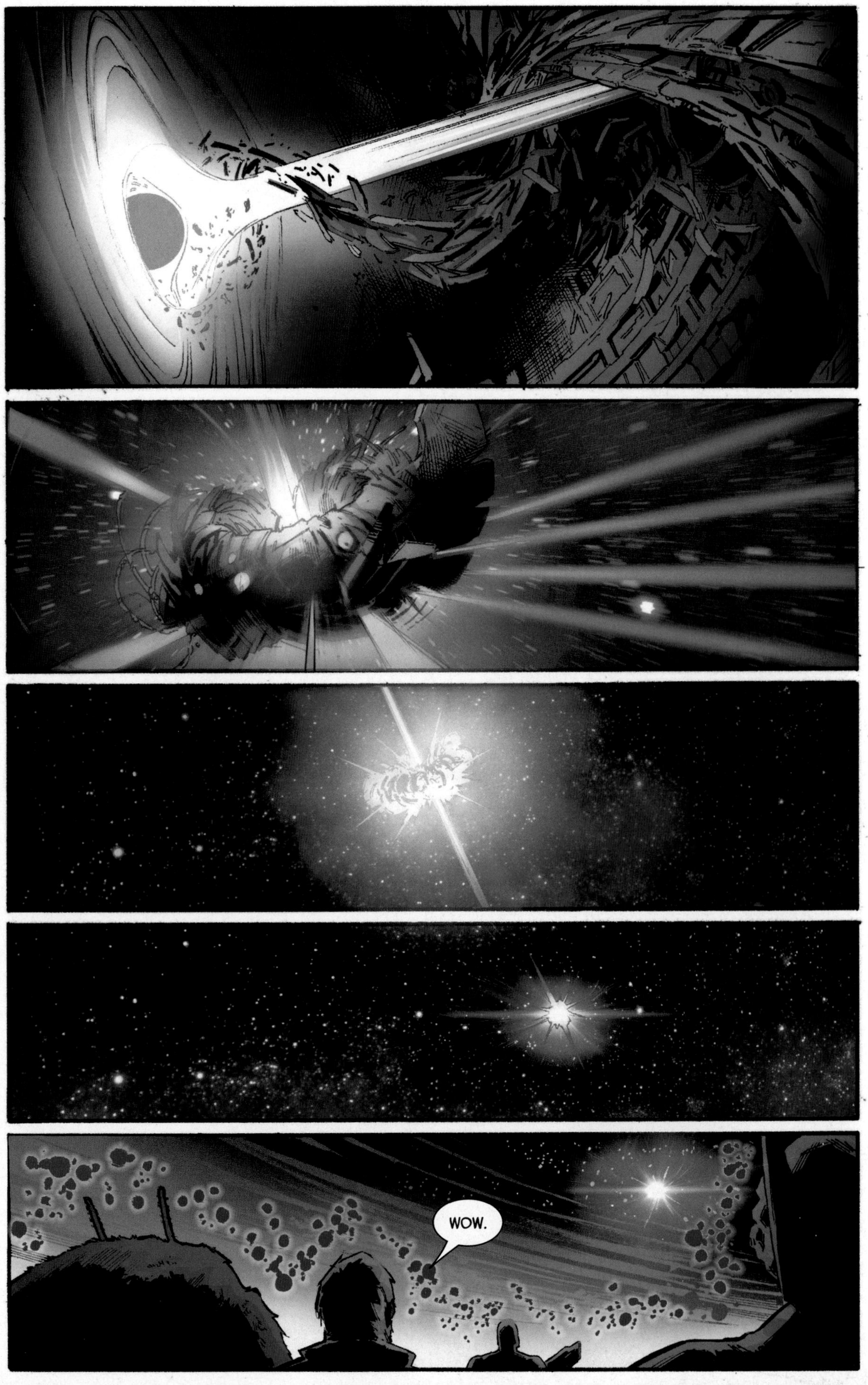
WOW.

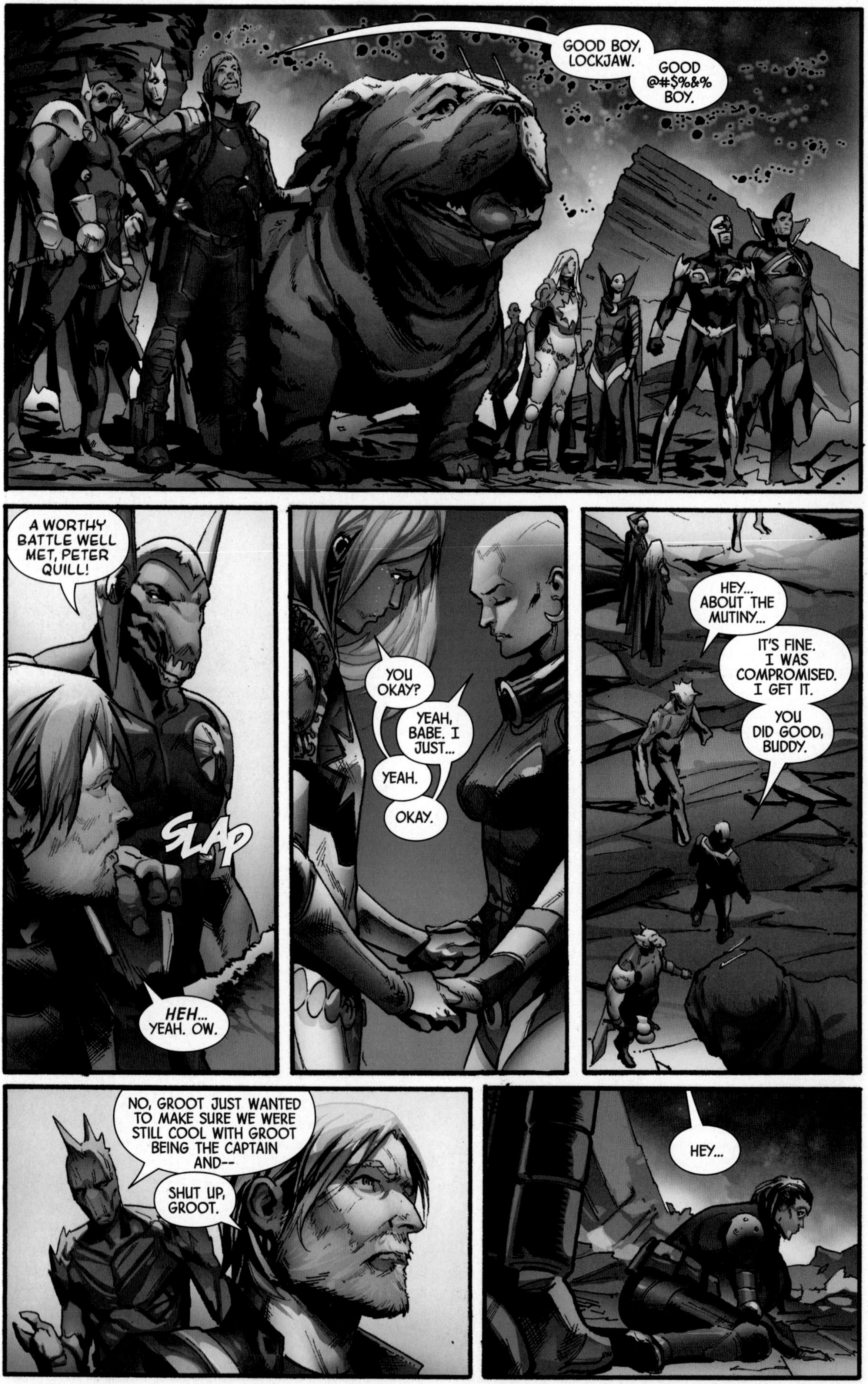
GOOD BOY, LOCKJAW.
GOOD @#$%&% BOY.
A WORTHY BATTLE WELL MET, PETER QUILL!
SLAP
HEH... YEAH. OW.
YOU OKAY?
YEAH, BABE. I JUST...
YEAH.
OKAY.
HEY... ABOUT THE MUTINY...
IT'S FINE. I WAS COMPROMISED. I GET IT.
YOU DID GOOD, BUDDY.
NO, GROOT JUST WANTED TO MAKE SURE WE WERE STILL COOL WITH GROOT BEING THE CAPTAIN AND--
SHUT UP, GROOT.
HEY...

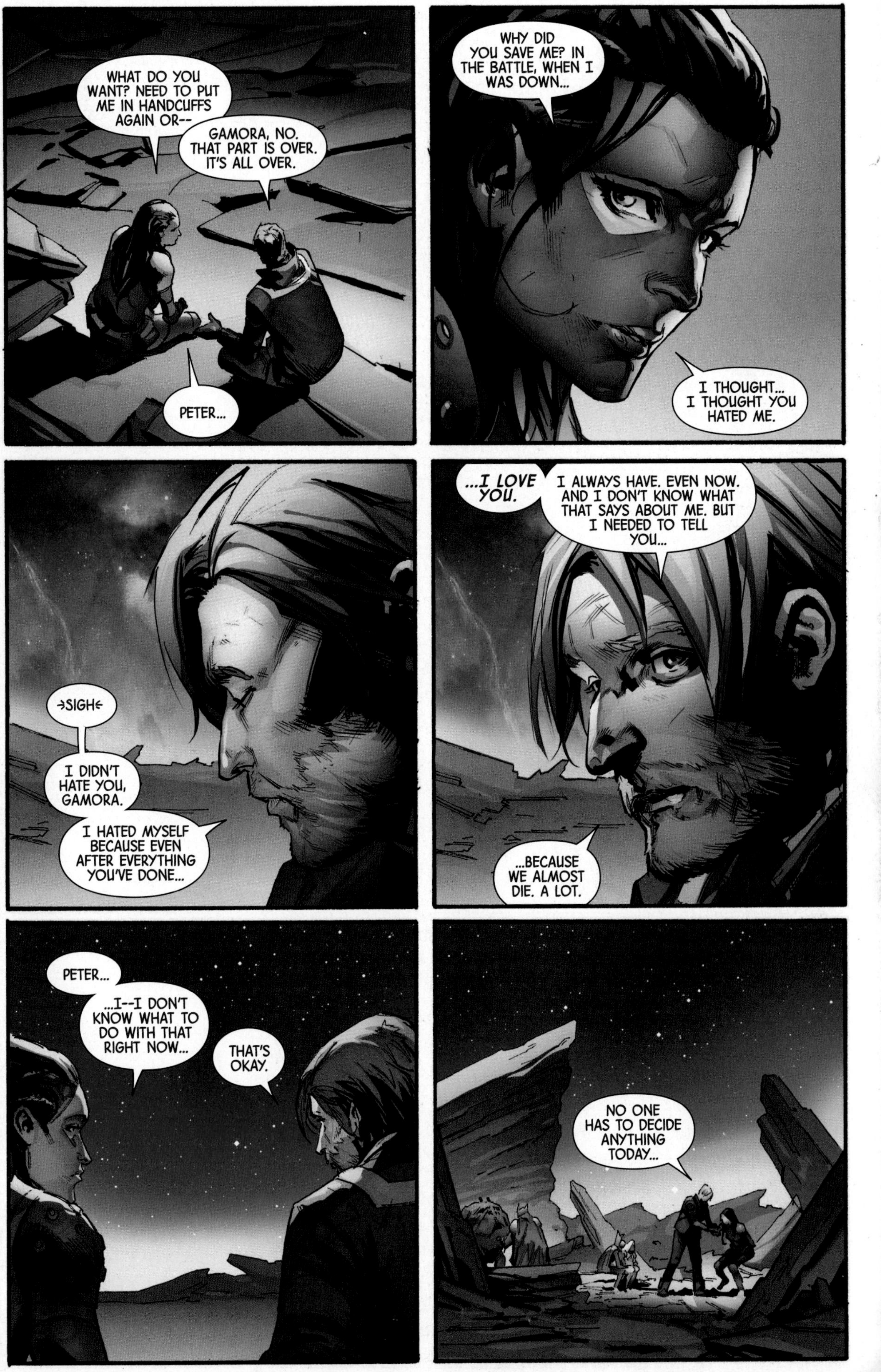

WHAT DO YOU WANT? NEED TO PUT ME IN HANDCUFFS AGAIN OR--
GAMORA, NO. THAT PART IS OVER. IT'S ALL OVER.
PETER...
WHY DID YOU SAVE ME? IN THE BATTLE, WHEN I WAS DOWN...
I THOUGHT... I THOUGHT YOU HATED ME.
→SIGH←
I DIDN'T HATE YOU, GAMORA.
I HATED MYSELF BECAUSE EVEN AFTER EVERYTHING YOU'VE DONE...
...I LOVE YOU.
I ALWAYS HAVE. EVEN NOW. AND I DON'T KNOW WHAT THAT SAYS ABOUT ME. BUT I NEEDED TO TELL YOU...
...BECAUSE WE ALMOST DIE. A LOT.
PETER...
...I--I DON'T KNOW WHAT TO DO WITH THAT RIGHT NOW...
THAT'S OKAY.
NO ONE HAS TO DECIDE ANYTHING TODAY...

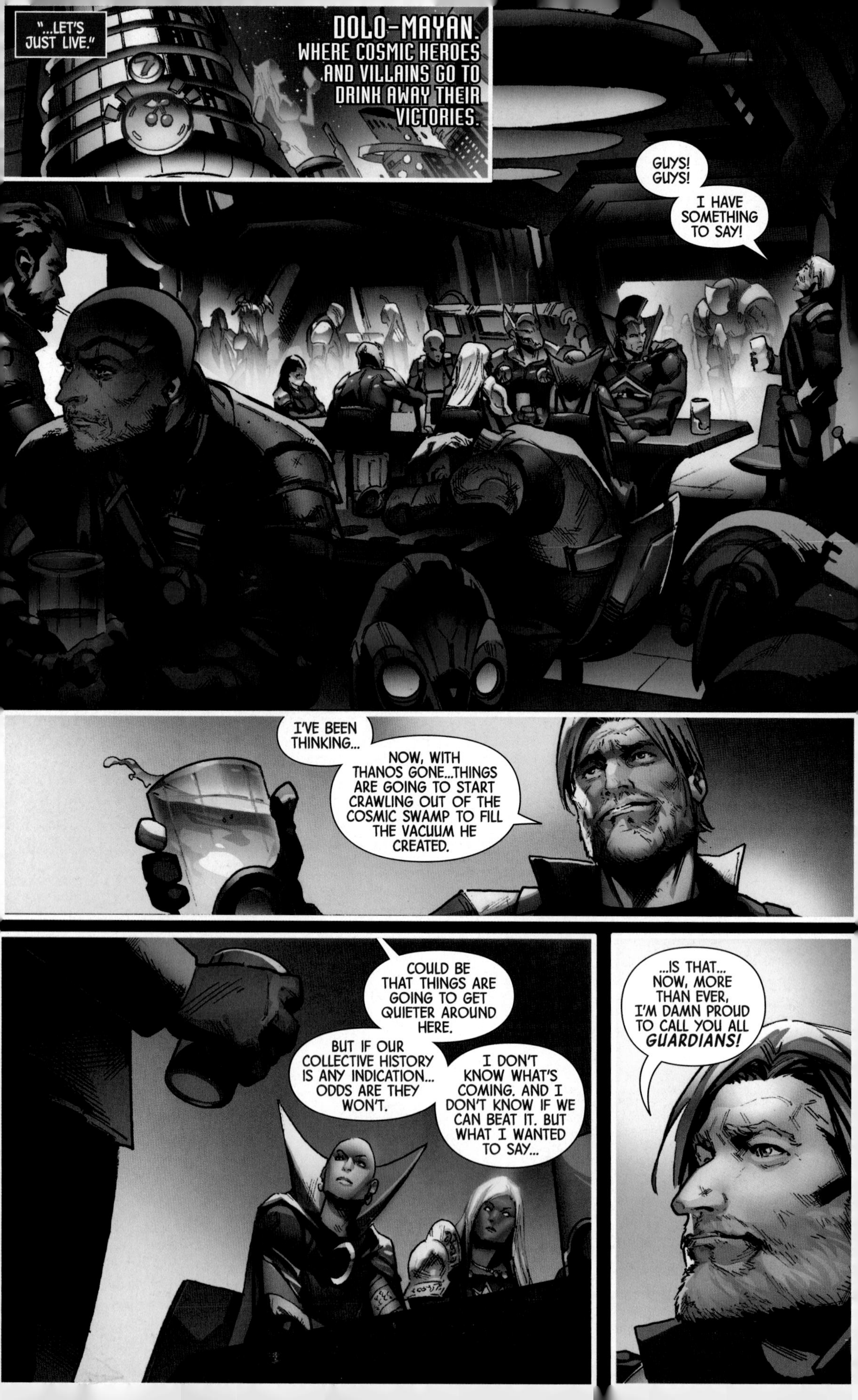
"...LET'S JUST LIVE."
DOLO-MAYAN. WHERE COSMIC HEROES AND VILLAINS GO TO DRINK AWAY THEIR VICTORIES.
GUYS! GUYS!
I HAVE SOMETHING TO SAY!
I'VE BEEN THINKING...
NOW, WITH THANOS GONE...THINGS ARE GOING TO START CRAWLING OUT OF THE COSMIC SWAMP TO FILL THE VACUUM HE CREATED.
COULD BE THAT THINGS ARE GOING TO GET QUIETER AROUND HERE.
BUT IF OUR COLLECTIVE HISTORY IS ANY INDICATION... ODDS ARE THEY WON'T.
I DON'T KNOW WHAT'S COMING. AND I DON'T KNOW IF WE CAN BEAT IT. BUT WHAT I WANTED TO SAY...
...IS THAT... NOW, MORE THAN EVER, I'M DAMN PROUD TO CALL YOU ALL GUARDIANS!

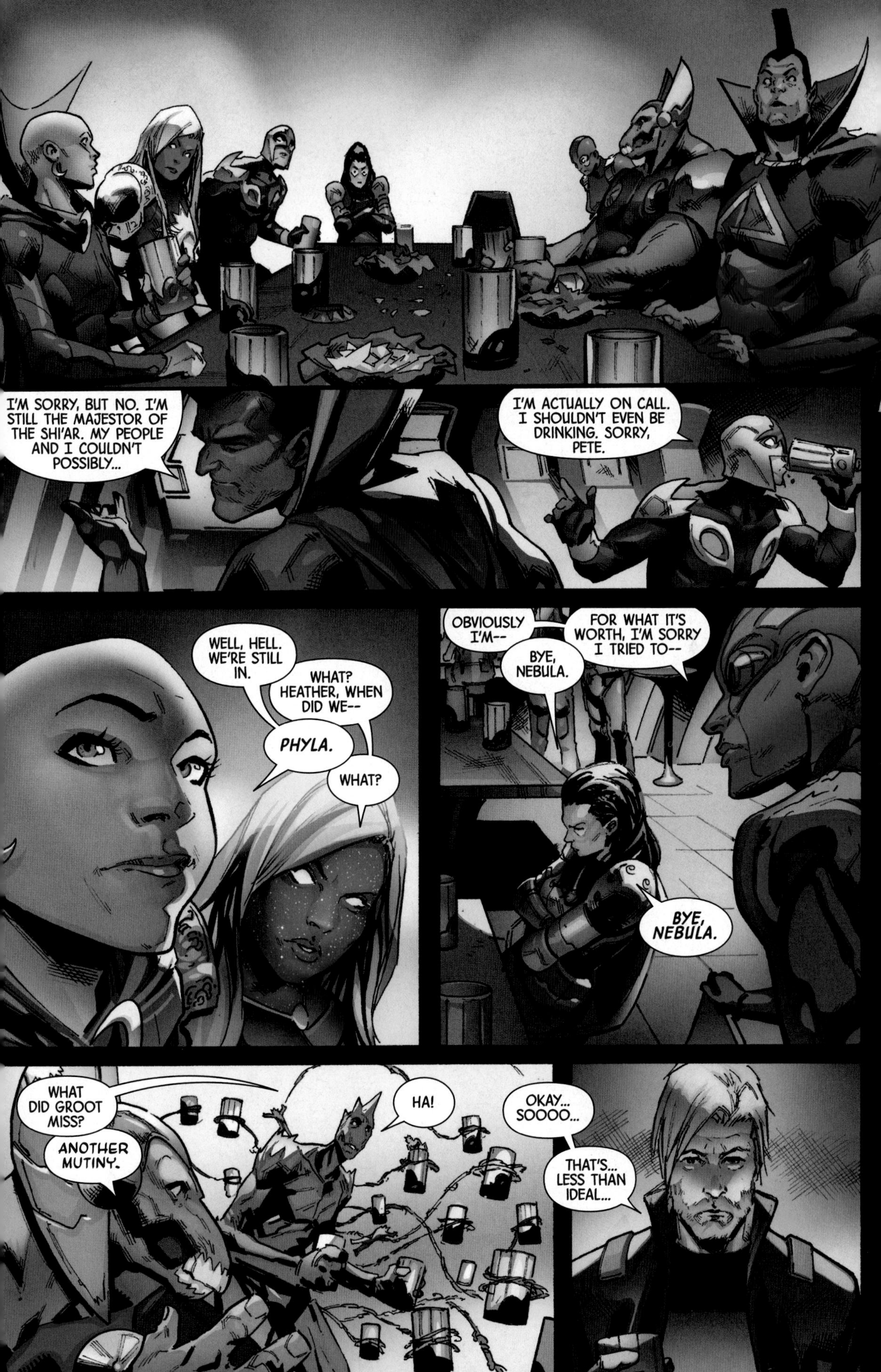
I'M SORRY, BUT NO. I'M STILL THE MAJESTOR OF THE SHI'AR. MY PEOPLE AND I COULDN'T POSSIBLY...
I'M ACTUALLY ON CALL. I SHOULDN'T EVEN BE DRINKING. SORRY, PETE.
WELL, HELL. WE'RE STILL IN.
WHAT? HEATHER, WHEN DID WE--
PHYLA.
WHAT?
OBVIOUSLY I'M--
FOR WHAT IT'S WORTH, I'M SORRY I TRIED TO--
BYE, NEBULA.
BYE, NEBULA.
WHAT DID GROOT MISS?
ANOTHER MUTINY.
HA!
OKAY... SOOOO...
THAT'S... LESS THAN IDEAL...

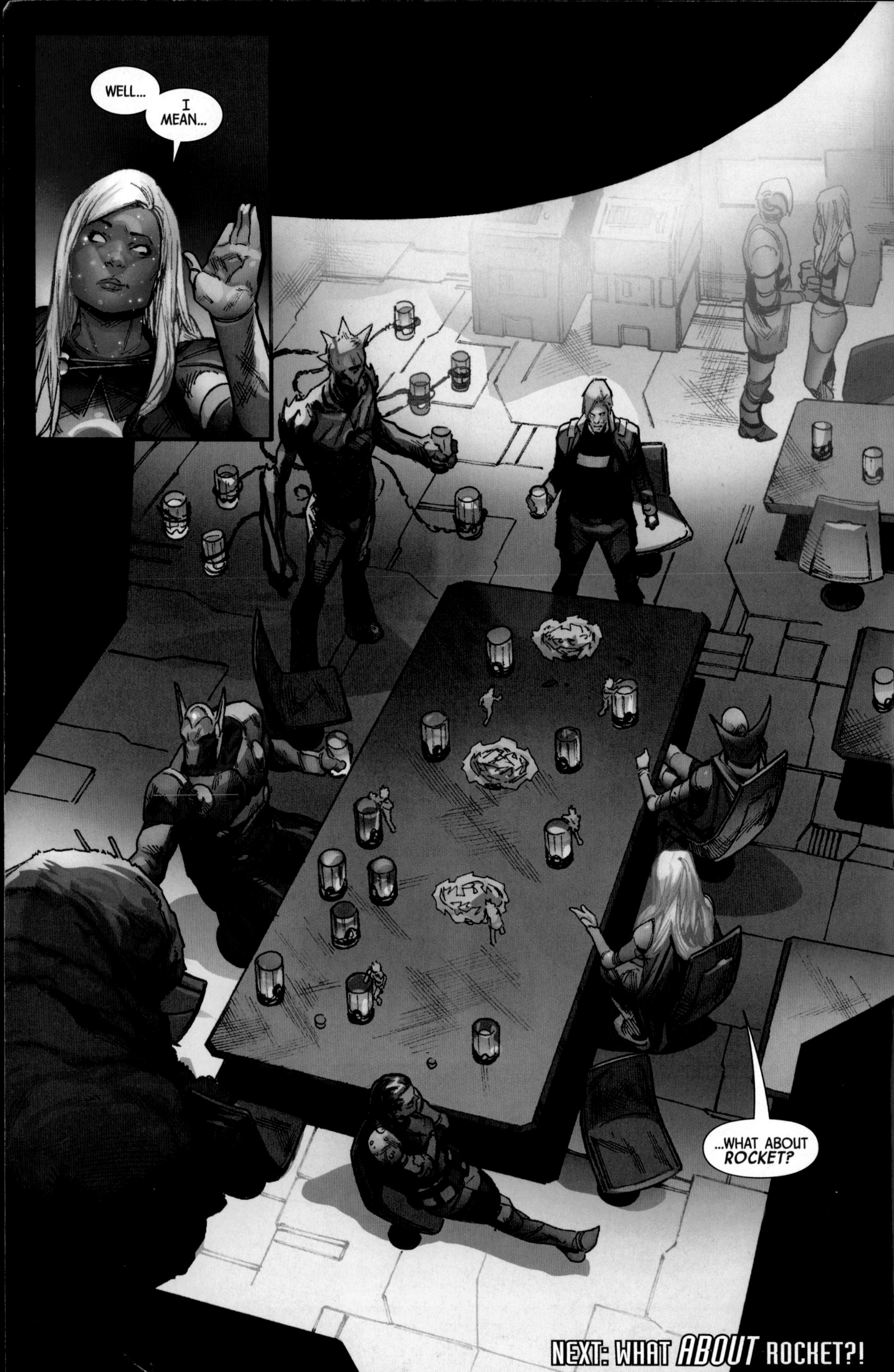
WELL...
I MEAN...
...WHAT ABOUT ROCKET?
NEXT: WHAT ABOUT ROCKET?!

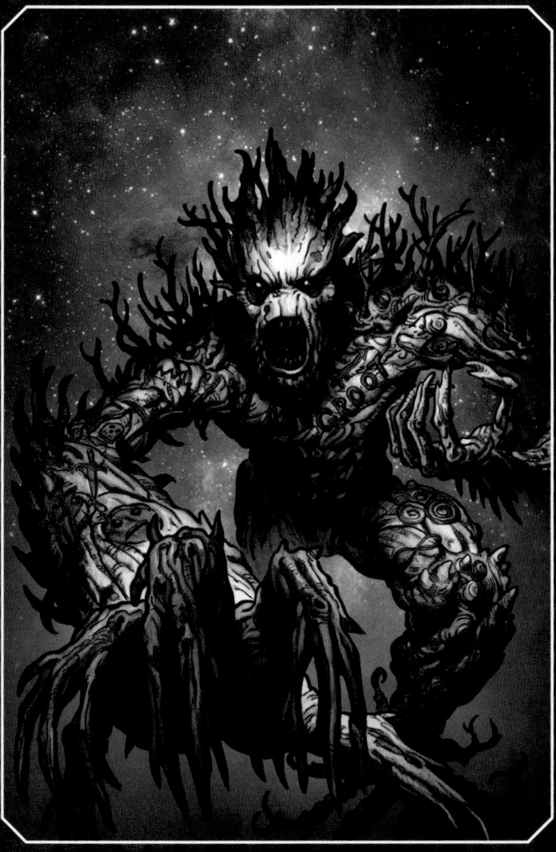

STEVE SKROCE & JASON KEITH
#1 variant

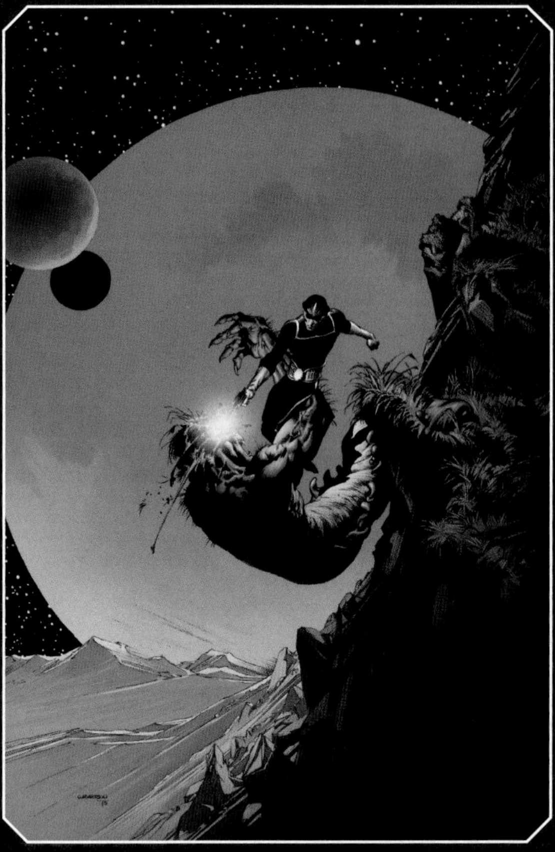

BERNIE WRIGHTSON & RICHARD ISANOVE
#1 Hidden Gem variant

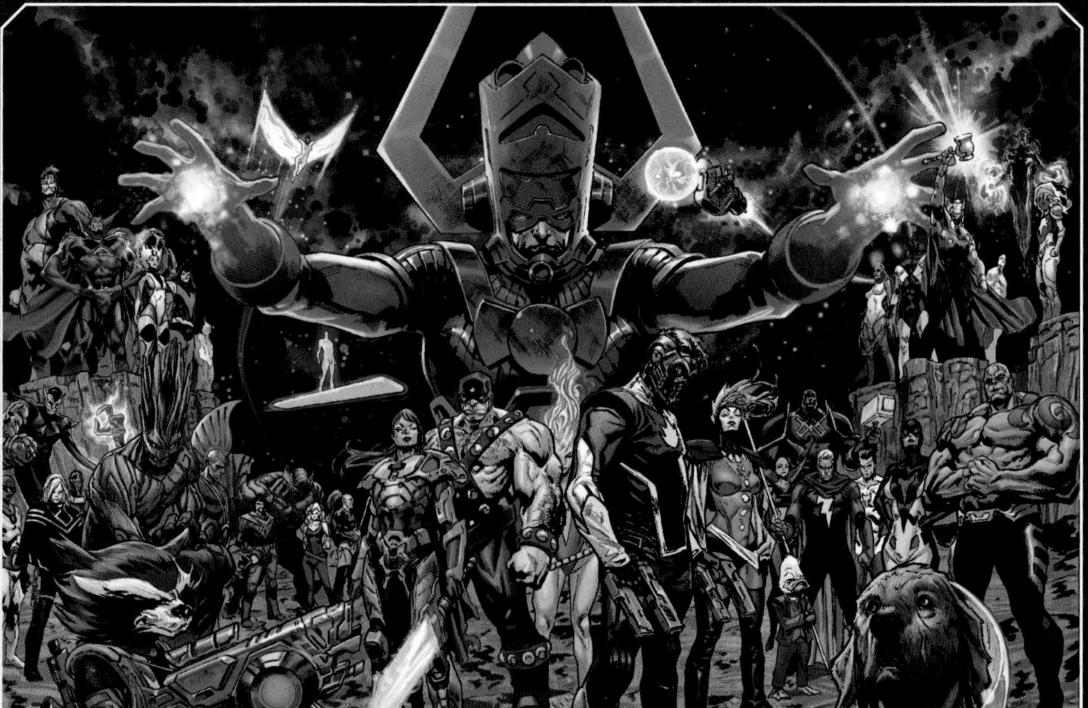
CCCP

GEOFF SHAW & DEAN WHITE
#1 variant

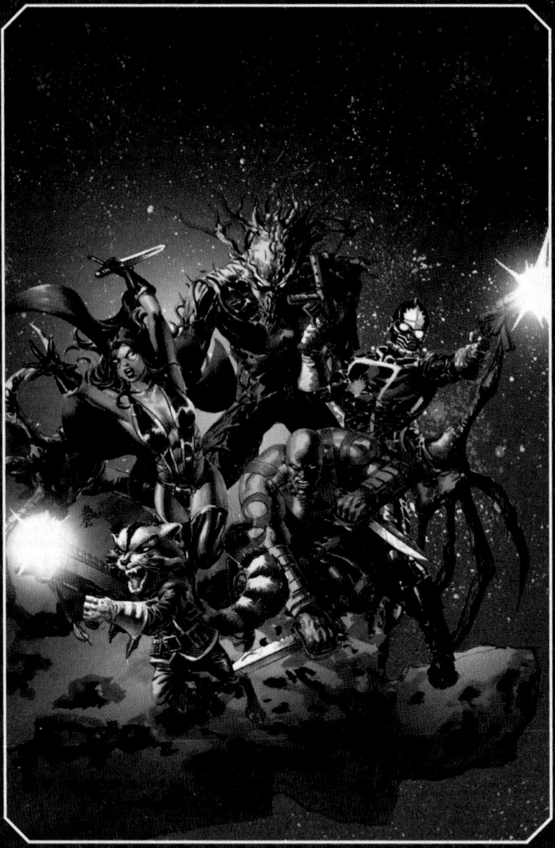

MIKE DEODATO JR. & RAIN BEREDO
#1 variant

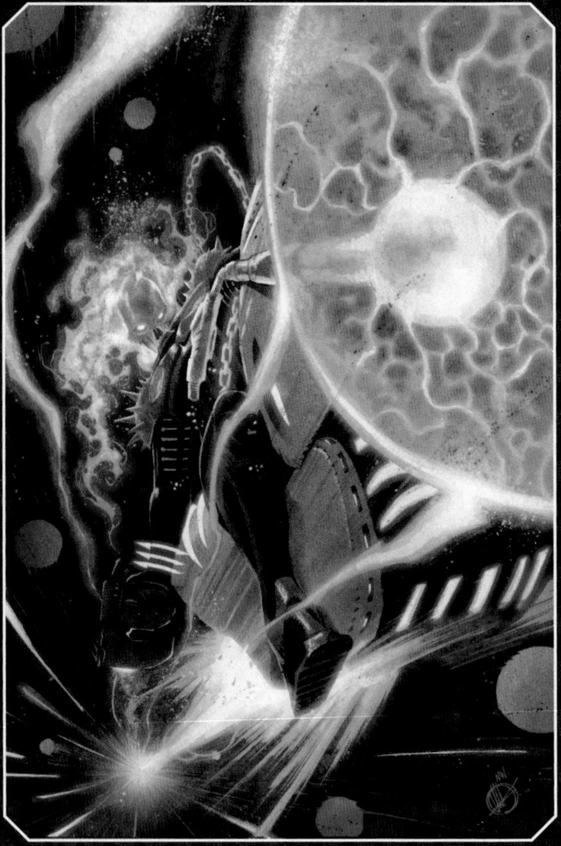

MATTEO SCALERA & MATTHEW WILSON
#2 variant

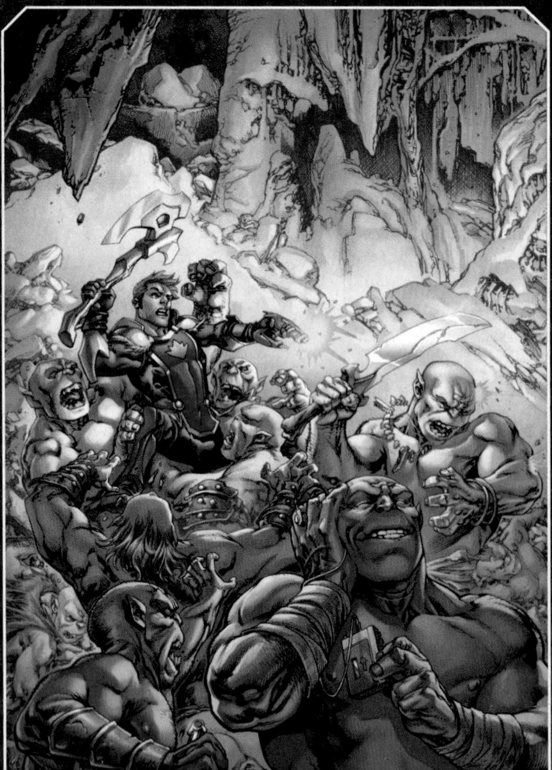

TOM RANEY & RACHELLE ROSENBERG
#4 Asgardian variant

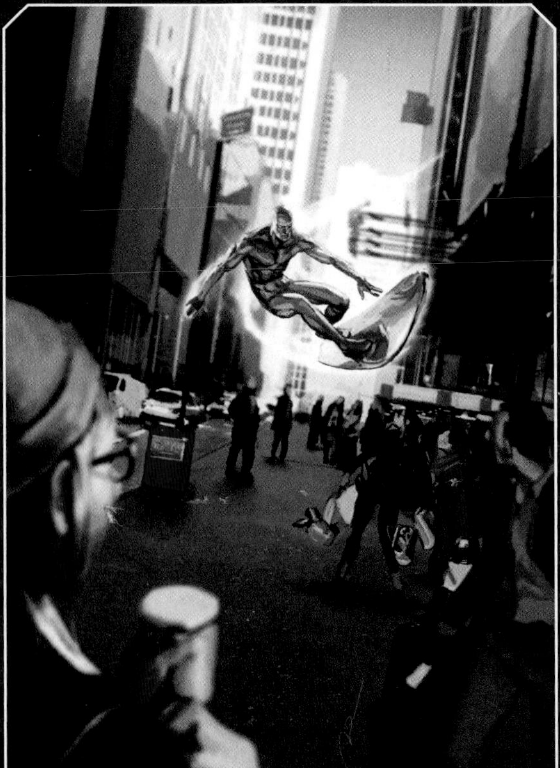

GERALD PAREL
#6 Marvels 25th Tribute variant